Lecture Notes in Computer Science 12636

More information about this subseries at http://www.springer.com/series/7412

Bertrand Kerautret · Miguel Colom ·
Adrien Krähenbühl · Daniel Lopresti ·
Pascal Monasse · Hugues Talbot (Eds.)

Reproducible Research in Pattern Recognition

Third International Workshop, RRPR 2021
Virtual Event, January 11, 2021
Revised Selected Papers

 Springer

Editors
Bertrand Kerautret (iD)
LIRIS
Université de Lyon 2
Bron, France

Adrien Krähenbühl (iD)
Laboratoire ICube
Illkirch, France

Pascal Monasse (iD)
Ecole des Ponts Paris Tech
Marne-la-Vallée, France

Miguel Colom (iD)
Centre Borelli
École Normale Supérieure Paris-Saclay
Gif-sur-Yvette, France

Daniel Lopresti (iD)
Department of Computer Science
and Engineering
Lehigh University
Bethlehem, PA, USA

Hugues Talbot (iD)
University of Paris-Saclay
Gif-sur-Yvette, France

ISSN 0302-9743   ISSN 1611-3349   (electronic)
Lecture Notes in Computer Science
ISBN 978-3-030-76422-7   ISBN 978-3-030-76423-4   (eBook)
https://doi.org/10.1007/978-3-030-76423-4

LNCS Sublibrary: SL6 – Image Processing, Computer Vision, Pattern Recognition, and Graphics

This Springer imprint is published by the registered company Springer Nature Switzerland AG
The registered company address is: Gewerbestrasse 11, 6330 Cham, Switzerland

Preface

This volume contains the original contributions presented during the third edition of the Workshop on Reproducible Research in Pattern Recognition (RRPR), which was held online on January 11, 2021, as a satellite workshop of ICPR2020. Following the two previous editions, this event continues to cover advances in platforms on reproducibility and new reproducible research results, which were covered by regular or short papers. Despite the global health crisis, the workshop was a success thanks to extended deadlines, which allowed authors more time to prepare their contributions.

The growing success of this event is evidenced by the larger number of authors who registered for this workshop (60 authors from 10 different countries), corresponding to an increase of 57%. The total number of submitted papers also increased, in this case by 28% (18 papers) compared to the previous edition. Each contribution was reviewed by three to four reviewers (for the regular papers) or by two reviewers (for the short papers, which we also call ICPR *companion papers*). The online-only audience (due to the COVID-19 pandemic) ranged from 25 to 30 attendees in each session.

The thirteen accepted papers were organized into three main categories. The first contributions focused on reproducible research frameworks. One paper introduced the *ReproducedPapers.org* platform, which opens new ways to share and validate reproducible research. This was complemented by a second contribution focused on the evaluation of reproducibility, including a survey of recommendations. A final article in this category introduced the *torchdistill* framework about knowledge distillation in the context of reproducible deep learning research. The second category of contributions focused on reproducible research results and addressed different topics including intrusion detection, emotion recognition algorithms, and biological structure modeling using tree defect analysis and vesselness filters. All of these contributing papers included source code or online demonstrations, which allow users to reproduce results easily by themselves. The last category included ICPR companion papers describing implementation and details that are an absolute requirement for reproducibility. This set of papers covered several topics such as 3D volume segmentation or properly deploying neural networks. Some of these short papers were awarded the *Reproduced Label in Pattern Recognition*. Videos of the pre-recorded presentations remain available on the workshop's website: https://rrpr2020.sciencesconf.org.

In this third edition, we were glad to invite Roberto Di Cosmo to present the *Software Heritage* project, which aims to establish a perpetual universal archive of software source code. This initiative is closely related to reproducibility, given that it ensures the availability of the source code in the long term and keeps important metadata. A second recent initiative in the computer graphics domain was presented by Nicolas Bonneel on *Code Replicability*. The evaluation of code replicability in computer graphics was presented along with http://replicability.graphics, the new platform they propose that encourages code sharing in this domain. We thank the two invited speakers for the high quality of their presentations and the meaningful discussions with the attendees.

We would like to thank all researchers who submitted contributions to RRPR and also the reviewers in the scientific committee. We address a special thank to the IAPR organizers, who have given their support once again to RRPR with the official IAPR endorsement. We also warmly thank the ICPR2020 general chairs, Rita Cucchiara, Alberto Del Bimbo, and Stan Sclaroff, along with the workshop chairs, Giovanni Maria Farinella and Tao Mei, who allowed us to handle these special post-proceedings in parallel to the several other workshops in the main conference. The publication of these post-proceedings was also made easier with the *EasyChair* platform and the involvement from Alfred Hoffman and his successor at Springer, Ronan Nugent. Finally, we also thank Audrey Bichet from the MMI department of the IUT de Saint-Dié-des-Vosges who made the nice poster for this third edition of RRPR.

March 2021

Bertrand Kerautret
Miguel Colom
Adrien Krähenbühl
Daniel Lopresti
Pascal Monasse
Hugues Talbot

Organization

Program Committee

Pablo Arias	Centre Borelli, ENS Paris-Saclay, France
Fabien Baldacci	LaBRI, Université de Bordeaux, France
Jenny Benois-Pineau	LaBRI, Université de Bordeaux, France
Partha Bhowmick	IIT, Kharagpur, India
Arindam Biswas	IIEST, Shibpur, India
Alexandre Boulch	Valeo.ai, France
Luc Brun	GREYC, Ensicaen, France
Leszek J Chmielewski	WZIM, University of Life Sciences, Warsaw, Poland
David Coeurjolly	LIRIS, CNRS, Lyon, France
Miguel Colom	Centre Borelli, ENS Paris-Saclay, France
Carlos Fernando Crispim-Junior	LIRIS, Université de Lyon 2, France
Isabelle Debled-Rennesson	LORIA, Université de Lorraine, France
Pascal Desbarats	LaBRI, Université de Bordeaux, France
Maxime Devanne	IRIMAS, Université de Haute-Alsace, France
Éléonore Dufresne	ICube, University of Strasbourg, France
Philippe Even	LORIA, Université de Lorraine, France
Yukiko Kenmochi	Laboratoire d'informatique Gaspard-Monge, CNRS, France
Bertrand Kerautret	LIRIS, Université de Lyon 2, France
Pierre Kraemer	ICube, University of Strasbourg, France
Adrien Krähenbühl	ICube, University of Strasbourg, France
Jacques-Olivier Lachaud	LAMA, University Savoie Mont Blanc, France
Daniel Lopresti	Lehigh University, USA
Vincent Mazet	ICube, University of Strasbourg, France
Enric Meinhardt	Centre Borelli, ENS Paris-Saclay, France
Nicolas Mellado	IRIT, CNRS, Université Paul Sabatier, France
Odyssée Merveille	CREATIS, INSA Lyon, France
Cyril Meyer	ICube, University of Strasbourg, France
Serge Miguet	LIRIS, Université de Lyon 2, France
Pascal Monasse	LIGM, École des Ponts ParisTech, France
Nelson Monzón López	Universidad de las Palmas de Gran Canaria, Spain
Jean-Michel Morel	Centre Borelli, ENS Paris-Saclay, France
Pierre Moulon	Zillow Group, Seattle, USA
Khadija Musayeva	Université Côte d'Azur, France
George Nagy	ECSE, Rensselaer Polytechnic Institute, USA
Benoît Naegel	ICube, University of Strasbourg, France
Phuc Ngo	LORIA, Université de Lorraine, France

Thanh Phuong Nguyen	University of Toulon, France
Nicolas Normand	LS2N, Université de Nantes, France
Nicolas Passat	CReSTIC, Université de Reims Champagne-Ardenne, France
Fabien Pierre	LORIA, Université de Lorraine, France
François Rousseau	LaTIM, IMT Atlantique, France
Loïc Simon	GREYC, Ensicaen, France
Isabelle Sivignon	GIPSA-lab, CNRS, France
Robin Strand	Centre for Image Analysis, Uppsala University, Sweden
Hugues Talbot	Center for Numerical Vision, CentraleSupelec, France
Iuliia Tkachenko	LIRIS, Université de Lyon 2, France
Laure Tougne	LIRIS, Université de Lyon 2, France
Antoine Vacavant	Institut Pascal, Université Clermont Auvergne, France
Paul Viville	ICube, University of Strasbourg, France
Jonathan Weber	IRIMAS, Université de Haute-Alsace, France
Laurent Wendling	LIPADE, Université Paris Descartes, France

Contents

RRPR Short Papers

Reproducible Research Framework

ReproducedPapers.org: Openly Teaching and Structuring Machine Learning Reproducibility

Burak Yildiz$^{(\boxtimes)}$, Hayley Hung, Jesse H. Krijthe , Cynthia C. S. Liem ,
Marco Loog , Gosia Migut, Frans A. Oliehoek , Annibale Panichella ,
Przemysław Pawełczak , Stjepan Picek , Mathijs de Weerdt ,
and Jan van Gemert

Delft University of Technology, Postbus 5, 2600 AA Delft, The Netherlands
b.yildiz@tudelft.nl

Abstract. We present ReproducedPapers.org: an open online repository for teaching and structuring machine learning reproducibility. We
evaluate doing a reproduction project among students and the added
value of an online reproduction repository among AI researchers. We use
anonymous self-assessment surveys and obtained 144 responses. Results
suggest that students who do a reproduction project place more value on
scientific reproductions and become more critical thinkers. Students and
AI researchers agree that our online reproduction repository is valuable.

Keywords: Machine learning · Reproducibility · Online repository

1 Introduction

Reproducibility is a cornerstone of science: if an experiment is not reproducible, we should question its conclusions. Yet, machine learning papers are
lacking reproductions [7,12]. Possible reasons may include a misaligned incentive between reproducing results and the short-term measures of career success
associated with more 'wins' [26] and publishing 'novel' work [15]. Nevertheless,
high-impact can be achieved, for instance, when a reproduction fails spectacu-
larly, e.g. [6,8,10,11,14,16,18,19,24]. Yet, these take colossal amounts of manual
effort [1,2,9,22] or massive resources [16,23]. There are venues for publishing
reproductions [3,4,25], which are typically peer-reviewed and thus uphold various selection standards to guarantee quality. We argue that this emphasis on
quality is a hurdle for sharing light-weight reproductions. Important and useful examples of light-weight reproductions include partial results, small variants
on the algorithm, hyperparameter sweeps, etc. Low-barrier options are indeed
available in workshop challenges [13,21] organized at conferences such as ICPR,
NeurIPS, ICLR, or ICML. However, such avenues are hard to maintain on a long-
term basis, as a workshop may or may not be organized. We argue that there is a
need for a low-barrier and long-term venue for machine learning reproductions.

© Springer Nature Switzerland AG 2021
B. Kerautret et al. (Eds.): RRPR 2021, LNCS 12636, pp. 3–11, 2021.
https://doi.org/10.1007/978-3-030-76423-4_1

A complementary angle on low-barrier reproductions is to improve university student training. We should teach the next generation of machine learning practitioners the importance of the reproducibility of research work, as done in other computer science domains such as computer networking, where results reproduction is the means to learn new material [30]. Doing a reproduction project in a course aligns with several important learning objectives for machine learning students. Among others, students (1) should be able to read, critique, and explain a scientific paper; (2) implement a method; (3) run, evaluate, investigate, and extend existing research or code; and (4) write clearly and concisely about code and methods. A reproduction project also lets students experience differences between published results and an implementation, which stimulates a critical attitude and allows reflections on the scientific process.

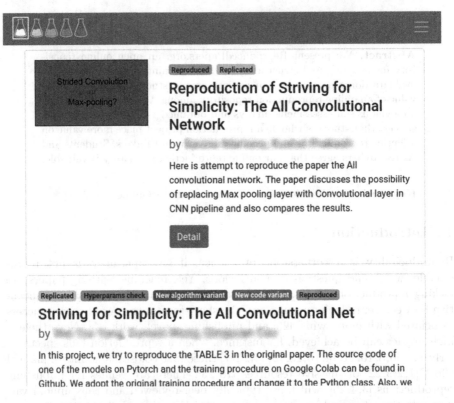

Fig. 1. A screenshot of ReproducedPapers.org. We allow multiple reproductions of the same original paper and investigations of several aspects, such as *Reproduced, Replicated, Hyperparameter check*, etc. Our online repository is user-centered: its sufficient if a user sees value in uploading some form of reproduction. Having such a repository is well-suited for students and adds structure to reproducibility in machine learning.

In this paper, we align the benefits of an online reproduction repository with those of teaching reproducibility. We introduce ReproducedPapers.org: an open, light-weight repository of reproduced papers which flexibly allows any sort of reproduction work, see Fig. 1. This repository benefits the research community while at the same time being well-equipped at accepting contributions from students. Although the standard of student reproductions might be lower than those required for peer reviewed reproductions, they can still give valuable insights such as clarifying which parts are difficult to implement or identifying the reproducibility level of elements. Such online reproductions are a low-threshold portfolio-building opportunity, which in turn may prove a valuable incentive to start doing more reproductions, as well as an opportunity to facilitate sharing reproductions that otherwise would not have been shared.

Our online repository shares traits with other light-weight, bottom-up, grass-roots community efforts such as *ArXiv* [5], *Open Review* [28], and *Papers with Code* [29]. Other efforts on facilitating reproducibility include software for reproducible and reusable experiments [20], open specification neural network diagrams [17], and a framework for automatic parsing of deep learning research paper to generate the implementation [27]. Similar to these approaches, in our work, we combine the traits from online repositories with those of tools facilitating reproducibility by providing an online repository that facilitates teaching as well as structuring reproducibility.

We make the following contributions. 1. We propose a new online reproduction repository; 2. We conduct a proof of concept with students from an MSc Deep Learning course to perform a reproduction project and populate the repository; 3. We evaluate the usefulness of the repository among AI researchers and the learning objectives among students by anonymous surveys.

2   The Online Reproduction Repository

We performed a proof of concept experiment with a reproducibility project for students of the MSc Deep Learning course taught by this paper's last author at Delft University of Technology (TU Delft). We solicited relevant papers among university staff and ensured that (i) data is available, (ii) it is clear which table or figure to reproduce, and (iii) the computational demands are reasonable. Students were also allowed to themselves suggest a paper to reproduce. On their paper of choice, they worked in groups of 2 to 4, for 8 weeks, for approximately one-third of their studying time (i.e., about 13 h a week). For grading, students submitted a blog in PDF and also the URL of an online version of their blog to ReproducedPapers.org to populate the repository. For students who do not wish to share a blog with the world, we offer a private option, which is only visible to course administrators. The option to publicly blog about reproducing machine learning provides an simple opportunity for students to build an online portfolio while simultaneously incentivizing making reproductions.

Table 1. Different aspects of reproduction which are highlighted as badges (see Fig. 1).

Aspect	Description
• Replicated	A full implementation from scratch without using any pre-existing code
• Reproduced	Existing code was evaluated
• Hyperparams check	New evaluation of hyperparameter sensitivity
• New data	Evaluating new datasets to obtain similar results
• New algorithm variant	Evaluating a different variant
• New code variant	Rewrote/ported existing code to be more efficient/readable
• Ablation study	Additional ablation studies

We explicitly allow for light-weight reproduction efforts such as evaluating existing code, checking only certain parts of the paper, proposing minor variations, doing hyperparameter sweeps, etc. Our current options (aspects) are shown in Table 1, and we will add others as the need arises. Authors label their reproduction with the relevant aspects themselves.

We developed ReproducedPapers.org in-house as a simple web application. It is implemented by this paper's first author, and its source code is available on GitHub[1]. Registering is necessary only when adding reproductions. Currently, the repository has 90 registered users and hosts 24 unique papers and 57 paper reproductions. Most papers have multiple reproductions, and only five reproductions are marked as private. The top-3 most-used aspects are *Replicated* (32 times); *Reproduced* (29 times) and *Hyperparams check* (17 times). Figure 2 whose data is derived from self-reported blog posts by users shows both success and failure rates to be around 40%.

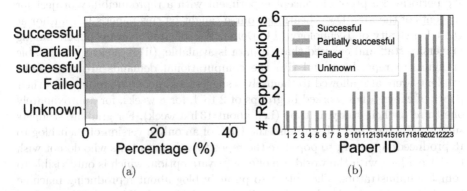

Fig. 2. Current ReproducedPapers.org statistics. (a) Reproduction success rates; (b) Number of reproductions per paper ID.

---

[1] https://github.com/CVLab-TUDelft/reproduced-papers.

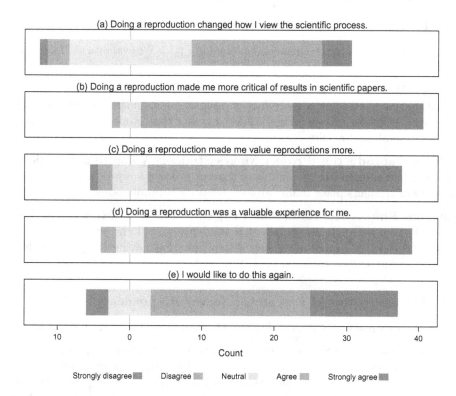

Fig. 3. Responses to survey questions from students who contributed to ReproducedPapers.org. Letting students themselves do a reproduction promotes a critical mindset (a and b), and teaches the value of scientific reproductions (c). In addition, the students considered it a positive experience (d, e). We conclude that these traits align with our learning objectives.

3 Survey Analysis

We evaluate student learning objectives and how AI researchers perceive our online reproduction repository by analyzing the results of small anonymous surveys for two groups: (i) students who recently added their reproduction to our repository and (ii) anybody identifying her/himself working in AI. The second group was invited to the survey through social media and emails. Both groups share the same questions, where the students have five additional questions to evaluate education. The survey data is available at ReproducedPapers.org[2].

We received a total of 144 responses: 43 from course students and 101 from third-party AI researchers all over the world. Of the latter, 87 identify themselves as a junior or senior researcher, and 14 as a student.

---

[2] https://reproducedpapers.org/survey-data.zip.

3.1   Evaluating Student Learning Objectives

The survey questions and results can be found in Fig. 3. We evaluate the following objectives.

Doing a Reproduction Project Increases Critical Thinking. Results in Fig. 3(a) show that doing a reproduction taught most students something new about the scientific process. Figure 3(b) suggests that students become more critical to published results.

Doing a Reproduction Project Makes Students Value Reproductions More. The results in Fig. 3(c) indicate that after doing a reproduction, a great majority of students place more value on scientific reproductions.

Students Find a Reproduction Project a Positive Experience. The results in Fig. 3(d,e) demonstrates that students valued the work and prefer to do a reproduction more often. Results suggest that having a reproducibility project teaches skills considered important by both student and teacher.

3.2   Evaluating the AI Researcher Survey Respondents

Figure 4 shows results for the third party AI researchers. We found the following.

The AI Researcher Survey Respondents Find Online Reproductions Valuable. Results in Fig. 4(a,d,g) show that students and, especially, researchers find an online reproduction valuable and useful. According to Fig. 4(i), there is no clear preference for doing a reproduction or writing a paper. Figure 4(e) suggests that the perceived value of reproduction by the community is smaller for researchers than for students.

The AI Researcher Survey Respondents Find an Online Reproduction Repository Valuable. Results in Fig. 4(b,c) show that students and researchers appreciate an online reproduction repository. Figure 4(f) shows that researchers are less likely than students to help contribute by doing reproductions.

The AI Researcher Survey Respondents See an Educational Role for Courses Where Students Do a Reproduction Project. Results in Fig. 4(h) show that researchers and students agree that reproduction projects should be used more often in courses.

Additionally, we make the following observations from Fig. 4:

(i) When compared to students, the *researchers think the community values reproductions less (e) and want their own team to work on reproductions less (f)*. This may suggest an inverse relationship between perceived value and willingness to contribute. Yet, when comparing researchers against themselves, most think the community values reproductions, and most researchers would like to contribute.

(ii) More researchers *want their work reproduced (g) than that they are willing to contribute (f)*. Can we place our hope on the students as future researchers, as they are much more willing to contribute?

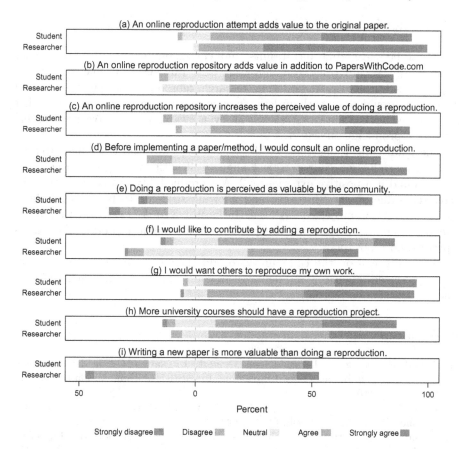

Fig. 4. Responses to survey questions by 57 students and 87 self-identified AI researchers. The survey question is in the sub-caption. Researchers and students agree that: Reproductions are valuable (a, d, g), that an online repository adds value (b, c), and that more courses should use a reproduction project (h). Researchers differ from students in that researchers more strongly find a reproduction valuable (a), and would consult online reproductions more (d). Researchers think a reproduction is valued less by the community (e) and are less likely to contribute with reproductions (f). Students and researchers both do not agree among themselves if a new paper is more valuable then a reproduction (i), suggesting that the answer is 'it depends'. We conclude that the respondents welcome an online repository for teaching and structuring reproducibility.

(iii) There is a clear consensus that *reproductions are valuable (a, d, g, i) but some researchers feel that the community does not reward it enough (e).* Therefore, an important question is how we can change the perception of a low reward for doing reproductions, beyond repositories as reported on here.

4   Discussion and Conclusions

It should be clear that our results and corresponding analysis are rather preliminary. We are convinced, however, that they warrant low-barrier and long-term solutions accommodating research reproduction. Our Reproduced Papers.org provides one such outlet. We hope that future analysis of the further accumulated survey data may sketch an even clearer picture. We hope others consider reproducing our effort.

The main conclusions that we draw at present are the following three. 1. Doing a reproduction course project aligns well with learning objectives, and students find it a positive experience. 2. A reproducibility project improves the perceived value of reproductions, and allowing students to blog online about their reproduction project offers an extra incentive to do a reproduction. 3. AI researcher survey respondents are positive about online reproductions and a reproduction repository.

We finally call on the community to add their reproductions to the website ReproducedPapers.org and deploy it in courses: may the next generation of machine learners be reproducers.

References

1. Anand, K., Wang, Z., Loog, M., van Gemert, J.: Black magic in deep learning: how human skill impacts network training. In: British Machine Vision Conference (BMVC) (2020)
2. Bonneel, N., Coeurjolly, D., Digne, J., Mellado, N.: Code replicability in computer graphics. ACM Trans. Graph. **39**(4) (2020)
3. Colom, M., Kerautret, B., Krähenbühl, A.: An overview of platforms for reproducible research and augmented publications. In: Kerautret, B., Colom, M., Lopresti, D., Monasse, P., Talbot, H. (eds.) RRPR 2018. LNCS, vol. 11455, pp. 25–39. Springer, Cham (2019). https://doi.org/10.1007/978-3-030-23987-9_2
4. Colom, M., Kerautret, B., Limare, N., Monasse, P., Morel, J.M.: IPOL: a new journal for fully reproducible research; analysis of four years development. In: 2015 7th International Conference on New Technologies, Mobility and Security (NTMS), pp. 1–5. IEEE (2015)
5. Cornell University Library: arxiv. https://arxiv.org, September 2011. Accessed 20 June 2020
6. Dacrema, M.F., Cremonesi, P., Jannach, D.: Are we really making much progress? A worrying analysis of recent neural recommendation approaches. In: Proceedings of the 13th ACM Conference on Recommender Systems (2019)
7. Drummond, C.: Replicability is not reproducibility: nor is it good science. In: Evaluation Methods for Machine Learning Workshop at the 26th ICML (2009)
8. Engstrom, L., et al.: Implementation matters in deep policy gradients: a case study on PPO and TRPO. arXiv preprint arXiv:2005.12729 (2020)
9. Fursin, G., Moreau, T., Reddi, V.: ASPLOS 2020 artifact evaluation report. In: Proceedings of the ASPLOS, pp. vi–vii. ACM (2020)
10. Gorman, K., Bedrick, S.: We need to talk about standard splits. In: Proceedings of the 57th Annual Meeting of the Association for Computational Linguistics, pp. 2786–2791 (2019)

11. Henderson, P., Islam, R., Bachman, P., Pineau, J., Precup, D., Meger, D.: Deep reinforcement learning that matters. In: Thirty-Second AAAI Conference on Artificial Intelligence (2018)
12. Hutson, M.: Artificial intelligence faces reproducibility crisis. Science **359**(6377), 725–726 (2018)
13. Kerautret, B., Colom, M., Lopresti, D., Monasse, P., Talbot, H. (eds.): RRPR 2018. LNCS, vol. 11455. Springer, Cham (2019). https://doi.org/10.1007/978-3-030-23987-9
14. Lin, J.: The neural hype and comparisons against weak baselines. ACM SIGIR Forum **52**(2), 40–51 (2019)
15. Lipton, Z.C., Steinhardt, J.: Research for practice: troubling trends in machine-learning scholarship. Commun. ACM **62**(6), 45–53 (2019)
16. Lucic, M., Kurach, K., Michalski, M., Gelly, S., Bousquet, O.: Are GANs created equal? a large-scale study. In: Advances in Neural Information Processing Systems, pp. 700–709 (2018)
17. Marshall, G., Freitas, A.: The Diagrammatic AI Language (DIAL): Version 0.1. arXiv preprint arXiv:1812.11142 (2018)
18. Melis, G., Dyer, C., Blunsom, P.: On the state of the art of evaluation in neural language models. In: International Conference on Learning Representations (2018). https://openreview.net/forum?id=ByJHuTgA-
19. Musgrave, K., Belongie, S., Lim, S.N.: A metric learning reality check. arXiv preprint arXiv:2003.08505 (2020)
20. Paganini, M., Forde, J.Z.: dagger: A Python Framework for Reproducible Machine Learning Experiment Orchestration (2020)
21. Pineau, J., Sinha, K., Fried, G., Ke, R.N., Larochelle, H.: ICLR reproducibility challenge 2019. ReScience C **5**(2), 5 (2019)
22. Raff, E.: A step toward quantifying independently reproducible machine learning research. In: NeurIPS,pp. 5486–5496 (2019)
23. Recht, B., Roelofs, R., Schmidt, L., Shankar, V.: Do imagenet classifiers generalize to imagenet? In: ICML, pp. 5389–5400 (2019)
24. Riquelme, C., Tucker, G., Snoek, J.: Deep Bayesian bandits showdown: an empirical comparison of Bayesian deep networks for Thompson sampling. In: International Conference on Learning Representations (2018). https://openreview.net/forum?id=SyYe6k-CW
25. Rougier, N.P., Hinsen, K.: ReScience C: a journal for reproducible replications in computational science. In: Kerautret, B., Colom, M., Lopresti, D., Monasse, P., Talbot, H. (eds.) RRPR 2018. LNCS, vol. 11455, pp. 150–156. Springer, Cham (2019). https://doi.org/10.1007/978-3-030-23987-9_14
26. Sculley, D., Snoek, J., Wiltschko, A., Rahimi, A.: Winner's curse? On pace, progress, and empirical rigor. In: ICLR Workshop (2018). https://openreview.net/forum?id=rJWF0Fywf
27. Sethi, A., Sankaran, A., Panwar, N., Khare, S., Mani, S.: DLPaper2Code: autogeneration of code from deep learning research papers. In: Thirty-Second AAAI Conference on Artificial Intelligence (2018)
28. Soergel, D., Saunders, A., McCallum, A.: Open scholarship and peer review: a time for experimentation. In: Proceedings of the ICML (2013)
29. Stojnic, R., Taylor, R.: Papers with code-a Facebook AI project, July 2018. https://paperswithcode.com. Accessed 20 June 2020
30. Yan, L., McKeown, N.: Learning networking by reproducing research results. SIGCOMM Comput. Commun. Rev. **47**(2), 19–26 (2017)

Reproducibility: Evaluating the Evaluations

Daniel Lopresti[1]([⊠]) [iD] and George Nagy[2] [iD]

[1] Lehigh University, Bethlehem, PA 18015, USA
`lopresti@cse.lehigh.edu`
[2] Rensselaer Polytechnic Institute, Troy, NY 12180, USA
`nagy@ecse.rpi.edu`

Abstract. Evaluation is at the heart of reproducibility in research, and the related but distinct concept of replicability. The difference between the two is whether the determination is based on the original author's source code (replicability), or is independent of the code and based purely on a written description of the method (reproducibility). A recent study of published machine learning experiments concluded that only two-thirds were reproducible, and that paradoxically, having access to the source code did not help with reproducibility, even though it obviously provides for replicability. Reproducibility depends critically, then, on the quality and completeness of both internal and external documentation. The growing popularity of competitions at pattern recognition conferences presents an opportunity to develop and disseminate new best practices for evaluating reproducibility. As an initial step forward, we collected the final reports and reviewed the competition websites associated with recent ICPR and ICDAR conferences. We used this data from 42 competitions to assess current practices and posit ways to extend evaluations from replicability (already checked by some competitions) to reproducibility on application-oriented data. We recommend empirical standards, monitoring competitions, and modified code testing to be considered and discussed by the research community as we all work together to advance the desirable goals of conducting and publishing research that achieves higher degrees of reproducibility. Competitions can play a special role in this regard, but only if certain changes are made in the way they are formulated, run, and documented.

Keywords: Pattern recognition research · Performance evaluation · Reproducibility

1 Background

Reproducibility and replicability are critical criteria for evaluating reports of experimental research. While the precise definitions of these two terms is open to debate, and different scientific disciplines have developed different preferences, here we will adopt the terminology attributed to the field of Computer Science in a recent National Academies consensus study [1], i.e., "reproducibility" refers to independent researchers arriving at the same results using their own data and methods, while "replicability" refers to a different team arriving at the same results using the original author's artifacts.

© Springer Nature Switzerland AG 2021
B. Kerautret et al. (Eds.): RRPR 2021, LNCS 12636, pp. 12–23, 2021.
https://doi.org/10.1007/978-3-030-76423-4_2

Interestingly, these definitions are the opposite of those specified for obtaining the "Reproducible Research" label at the RRPR 2021 workshop [2], an apparent contradiction anticipated in the National Academics consensus study, which notes that the fields of Signal Processing and Scientific Computing tend to use this other, flipped set of definitions. While a seemingly minor detail, this observation can, at times, take on major significance.

Determining if two sets of experiments obtained the "same" results, mostly similar results, or significantly different results hinges, of course, on the way the experiments are evaluated. And while it would be convenient to assume that evaluation is a mechanical process that is itself practiced uniformly by everyone working in research, this is most certainly not the case. This has implications for reproducibility as well.

Best practices in reproducibility in the pattern recognition community can be summarized based on papers presented at conferences like ICPR, and also in the competitions that are now becoming common at conferences. For the most part, published work contains hints of this when the authors of Paper A write that they have used published code from the authors of Paper B for comparison purposes, or, alternatively, that they were "forced" to reimplement an algorithm because the code was not available. We note that this is a commentary not on the first paper in question (Paper A), but rather on the paper that it references (Paper B); i.e., it is an indirect measure of reproducibility that, so far as we know, no one has attempted to study or quantify. Instead of viewing this as a criticism of the authors of Paper B (for not publicizing their code), it can be considered a complement (publishing a paper that is clear enough that the idea can be reimplemented by others). There is also a tacit assumption that the authors of Paper A have done a good enough job reimplementing the algorithm from Paper B to make for a "fair" comparison, although, of course, there is an inherent conflict of interest, and doubts have sometimes been raised about this, often by the (outraged) authors of Paper B. Sometimes authors point out that they are not able to achieve the same level of performance as was previously published by the original authors; this can be seen as a positive (operating in the interests of full disclosure), or as a complaint (a suggestion that the authors of Paper B did not do a good enough job making their work reproducible). We should also note that simply providing code and data online in a public repository does not by itself satisfy the definition of reproducibility because, as we have noted, this requires "independent researchers arriving at the same results using their own data and methods" (more on this later), although it may very well satisfy the definition of replicability ("a different team arriving at the same results using the original author's artifacts").

2   A Relevant Experiment on Reproducibility

The issue of reproducibility (and the lack thereof) was the focus of a recent study by Edward Raff [3]. Raff uses "reproducible" and "replicable" interchangeably in his writing, but performed his initial analysis of 255 published machine learning papers without looking at the original source code, which satisfies the definition we have adopted for "reproducible." Hence, this is the terminology we will use in summarizing his conclusions here.

Raff found that reported results could be successfully reproduced in only 63.5% of the cases, a somewhat disturbing outcome for those of us working as researchers in pattern recognition. He used 26 different features to characterize the selected papers, broken into three different broad categories: unambiguous features (e.g., features that are well defined and can be easily counted, like the number of authors, the number of references, or the publication type: book, journal, conference, workshop, or tech report), mildly subjective features (e.g., the total number of tables in the paper, which as we know can be somewhat difficult to count, or whether all of the hyperparameters are completely specified), and subjective features (e.g., the number of "conceptualization" figures, the algorithm's difficulty, or the paper's readability). Raff found 10 features to be important at a level of statistical significance for predicting reproducibility: readability had the largest impact, but also significant were rigor vs. empirical (whether a paper is more theoretical or more practical), algorithm difficulty, the presence of pseudo code, the broad subject area of the paper (e.g., the specific branch of machine learning), the number of tables (positively correlated with reproducibility) and the number of equations (negatively correlated with reproducibility), and the computing environment (higher reproducible rates for work run on a GPU, and lower reproducible rates for work run on a cluster). The responsiveness of authors to email queries was also significant in predicting the reproducibility of work reported in their paper.

With some additional work, these observations could form the basis for new evaluation paradigms for reproducibility, a topic worthy of discussion within the pattern recognition research community, and one of our primary recommendations. But perhaps the most counter-intuitive conclusion from Raff's work is his discovery that whether or not a paper's authors released their code had no significant relationship to the paper's independent reproducibility. He posits that perhaps such authors include less detail in their papers because they assume readers will find it in their code. It might seem like authors who release code are signaling that they care more about reproducibility, which makes the lack of a correlation especially surprising. Our conclusion for efforts such as RRPR's "Reproducible Label" initiative is that access to and confirmation of a paper's source code demonstrates replicability, but cannot make claims regarding a work's reproducibility. This same point is almost certainly true of the competitions that have proliferated in the pattern recognition research community. Acknowledging this, we believe it would be useful for the community to have an ongoing discussion regarding the relative importance of reproducibility and replicability, and to take actions designed to take quantifiable steps in the direction of improving both of these measures in our work.

3 Examining Community Practices via Competitions

When it comes to measuring the "status quo" in the community, we have made the decision, for now, to focus on the competitions (sometimes called "contests") that take place at major conferences rather than on individual published papers. Competitions can play an important role in fostering reproducibility, but to do so, certain changes must be made in the way they are organized, run, and documented. We survey current practices and make recommendations for adapting them. This is based on the premise that extra care is exercised by authors and by evaluators in setting up and running competitions, so in some sense they should reflect the "best case" scenario, and also because there are far fewer competitions than published papers to survey, reducing the need to find an unbiased way to sample a very large population.

Competitions do not have as their traditional focus reproducibility, but they may insist on replicability by, for example, requiring submission of working code in order to participate. It could be argued there is little reason to replicate or reproduce a method that yielded poor results on the tasks set by the competition. This is a different scenario from *publication*, where the presumption is that the proposed method is, in some sense, the best known so far, at least according to the proposers. We see, however, no reason why competitions could not more explicitly encourage and measure reproducibility in pattern recognition research, and this is another of the suggestions we offer. In doing so, competitions could lead the way in establishing best practices that will be more broadly followed once understood and accepted by the community.

We have gathered data on competitions and contests organized at two of the largest, most important conferences in our field: The International Conference on Pattern Recognition (ICPR) and The International Conference on Document Analysis and Recognition (ICDAR). Both take place every two years, in alternating years (under normal circumstances). Interestingly, while ICPR is the larger conference often drawing over 1,000 attendees, ICDAR, with around 500 attendees, fields many more competitions: for example, ICDAR 2019 had 27 competitions vs. 4 for ICPR 2018, and ICDAR 2017 had 25 competitions vs. 7 for ICPR 2016. These large differences can, of course, be explained by the traditions of the two conference series.[1]

Here we report what we have discovered about the practices of ICPR and ICDAR competitions. Our focus is on issues relating to reproducibility and replicability, and opportunities to inject more of these two considerations into competitions. Prior to doing our survey, we expected that we would find two common models. In one model, all of the experiments are performed by the competitors. There is a training set released well in advance, and a test set that is distributed with a limited amount of time to report results back to the competition organizers. The other model is that competitors must submit their code to the conference organizers who will then run it on new, previously unseen data. Even the latter is, at best, evidence of replicability, not reproducibility. The former tells us nothing, really, about either. However, it is possible the competition organizers will have made a separate effort to read and analyze an accompanying paper to try to verify whether the reported experimental results are "plausible." We looked for evidence of this in the published competition reports and on associated websites.

Since it seems unlikely competition organizers would independently implement methods published in a paper due to the amount of work that would be involved, what might it mean when they take code provided by a competitor and run in on new data, obtaining results that appear consistent with what the competitor has demonstrated through their own experiments? Could this be called a weak form of "reproducibility"? Perhaps a better term would be "robustness" or "generalizability." This makes a case for competitions that push algorithms to the edge of breaking, otherwise what is learned from the competition does not substantially improve on what already appears in published work by the competitors or other authors.

---

[1] While ICPR and ICDAR seemed to us to be two obvious candidates to study, as noted by one of the reviewers there are, of course, many other relevant examples that may be instructive to consider, including Kaggle, the KITTI Vision Benchmark Suite, ImageNet, and reproducedpapers.org, among others.

It is also possible to imagine competitions that truly measure reproducibility. While requiring more work, this would likely provide much more value to the community. Much of the programming required by participation in a competition already devolves to Ph.D. students. Attempting to reproduce published work seems like another ideal task for students and early career researchers, many of whom are already doing this anyway as part of their entry into the field (perhaps such efforts could also include retired experts who still wish to remain connected to the community, as suggested by one of the reviewers of this paper). As of now, important work like this receives little credit within the research community, but new forms of recognition seem possible, maybe even publication credit or awards, for those who support competitions by evaluating and reporting on the reproducibility of published methods. This is another one of our suggestions for advancing the field.

Our survey results for the ICPR and ICDAR competitions are presented in Table 1. We evaluated the following features in each case:

- Announced Competitions: as per the main conference website.
- Held Competitions: competitions that actually took place, as evidenced by a written report. As can be seen, of the announced competitions, only 67% were actually held. The remainder were cancelled. In most cases the cancellations are indicated explicitly, often on the competition webpage, but sometimes even this minimal information is missing and it is only the lack of a website or a report that indicates it was cancelled.

All the rest of the percentages below are calculated relative to the competitions that were held, not the number that was originally announced:

- Competition Website - Active: whether the competition website still responds with valid information about the competition. This is true for 78% of the competitions.
- Competition Website - Competition Reproducible: whether (in our judgement) the competition protocol could be reproduced based purely on information present on the website. This is true for 71% of the competitions (clearly if the website is no longer responsive, the competition cannot be reproduced from the website).
- Final Report - In Proceedings: whether the final report was published in the conference proceedings. This is true for 93% of the competitions. While clearly it is desirable for 100% of the reports to be published in the proceedings, whether it is feasible depends on the interplay between publication deadlines and the timing of the competitions.
- Final Report - On Website: even with the report appearing in the conference proceedings, it would seem to be valuable to also include it on the website, but we found only 14% of the final reports are on the competition websites. (Sometimes there are graphs of the final results on the website, but no written analysis – we counted this only if the final written report, or something close to it, was on the website.)
- Final Report - Competition Reproducible: a companion to the information appearing on the website, this answers the question whether the competition can be reproduced by what appears in the written report. This was true for 83% of the competitions. We found that sometimes the written report does a better job in this regard, and other times the website does a better job.

Table 1. Survey of ICDAR and ICPR competitions.

	Conference	ICDAR		ICPR		Total
		2019	2017	2018	2016	
Status	Announced Competitions	27	25	4	7	**63**
	Held Competitions	**18**	**17**	**3**	**4**	**42**
Competition Website	Active	16	11	2	4	**33**
	Competition Reproducible	15	9	2	4	**30**
Final Report	In Proceedings	17	17	3	2	**39**
	On Website	3	3	0	0	**6**
	Competition Reproducible	17	14	2	2	**35**
Entries Reproducible	Some	16	11	2	2	**31**
	All	1	0	0	1	**2**
Tests Run By?	Participants	16	15	3	2	**36**
	Organizers	2	2	0	2	**6**
	Code Required?	5	4	0	2	**11**
Public Data?	Some Data	8	6	1	3	**18**
	All Data	5	6	1	3	**15**
	With Registration	10	7	1	0	**18**
Public Source Code?	Some Code	6	5	0	0	**11**
	All Code	0	0	0	0	**0**

- Entries Reproducible - Some: whether, in our judgement, sufficient information is included for at least some of the contest entries to be able to reproduce them. This will often mean a reference to a full-length published paper describing the method, sometimes supplemented by the source code on a public repository. Entries judged not to be reproducible are described only very briefly – often in a short paragraph using only very general terms (e.g., "we used a Recurrent Neural Network"). In a few cases, there is no description of a method whatsoever. We determined that for 74% of the competitions, at least some of the entries were reproducible. If just one entry in a competition was judged reproducible, we would count it here.
- Entries Reproducible - All: using the same criteria as above, but requiring all of the entries to be described in sufficient detail to be able to reproduce each one of them. Of the 42 competitions we studied, only two of them provided enough information to reproduce all of the entries (one each from ICDAR 2019 and ICPR 2016). This is a major area for improvement we recommend moving forward.
- Tests Run By? Participants: the competition participants ran their own code and submitted results to the organizers to be judged.
- Tests Run By? Organizers: in a few notable cases, the competition required entrants to submit code in one of a number of standard formats to the organizers which they then ran. This was true for 14% of the competitions.

- Tests Run By? Code Required?: in this case, the competition rules state that entrants must provide their code to the organizers. While this might seem to be identical to the previous measure, some competitions require participants to run their own code and submit results for judging, and also to submit their code for "verification." This is a good idea. However, we were unable to find explicit statements in the reports or on the websites for those competitions suggesting that the code had actually been verified. We believe it would be improper to take the lack of any sort of comment as confirmation the verification had been performed and passed. We suggest an explicit affirmation should always be included.
- Public Data? Some Data: at least some of the data used for the competition is public via links on the website or in the report. In some cases, competitions claim to be using public data, and this may in fact be true, but if a link was not provided to confirm accessibility, we did not call it public.
- Public Data? All Data: all of the data used for the competition is public via links on the website or in the report. Only 36% of the competitions make all of their data public, at least at the time of this writing.
- Public Data? With Registration: a number of the competition websites state that the data can be obtained only after registering for the competition. This may or may not be accompanied by a claim that public data is being used (e.g., it is data from a digital library), but if registration is required, then the data is hidden behind a "wall" and not truly public.
- Public Source Code? Some Code: source code for at least some of the entrants is available on a public website (e.g., GitHub) linked by the competition. This is true for 26% of the competitions. Note that just because code is required by the competition, the code is not necessarily made public. (In some cases, the organizers took executable code and not source code.)
- Public Source Code? All Code: source code from all of the competitors is available on a public website linked by the competition. This was not the case for any of the 42 competitions. There is, of course, a tension here between allowing companies to participate in competitions while protecting their intellectual property on the one hand, and encouraging the open sharing of ideas which is the hallmark of reproducible research on the other.

In conducting our survey, we experienced a number of frustrations that can also be seen as negatively impacting reproducibility. This included links to competition websites that no longer work, and links that work but now point to new, completely different activities with no hint of the previous competition. We found one published report that described the setup of the competition, but did not provide any of the results. Another final report was published in an unrelated journal, but not in the associated conference proceedings. We saw reports that only vaguely identified the contest participants, let alone provide sufficient details for reproducibility. Finally, there were a couple competitions that failed to generate outside interest for some of the tasks, so there was no real "contest," but the organizers still produced results to include in the report by running their own code.

While all the competitions did a good job describing their evaluation metrics, many of them were not completely clear on the data they used, often only generally referencing drawing it from a larger collection (e.g., a digital library) and sometimes including a small set of sample images on the website. Surprisingly, it also sometimes required some digging to determine that participants ran their own code – this seems to be a tacit assumption that was not always explained clearly.

Our survey was admittedly simple and limited in its scope to what was publicly visible at a time well after the competitions took place. We suspect some important information was only conveyed via email exchanges between the organizers and the competitors, and never recorded anywhere else. This seems like a reasonable expediency, but it hurts later reproducibility; all of the details ought to be fully documented.

Competitions are becoming increasingly popular and play a valuable role in conferences such as ICPR and ICDAR. They have the power to focus attention on problems the community considers important, and to drive the field forward. Our colleagues who devote substantial time and effort to organizing these activities rarely receive credit commensurate with the workload they take on. Nothing in our analysis is meant to be critical of the contributions that have been made so far, but rather an attempt to rally the community around developing best practices for reproducibility. Competitions could play a valuable role in this regard, if more attention is focused on the details.

4 Empirical Standards Favoring Reproducibility

As we have noted, readability was found to be the most critical factor by Raff in his work on reproducibility. Building on this, we might imagine developing a "best practices checklist" to be used by authors when they writeup their results, and by reviewers when evaluating submissions for conferences and journals.

In our search for additional clarity, we find it instructive to turn to a series of recent best practices discussions that have taken place in the programming language community (ACM SIGPLAN), resulting in a set of Empirical Evaluation Guidelines which are formulated as a single page (poster-format) "checklist" proposed for use when evaluating papers for publication [4]. Similar discussions having been taking place in the fields of software engineering [5] and computer graphics [6].

One community exercise that is interesting to ponder would be building on the SIGPLAN checklist, keeping aspects considered useful in pattern recognition research, and deleting or modifying those which do not apply as currently stated. The goal would be to advance reproducibility beyond its current levels, without creating too great an added burden on already busy reviewers, conference chairs, and editors.

5 Program Integrity and External Dependencies

Program bugs can, of course, introduce security risks as well as hamper reproducibility. They are seldom revealed by replication on the same data. Among the many tools available for detecting bugs, fuzz testing with random inputs is attracting much current attention [7]. These tools are not specific to document image analysis, where more targeted variations in input are desirable. For example, egregious paragraphs consisting of only a few words, mathematical formulas or unusual page-breaks may affect segmentation and layout analysis. Some scanners exhibit ambient light leaks resulting in border noise. (Even the same scanner generates different bitmaps on successive scans of the same page.)

Classification results may depend on language-specific libraries like equation solvers. Therefore, reproducibility studies should include, beside broad test data, diverse transducers (scanners or cameras) and platforms (languages and compilers). Should they also require directions for sampling a new data source, dividing the sample into training, validation, and test sets, and rebuilding the classifier from scratch? Experiments involving human-computer interaction add further dimensions of subject, training, and protocol variability. Similar observations apply beyond the field of document analysis, of course, extending across the broad domain of pattern recognition research.

6 Suggestions for Further Action

Note that these recommendations are intended as jumping off points for further discussion, not set-in-stone policies for changing the community's current practices. Suggestions like this can serve as a basis for organizing competitions and reviewing papers, as well as for conducting experiments and writing them up for publication. As noted by the members of the SIGPLAN community [4]: "The goal of the checklist is to help authors produce stronger scholarship, and to help reviewers evaluate such scholarship more consistently. Importantly, the checklist is … meant to support informed judgment, not supplant it. The committee's hope is that this checklist can put all members of the community literally on the same page." We would echo the same goal for any similar effort within our own community.

We also note that not all attempts at building evaluation check-lists are equally helpful: if verbosity is not carefully managed, then simply attempting to read, understand, and apply the checklist becomes a chore in itself; this is one reason the authors of the SIGPLAN effort strove to fit their checklist on a single (albeit dense) page (for comparison, contrast this with the 59-page SIGSOFT effort [6]). At its heart, evaluation for reproducibility is a human factors activity, and consideration for the reviewer must be front and center.

The concept of reproducibility overlaps that of *generalizability*. Will a method that gives satisfactory results on selected data also work well enough on hitherto unseen application streams? All test data samples that we have seen are basically convenience samples, not population samples. The multitude of digital images, even when considering only document images in a specific category, discourages credible sampling. Web crawls collect huge samples, but cannot yet formulate descriptors accurate enough for reliable evaluations of generalizability beyond tiny and arbitrary test sets. Is it time to design and develop a web-scale census?

Finally, as we noted in our competition survey, evaluations for evaluating reproducibility must themselves be reproducible via archival publication of clear, complete, objective protocols. As much experimental science proceeds without theoretical foundations, the evaluation of any such process (the original experiment, assessment of its reproducibility, evaluation of this assessment …) must be open to external scrutiny. Empirical standards for evaluating the evaluations, *ad libitum*?

With these various points in mind, we offer the following specific suggestions for strengthening the role that competitions play in fostering reproducibility:

- Organizers should commit to completely and openly documenting all aspects of their competition in sufficient detail that the competition itself can be reproduced at an arbitrary later date. This means using URL's that are active indefinitely, recording all aspects of the competition protocol (including important details that may have been conveyed only via emails during the competition), and making sure the evaluation measures are both reproducible and replicable; as we have noted, these are two fundamentally different concepts. Full written reports should be included both in the conference proceedings and also on the competition website.
- Assurance of the reproducibility of an entry in the competition should be a requirement for participation. Brief one-paragraph descriptions written in general terms are not enough, nor is the release of course code by itself necessarily sufficient. Presumably competitions come toward the end of a line of research, so there should already be publications to assure authors receive proper credit for their work; secrecy and proprietary interests have no place in competitions conduced in an open research community.
- Public data should be used for competitions whenever possible. In any case, the precise data that is used, both the raw inputs and the associated ground truth, should be carefully recorded and documented. Long-lived URL's or DOI's and/or the use of public repositories should be encouraged. If the actual data cannot be made public due to usage restrictions, then sufficient meta-data should be provided that someone without privileged access to the actual data can still fully understand the nature of the competition, including the target population, the set of inputs chosen from it, and the manner in which the selection was made (i.e., which of the possible inputs were included, which were excluded, and why).
- The public release of source code is admittedly problematic when there is a desire to protect intellectual property rights. Moreover, as Raff has noted, access to source code by itself does not make a work reproducible. Competitions that do not require the public release of source code should demand a complete written description of the method sufficient to make it independently reproducible. When source code is released, a separate review should be performed to confirm that the method can still be reproduced in the event the code cannot be run for whatever reason (i.e., assuring that the code is self-documenting, or that there is a separately published paper that describes the method in sufficient detail).
- Conference organizers (competition chairs) should enforce strong documentation requirements, both as a first step toward approval and also as a final check before a competition's results are "accepted" for publication. If a competition falls short at any point in the process, it should be removed from the conference website and treated as a rejected paper is treated.

These suggestions are offered as feasible improvements; following them does not guarantee reproducibility. Nor do we suggest mandatory standards for every entry. There is no doubt, however, that better documentation enhances the value of competitions.

In this analysis we have ignored several important issues that can be problematic, including whether competitors should be allowed to run their own code (especially when methods are not reproducible), and the value in a "winner takes all" approach when differences between top-ranked entries may be slight and a simple resampling of the test data could easily change the results. Organizers should carefully consider these questions and justify their answers to the community.

It is also important to step back from time-to-time and try to answer the question "why?" Reproducibility is a mantra in the laboratory sciences, but more difficult in the social sciences. Strains of white mice are far more homogenous than samples of students, shoppers, or voters. Information sciences occupy an intermediate position in this spectrum. Control groups of mice or cultures of bacteria are relatively easy to prepare, but control groups for most interesting pattern recognition problems are not.

For example, in the field of document analysis we do not yet have methods of collecting random samples of documents that are representative of any significant population. Yet reproducibility depends critically on a test set "similar in all relevant aspects" to the data used in the competition (and, in some competitions, also on the training and validation sets). What would this even mean? Has any publicly available dataset been claimed to be comparable to the now-famous UW-1 or MNIST datasets? What is a random sample of historical documents, or even of 17th Century English literature? *Naked Statistics* by Whelan lists a dozen subtle yet well-known possible sources of biased samples and inappropriate metrics [8].

Nor is reproducibility important for every entry in a competition when there is knowledge to be gained purely through participating. Why discourage a pair of students with a clever idea from trying their luck against large teams of professional researchers? The million-dollar Netflix Prize was won by just such a team, but the thousands of participants in the contest undoubtedly learned valuable lessons along the way.

Competitions at ICDAR extend back at least as early as 2001 [9], and as least as early as 2000 at ICPR [10]. ICDAR 2021 promises to offer three "long-term" competitions and 10 "short-term" competitions [11]. The former is described as "open for a longer time period and address challenges which could continue over the next years." Best practices are evolving, albeit slowly. It would benefit all in the community if the same degree of rigor now applied to research paper submissions was carried over to proposed competitions and their implementation.

We expect topics like these will remain an ongoing, productive discussion within the pattern recognition research community, as reflected by the RRPR workshop.

Acknowledgements. We thank the reviewers for their carefully considered feedback and helpful comments, many of which we have included in the present version of this paper.

References

1. National Academies of Sciences, Engineering, and Medicine: Reproducibility and Replicability in Science. The National Academies Press, Washington, DC (2019). https://doi.org/10.17226/25303
2. Third Workshop on Reproducible Research in Pattern Recognition (RRPR 2020). Reproducible Label. https://rrpr2020.sciencesconf.org/resource/page/id/5. Accessed 16 Oct 2020
3. Raff, E.: A step toward quantifying independently reproducible machine learning research. In: Proceedings of the 33rd Conference on Neural Information Processing Systems (NeurIPS), pp. 5,485–5,495. Curran Associates, Inc., Vancouver (2019). https://papers.nips.cc/paper/8787-a-step-toward-quantifying-independently-reproducible-machine-learning-research. Accessed 16 Oct 2020

4. Berger, E.D., et al.: ACM SIGPLAN Empirical Evaluation Guidelines (2018). https://www.sigplan.org/Resources/EmpiricalEvaluation/. Accessed 13 Oct 2020

5. Ralph, P., et al.: ACM SIGSOFT Empirical Standards (2020). https://github.com/acmsigsoft/EmpiricalStandards. Accessed 1 Nov 2020

6. Bonneel, N., et al.: Code replicability in computer graphics. ACM Trans. Graph. **39**, 4. https://replicability.graphics/. (Proceedings of SIGGRAPH 2020)

7. Klees, G., et al.: Evaluating fuzz testing. In: Proceedings of the 2018 ACM SIGSAC Conference on Computer and Communications Security, Association for Computing Machinery (2018). https://dl.acm.org/doi/proceedings/10.1145/3243734. Accessed 1 Nov 2020

8. Wheelan, C.: Naked Statistics. W. W. Norton & Company, New York/London (2013)

9. Competitions, University of Salford Manchester. https://www.primaresearch.org/competitions. Accessed 17 Jan 2021

10. Aksoy, S., et al.: Algorithm performance contest. In: Proceedings of the 15th International Conference on Pattern Recognition, vol. 4, pp. 4870–4876, September 2020

11. ICDAR 2021 Competitions. https://icdar2021.org/competitions/. Accessed 17 Jan 2021

torchdistill: A Modular, Configuration-Driven Framework for Knowledge Distillation

Yoshitomo Matsubara(✉) ⓘ

University of California, Irvine, CA 92697, USA
yoshitom@uci.edu

Abstract. While knowledge distillation (transfer) has been attracting attentions from the research community, the recent development in the fields has heightened the need for reproducible studies and highly generalized frameworks to lower barriers to such high-quality, reproducible deep learning research. Several researchers voluntarily published frameworks used in their knowledge distillation studies to help other interested researchers reproduce their original work. Such frameworks, however, are usually neither well generalized nor maintained, thus researchers are still required to write a lot of code to refactor/build on the frameworks for introducing new methods, models, datasets and designing experiments. In this paper, we present our developed open-source framework built on PyTorch and dedicated for knowledge distillation studies. The framework is designed to enable users to design experiments by declarative PyYAML configuration files, and helps researchers complete the recently proposed ML Code Completeness Checklist. Using the developed framework, we demonstrate its various efficient training strategies, and implement a variety of knowledge distillation methods. We also reproduce some of their original experimental results on the ImageNet and COCO datasets presented at major machine learning conferences such as ICLR, NeurIPS, CVPR and ECCV, including recent state-of-the-art methods. All the source code, configurations, log files and trained model weights are publicly available at https://github.com/yoshitomo-matsubara/torchdistill.

Keywords: Knowledge distillation · Open source framework · Reproducibility

1 Introduction

Deep learning methods have been achieving state-of-the-art performances, contributing to the rapid development of applications for a variety of tasks such as image classification [11,23,41,43] and object detection [4,10,35]. One of the critical problems with such state-of-the-art models is their complexity, thus the complex models are difficult to be deployed for real-world applications. In general, there is a trade-off between model complexity and inference performance (*e.g.,*

© Springer Nature Switzerland AG 2021
B. Kerautret et al. (Eds.): RRPR 2021, LNCS 12636, pp. 24–44, 2021.
https://doi.org/10.1007/978-3-030-76423-4_3

Table 1. Knowledge distillation frameworks. **torchdistill** supports modules in PyTorch and torchvision such as loss, datasets and models. ImageNet: ILSVRC 2012 [37], YT Faces: YouTube Faces DB [47], MIT Scenes: Indoor Scenes dataset [32], CUB-2011: Caltech-UCSD Birds-200-2011 [45], Cars: Cars dataset [18], SOP: Stanford Online Products [27]. P: Pretrained models, M: Module abstraction, D: Distributed training.

Framework	Supported datasets	Models	P	M	D
Zagoruyko & Komodakis [52]	CIFAR-10, ImageNet	Hard-coded	✓		
Passalis & Tefas [29]	CIFAR-10, YT Faces	Hard-coded			
Heo *et al.* [12]	CIFAR-10, MIT scenes	Hard-coded	✓		
Park *et al.* [28]	Cars, CUB-2011, SOP	Hard-coded			
Tian *et al.* [42]	CIFAR-100	Hard-coded	✓		
Yuan *et al.* [51]	CIFAR-10, -100, Tiny ImageNet	Hard-coded	✓		
Xu *et al.* [49]	CIFAR-100	Hard-coded	✓		
torchdistill	torchvision*	torchvision*	✓	✓	✓

* **torchdistill** supports those implemented with PyTorch. In this paper, our focus is on torchvision.

measured as accuracy), and there are three different types of method to make models deployable: 1) designing lightweight models, 2) model compression/pruning, and 3) knowledge distillation. Lightweight models such as MobileNet [14,38], MnasNet [40] and YOLO series [33,34] often sacrifice inference performance to reduce inference time, compared to complex models *e.g.*, ResNet [11] and Mask R-CNN [10]. Model compression and pruning [9,21] techniques reduce model size by quantizing parameters and pruning redundant neurons, and such methods are covered by Distiller [54], an open-source library for model compression.

In this paper, our focus is on the last category, knowledge distillation, that trains a simpler (student) model to mimic the behavior of a powerful (teacher) model. Knowledge distillation [13] stems from the study by Buciluă *et al.* [3], that presents a method to compress large, complex ensembles into smaller models with small loss in inference performance. Interestingly, Ba and Caruana [2] report that student models trained to mimic the behavior of the teacher models (*soft-label*) significantly outperform those trained on the original (*hard-label*) dataset. Following these studies, knowledge distillation and transfer have been attracting attention from the research communities such as computer vision [36] and natural language processing [39].

As summarized in Table 1, some researchers voluntarily publish their knowledge distillation frameworks *e.g.*, [12,28,29,42,49,52] to help other researchers reproduce their original studies. However, such frameworks are usually not either well generalized or maintained to be built on. Besides, Distiller [54] supports only one method for knowledge distillation, and Catalyst [17] is a framework built on PyTorch with a focus on reproducibility of deep learning research. To support various deep learning methods, these frameworks are well generalized, yet require users to *hardcode* (reimplement) critical modules such as models and datasets, even if the implementations are publicly available in popular libraries, to design complex knowledge distillation experiments. As pointed out by Gardner *et al.* [6], reference methods and models are often re-implemented from scratch, and this makes it difficult to reproduce the reported results. For further advancing the deep learning research, a new generalized framework is therefore needed, and the framework should be able to allow researchers to easily try different modules (*e.g.*, models, datasets, loss configurations), implement various approaches, and take care of reproducibility of their work.

The concept of our framework, **torchdistill**,[1] is highly inspired by AllenNLP [6], a platform built on PyTorch [30] for research on deep learning methods in natural language processing. Similar to AllenNLP, **torchdistill** supports the following features:

- module abstractions that enable researchers to write higher-level code for experiments *e.g.*, model, dataset, optimizer and loss;
- declarative PyYAML configuration files, which can be seen as high-level summaries of experiments (training and evaluation), enable to use anchors and aliases in the file to refer to the same object (*e.g.*, file paths) and simplify themselves, and make it easy to change the abstracted components and hyper-parameters; and
- generalized reference code and configurations to apply knowledge distillation methods to PyTorch and torchvision models pretrained on well-known complex benchmark datasets: ImageNet (ILSVRC 2012) [37] and COCO 2017 [22].

Furthermore, **torchdistill** supports 1) seamless multi-stage training, 2) caching teacher's outputs, and 3) redesigning (pruning) teacher and student models without hard-coding (reimplementation). To the best of our knowledge, this is the first, highly generalized open-source framework that can support a variety of knowledge distillation methods, and lower barriers to high-quality, reproducible deep learning research [8]. Researchers can explore methods and shape new approaches, building on this generalized framework that makes it easy not only to customize existing methods and models, but also introduce completely new ones. Using some of our reimplemented methods, we also reproduce the experimental results on ILSVRC 2012 and COCO 2017 datasets reported in the original studies.

2   Framework Design

Our developed framework, **torchdistill**, is an open source framework dedicated for knowledge distillation studies, built on PyTorch [30]. For vision tasks such as image classification and object detection, the framework is designed to support torchvision, that offers a lot of options for datasets, model architectures and common image transformations. The collection of supported reference models and datasets in our framework are dependent on the version of user's installed

---

[1] https://github.com/yoshitomo-matsubara/torchdistill

torchvision. For instance, when users find new models in the latest torchvision, they can shortly try the models simply by updating the torchvision and configuration files for their experiments with our framework.

2.1   Module Abstractions

An objective of module abstractions in our framework is to enable researchers to experiment with various modules by simply changing a PyYAML configuration file described in Sect. 2.3. We focus abstraction on critical modules to experiment, specifically model architectures, datasets, transforms, and losses to be minimized during training. These modules are often hard-coded (See Appendix A) in authors' published frameworks [12,28,29,42,49,52], and many of the hyperparameters are hard-coded as well.

Model Architectures: torchvision offers various model families for vision tasks from AlexNet [20] to R-CNNs [10,35], and many of them are pretrained on large benchmark datasets. Specifically, the latest release (v0.8.2) provides about 30 image classification models pretrained on ImageNet (ILSVRC 2012) [37] and 4 object detection models pretrained on COCO 2017 [22]. As our framework supports torchvision for vision tasks, researchers can use such pretrained models as teacher and/or baseline models (*e.g.*, student trained without teacher). In addition to the pretrained models available in torchvision, they can use their own pretrained model weights and any model architectures implemented with PyTorch. Moreover, **torchdistill** supports PyTorch Hub[2] and enable users to import modules via the hub by specifying repository names in a PyYAML configuration file.

Datasets: As described above, torchvision also supports a variety of datasets, and previous studies [1,12,16,24,28,29,31,36,42,44,46,50,52] use many of them to validate proposed distillation techniques such as ImageNet [37], COCO [22], CIFAR-10 and -100 [19], and Caltech101 [5]. Similar to model architectures, **torchdistill** supports such datasets and can collaborate with any datasets implemented with PyTorch.

Transforms: In vision tasks, there are de facto standard image transform techniques. Taking image classification on the ImageNet dataset as an example, a standard transform pipeline for training with torchvision[3] consists of 1) making a crop of random size of the original size and with a random aspect ratio of the original aspect ratio, 2) horizontal reflection with 50% chance for data augmentation to reduce a risk of overfitting [20], 3) PIL-to-Tensor conversion, and 4) channel-wise normalization using (0.485, 0.456, 0.406) and (0.229, 0.224, 0.225) as means and standard deviations, respectively. In **torchdistill**, users can define their own transform pipeline in a configuration file.

---

[2] https://pytorch.org/hub/.

[3] https://github.com/pytorch/vision/blob/master/references/classification/train.py.

Losses: In distillation process, student models are trained using outputs from teacher models, and the research community has been proposing a lot of unique losses with/without task-specific losses such as cross entropy loss for classification tasks. PyTorch [30] supports various loss classes/functions, and simple distillation losses can be defined in a configuration file by combining such supported losses using **torchdistill**'s customizable loss module (See Sect. 2.6).

2.2 Registry

The registry is an important component in **torchdistill** as abstracted modules are instantiated by mapping strings in the configuration file to the objects in code. Furthermore, it would make it easy for users to collaborate their implemented modules/functions with this framework. Similar to AllenNLP [6] and Catalyst [17], this can be done even outside the framework by using a Python decorator. The following example shows that a new model class, *MyModel*, is added to the framework by simply using *@register_model* (defined in the framework), and the new class can be instantiated by defining "MyModel" with required parameters at designated places in a configuration file.

```
@register_model
class MyModel(nn.Module):
    def __init__(self, *args, **kwargs):
        super().__init__()
        self.conv1 = nn.Conv2d(**kwargs['conv1_kwargs'])
        ...
```

2.3 Configurations

An experiment can be defined by a PyYAML configuration file (See Appendix B), that allows users to tune hyperparameters, and change methods/models without hard-coding. With PyYAML's features, configuration files allow users to leverage anchors and aliases, and these features would be helpful to simplify the configurations in cases that users would like to reuse parameters defined in the configuration file such as root directory path for datasets, parameters and model names as part of checkpoint file paths for better data management. In a configuration file, there are three main components to be defined: datasets, teacher and student models, and training. Each of the key components is defined by using abstracted and registered modules described in Sects. 2.1 and 2.2. A configuration file gives users a summary of the experiment, and shows all the parameters to reproduce the experimental results except implicit factors such as hardware specifications used for the experiment.

The following example illustrates how to define a global teacher model declared in a PyYAML configuration file. As described in the previous sections, various types of modules are abstracted in our framework, and such modules (classes and functions) in user's installed torchvision are registered. In this example, 'resnet34' function[4] is used to instantiate an object of type *ResNet* by using

---

[4] https://pytorch.org/docs/stable/torchvision/models.html#torchvision.models.resnet34.

a dictionary of keyword arguments (***params*). *i.e. num_classess* = 1000 and *pretrained* = True are given as arguments of 'resnet34' function. For image classification models implemented in torchvision or those users add to the registry in our framework, users can easily try different models by changing 'resnet34' *e.g.*, 'densenet201' [15], 'mnasnet1_0' [40]. Besides that, *ckpt* indicates the file path of checkpoint, that is './resnet34.pt' in the example defined by leveraging some of YAML features: anchors (&) and aliases (*). For teacher model, the checkpoint will be used to initialize the model with user's own model weights if the checkpoint file exists. Otherwise, 'resnet34' in this example will be initialized with torchvision's pretrained weights for ILSVRC 2012.

```
teacher_model:
    name: &teacher 'resnet34'
    params:
        num_classes: 1000
        pretrained: True
    ckpt: !join ['./', *teacher, '.pt']
```

Furthermore, **torchdistill** offers an option to generate log files that monitor the experiments. For instance, a log file presents what parameters were used, when executed, the trends of training behavior (*e.g.*, training loss, learning rate and validation accuracy) at a frequency set in the configuration file, and evaluation results.

These configuration and log files[5] will also help the researchers complete *ML Code Completeness Checklist*,[6] that was recently proposed to facilitate reproducibility in the research community as part of the official code submission process at major machine learning conferences *e.g.*, NeurIPS, ICML and CVPR.

2.4   Dataset Wrappers

To support a wide variety of knowledge distillation methods, dataset is an important module to be generalized. Usually, the dataset module in PyTorch and torchvision returns a pair of input batch (*e.g.*, collated image tensors) and targets (ground-truth) at each iteration, but some of the existing knowledge distillation approaches require additional information for the batch. For instance, contrastive representation distillation (CRD) [42] requires an efficient strategy to retrieve a large number of negative samples in the training session, that requires the dataset module to return an additional object (*e.g.*, negative sample indices). To support such extensions, we design dataset wrappers to return input batch, targets, and a supplementary dictionary, that can be empty when not used. For the above case, the additional object can be stored in the supplementary dictionary, and used when computing the contrastive loss. This design also enables us to support caching teacher model's outputs against data indices in the original dataset so that teacher's inference can be skipped by caching (serializing) outputs of the teacher model given a data index at the first epoch, and reading and collating the cached outputs given batch of data indices at the following epochs.

---

[5] Available at https://github.com/yoshitomo-matsubara/torchdistill/tree/master/configs/.

[6] https://github.com/paperswithcode/releasing-research-code.

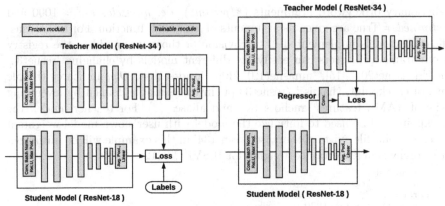

(a) Knowledge distillation [13] using ResNet-34 and ResNet-18 as teacher and student models, respectively.

(b) Hint-training with an auxiliary module (convolutional regressor) as stage 1 of FitNet method [36]. Its stage 2 is knowledge distillation as illustrated in Figure 1a.

Fig. 1. Knowledge distillation and FitNet methods. Yellow and blue modules indicate that their parameters are frozen and trainable, respectively (Color figure online).

Table 2. Epoch-level training speed improvement by **caching teacher's outputs** at the 1st epoch, using ResNet-18 as student model for knowledge distillation [13].

Teacher	ResNet-34	ResNet-50	ResNet-101	ResNet-152
No cache	801 sec	1,030 sec	1,348 sec	1,944 sec
Cache (1st)	859 sec	1,079 sec	1,402 sec	1,966 sec
Cache (2nd)	**651 sec**	**649 sec**	**656 sec**	**917 sec**

To demonstrate that caching improves training efficiency, we perform an experiment with knowledge distillation [13] illustrated in Fig. 1a that caches outputs of the teacher model at the first epoch for training ResNet-18 (student) on ILSVRC 2012 dataset, and skips the teacher model's inference by loading and feeding the outputs cached on disk to the loss module. Table 2 suggests that spending an extra one-minute at the 1st epoch to serialize teacher's outputs, the caching strategy makes the following training process (*i.e.* from the 2nd epoch) approximately 1.23 – 2.11 times faster at epoch-level when using 3 NVIDIA GeForce RTX 2080 Ti's with batch size of 256. Also, this improvement becomes more significant when using a larger teacher model such as ResNet-152 (approximately 2.11 times faster than training without cache). The ILSVRC 2012 training dataset consists of approximately 1.3 million images, and the cached files consumes only 10GB whereas the original training dataset uses about 140GB. Note that caching may not improve the training efficiency if teacher's outputs to be cached are much larger *e.g.*, hint-based training [36] requires intermediate

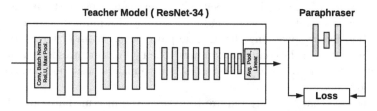

(a) 1st stage: training *paraphraser* for teacher model.

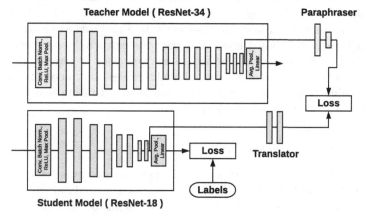

(b) 2nd stage: training student model and *translator*, using labels and outputs of *paraphraser*'s middle layer.

Fig. 2. Factor transfer with two auxiliary modules.

outputs from teacher and student models. Also, this mode should be turned off when applying data augmentation strategies.

2.5 Teacher and Student Models

Teacher-Student pairs are keys in knowledge distillation experiments, and recently proposed approaches [1,12,31,36,42,49,50,52,53] introduce auxiliary modules, which are used only in training session. Such auxiliary modules use tensors from intermediate layers in models, and introducing the modules to the models often results in branching their feedforward path as shown in Figs. 1 and 2. This paradigm, however, is also one of the backgrounds that researchers decide to hard-code the models (*e.g.*, modify the original implementations of models in torchvision every time they change the placement of auxiliary modules for preliminary experiments) to introduce such auxiliary modules used for their proposed methods, and make it difficult for other researchers to build on the published frameworks [12,28,29,42,49,52].

Taking an advantage of forward hook paradigm in PyTorch [30], **torchdistill** supports introducing such auxiliary modules without altering the original implementations of the models. Specifically, users can register the framework's provided *forward hooks* to specific modules to store its input and/or output in a I/O dictionary by specifying the module paths (*e.g.*, "conv1" for a MyModel object in Sect. 2.2) in the configuration files. The I/O dictionaries for teacher and student models will be fed to a generalized, customizable loss module described in Sect. 2.6.

For methods that not only require to extract the intermediate outputs (See Fig. 1) but also feed the extracted outputs to trainable auxiliary modules in different branches to be processed (See Fig. 2b), we define a *special* module in the framework, that is designed to have a *post-forward* function. In Fig. 1, for instance, the framework first executes ResNet-18 and extracts intermediate output by a registered forward hook, and then the extracted output stored in the student's I/O dictionary will be fed to the regressor as part of the *post-forward* process. The concept of the special module gives users more flexibility in designing training methods while leaving the original implementations of models (ResNet-34 and ResNet-18 in Fig. 2) unaltered.

2.6   Customizable Loss Module

Leveraging the I/O dictionaries that contain input/output of specific modules with registered forward hooks, **torchdistill** provides a generalized customizable loss module that allows users to easily combine different loss modules with balancing factors by configuration files such as those in Fig. 2b. Given a pair of input x and ground-truth y, the I/O dictionaries consist of a set of keys J and the values z_j^S and z_j^T ($j \in J$) extracted from student and teacher models respectively. Using the I/O dictionaries and the ground-truth, the generalized loss is defined as

$$\mathcal{L} = \sum_{j \in J} \lambda_j \cdot \mathcal{L}_j(z_j^S, z_j^T, y), \tag{1}$$

where λ_j is a balancing weight (hyperparameter) for $\mathcal{L}_j$, which is either a loss module implemented in PyTorch [30] or user's defined loss module in registry.

For instance, the loss function to train student model on ILSVRC 2015 dataset [37] at the 2nd stage of factor transfer (Fig. 2b) can be defined as:

$$\mathcal{L} = \lambda_{cls} \cdot \mathcal{L}_{cls}(z_{cls}^S, z_{cls}^T, y) + \lambda_{FT} \cdot \mathcal{L}_{FT}(z_{FT}^S, z_{FT}^T, y) \tag{2}$$

$$\mathcal{L}_{cls}(z_{cls}^S, z_{cls}^T, y) = \text{CrossEntropyLoss}(z_{cls}^S, y)$$

$$\mathcal{L}_{FT}(z_{FT}^S, z_{FT}^T, y) = \left\| \frac{z_{FT}^S}{\|z_{FT}^S\|_2} - \frac{z_{FT}^T}{\|z_{FT}^T\|_2} \right\|_p,$$

where $\lambda_{cls} = 1$, $\lambda_{FT} = 1,000$ and $p = 1$, following [16].

2.7   Stage-wise Training Configuration

In the previous sections, we describe the main features of **torchdistill**, and what modules are configurable in the framework. We emphasize that all the training configurations described above can be defined stage-wisely.

Seamless Multi-stage Training Configurations: Specifically, the framework is designed to enable users to configure critical components such as 1) number of epochs, 2) training and validation datasets, 3) teacher and student models, 4) modules (layers) to be trained/frozen, 5) optimizer, 6) learning rate scheduler, 7) loss module. These components can be re-defined at each of training stages, otherwise the framework reuses those from the previous stage. Notice that these training configurations can be declared in a configuration file, and this design enables to support not only two-stage training strategies [12,16,36,50], but also more complicated distillation methods such as teacher assistant knowledge distillation (TAKD) [26], that trains TAs to fill the gap between student and teacher models. Transfer learning also can be supported by changing models and datasets from stage to stage, and users would execute code with a configuration file only once. Therefore, they will not need to execute code multiple times to perform multi-stage training, including transfer learning.

Redesigning Models for Efficient Training: Furthermore, our framework gives users an option to redesign teacher and student models at each stage by specifying the required modules in a configuration file. Specifically, users are allowed to rebuild models by reusing modules in the models optionally with auxiliary modules. Figure 1 shows an example that modules after the 8th and the 5th blocks of the teacher and student models respectively can be pruned as the outputs of the modules are not used in the hint-training (1st stage), thus not required to be executed. In this specific case, the redesigned student model will consist of the trainable (blue) modules and a regressor (auxiliary module) as illustrated in Fig. 3, and the teacher and student architectures at the 2nd stage will be reverted to the original ones (Fig. 1a) with parameters learnt at the 1st stage. Also, the redesigned teacher/student model can be an empty module to save execution time. In Fig. 2a, for instance, there is no need to feed input batch to the student model (thus, can be empty) as at the 1st stage of factor transfer, only the teacher model is executed to train the paraphraser.

As introduced in Sect. 2.4, when the teacher's outputs are cacheable (*e.g.*, in terms of available disk space), teacher's inference can be skipped by loading the cache files produced at previous epoch. Redesigning models help users shorten training sessions even when teacher's outputs are not cacheable. Note that student model's outputs, however, cannot be cached as the model's parameters are updated every iteration. Table 3 suggests that redesigning models using only modules to be executed for training would be an effective approach to saving training time, and this improvement would be more critical for training models on large datasets and/or with a lot of epochs. We emphasize that users can redesign (minimize) the models by specifying the required modules in a configuration file rather than hardcode (reimplement) the pruned models.

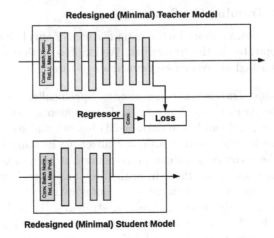

Fig. 3. Hint-training with teacher and student models pruned simply by specifying required modules in a configuration file for further efficient training, compared to a naive configuration in Fig. 1.

3   Reference Methods

Here, we describe the reimplementations of knowledge distillation methods and experiments to reproduce the reported results on ImageNet and COCO datasets.

Table 3. Epoch-level training speed improvement by **redesigning teacher and student (ResNet-18) models** with required modules only for hint-training shown in Fig. 3.

Teacher	ResNet-34	ResNet-50	ResNet-101	ResNet-152
Original	934 sec	1,175 sec	1,468 sec	1,779 sec
Minimal	**786 sec**	**929 sec**	**936 sec**	**1,022 sec**

3.1   Reimplementations

Given that the pretrained models in torchvision are trained on large benchmark datasets, ImageNet (ILSVRC 2012) [37], and COCO 2017 [22], we focus our implementations on these datasets as the pretrained models can be used as teacher models and/or baseline student models (naively trained on human-annotated datasets). Note that some of the methods are not validated on these datasets in their original work.

Table 4 shows a brief summary of reference distillation methods reimplemented with **torchdistill**, and indicates what additional modules were implemented and added to the registry for reimplementing the methods. We emphasize that methods without any check marks ($\checkmark$) in the *Required additional modules* columns such as KD, AT, PKT, RKD, HND, SPKD, Tf-KD, GHND and L_2 can be reimplemented simply by adding the new loss modules to the registry in the framework (Sect. 2.2).

Different from the existing frameworks [12,28,29,42,49,52], all the methods in Table 4 are reimplemented independently from models in torchvision so that users can easily switch models by specifying a model name and its parameters in a configuration file. Taking image classification as an example, the shapes of inputs and (intermediate) outputs for the models are often fixed (*e.g.*, $3 \times 224 \times 224$ and 1,000 respectively, for models trained on ImageNet dataset), that makes it easy to match the shape of student's output with that of teacher when computing loss values to be minimized.

3.2   Reproducing ImageNet Experiments

In this section, we attempt to reproduce some experimental results with their proposed distillation methods. In particular, we choose the attention transfer (AT), factor transfer (FT) [16], contrastive representation distillation (CRD) [42], teacher-free knowledge distillation (Tf-KD) [51], self-supervised knowledge distillation (SSKD) [49], L_2 and prime-aware adaptive distillation (PAD-L_2) methods [53] for the following reasons:

– these methods are validated with the ImageNet datasets for ResNet-34 and ResNet-18 as teacher and student models in their original work;[7]
– the hyperparameters used in the ImageNet experiments are described in the original studies and/or their published source code; and
– we did not have time to tune hyperparameters for other methods that are not validated on the ImageNet dataset in their original papers.

In addition to the methods, we apply knowledge distillation (KD) [13] to the same teacher-student pair. Note that except KD[8], we reuse the hyperparameters (*e.g.*, number of epochs) for ImageNet given in their original work to reproduce their experimental results, and we provide the configuration and log files, and trained model weights (See footnote 5).

We also should note that Zagoruyko and Komodakis [52] propose attention transfer (AT), and define the following total loss function for their ImageNet experiment:

$$\mathcal{L}_{AT} = \mathcal{L}(\mathrm{W}_S, x) + \frac{\beta}{2} \sum_{j \in \mathcal{I}} \left\| \frac{Q_S^j}{\left\| Q_S^j \right\|_2} - \frac{Q_T^j}{\left\| Q_T^j \right\|_2} \right\|_p, \tag{3}$$

---

[7] The teacher model for Tf-KD is the pretrained ResNet-18 [51].
[8] For KD, we set hyperparameters as follows: temperature $T = 1$ and relative weight $\alpha = 0.5$.

Table 4. Reference knowledge distillation methods implemented in **torchdistill**.

Methods	Multi-stage training	Required additional modules		
		Auxiliary	Special	Custom dataset
KD [13]				
FitNet [36]	✓	✓		
FSP [50]	✓	✓		
AT [52]				
PKT [29]				
FT [16]	✓	✓	✓	
DAB [12]	✓	✓	✓	
RKD [28]				
VID [1]		✓	✓	
CCKD [31]		✓	✓	
HND [24]				
SPKD [44]				
CRD [42]		✓	✓	✓
Tf-KD [51]				
GHND [25]				
SSKD [49]	✓	✓	✓	✓
L_2 [53]				
PAD-L_2 [53]	✓	✓	✓	

where $\mathcal{L}(W_S, x)$ is a standard cross entropy loss, and Q_S^j and Q_T^j denote the vectorized forms of the j-th pair of student and teacher attention maps, respectively (Refer to their work [52] for more details). In their published framework[9], they set β and p to 1,000 and 2 respectively. However, we find a discrepancy between their defined loss function (Eq. (3)) and their implemented loss function (Eq. (4)), that computes mean squared error (MSE) between the teacher and student attention maps.

$$\mathcal{L}_{AT} = \mathcal{L}(W_S, x) + \frac{\beta}{2} \sum_{j \in \mathcal{I}} MSE\left(\frac{Q_S^j}{\left\| Q_S^j \right\|_2}, \frac{Q_T^j}{\left\| Q_T^j \right\|_2} \right) \tag{4}$$

In our preliminary experiment with hyperparameters the authors provide, the student model did not train well with the loss module based on Eq. (3). For this reason, we used Eq. (4) instead for AT in our experiments.

Table 5 summarizes the results of the experiments with the training configurations (*e.g.*, teacher-student pair, hyperparameters) described in each of the original studies and/or verified by the authors. In addition to experiments with a single GPU, we perform experiments with a distributed training strategy supported by PyTorch (reported with a dagger mark †) to demonstrate that our framework supports the strategy for saving training time. As for the L_2 and

---

[9] https://github.com/szagoruyko/attention-transfer.

Table 5. Validation accuracy of ResNet-18 (student) trained on ILSVRC 2012 dataset with ResNet-34 (teacher), using eight different distillation methods. With the hyperparameters (*e.g.*, # Epochs) either described in the original work or given by the authors, all the reimplemented methods outperform the student model trained without teacher.

	Accuracy[%]		# Epochs	Training time
	Top-1	Diff.		
Teacher: ResNet-34	73.31	+3.56	N/A	N/A
Student: ResNet-18	69.75	0.00	N/A	N/A
KD	71.23	+1.48	100	60 hr 04 min
KD †	71.37	+1.62	100	23 hr 07 min
AT	70.90	+1.15	100	59 hr 07 min
AT †	70.55	+0.80	100	23 hr 11 min
FT	71.56	+1.81	91	55 hr 06 min
FT †	71.13	+1.38	91	22 hr 15 min
CRD	70.81	+1.06	100	356 hr 31 min
CRD ‡	70.93	+1.18	100	179 hr 12 min
Tf-KD	70.52	+0.77	90	46 hr 34 min
Tf-KD †	70.21	+0.46	90	18 hr 50 min
SSKD ‡	70.09	+0.34	130	113 hr 12 min
L_2 ‡	71.08	+1.33	90	21 hr 25 min
PAD-L_2 ‡	71.71	+1.96	(90 +) 30	28 hr 34 min

† Distributed training on 3 GPUs with linear scaling rule [7]: Learning rates are modified according to the number of distributed training processes. (*i.e.* multiplied by the number of GPUs).

‡ Distributed training on 3 GPUs with total batch size used in original work.

PAD-L_2 methods, the original study [53] uses batch size of 512 for their ImageNet experiments, which did not fit in our single GPU. Thus, we split the batch size into 171 per GPU, and report only the results with the distributed training (marked with ‡). The same strategy is applied to SSKD (total batch size of 256 and 768 for normal and augmented samples, respectively [49]) as it takes at least 4 times as long at epoch-level to train a model, compared to the other methods due to their 4x augmented training data, and our batch size per GPU is 85 (for normal samples + 255 for augmented samples). Similarly, we apply the same strategy for CRD due to the limited time. We also note that Zhang *et al.* [53] applied their proposed PAD-L_2 to the student model trained with their proposed L_2 as a pretrained model, and train the student model with the PAD-L_2 method for 30 more epochs (*i.e.*, 120 epochs).[10]

Based on the methods we reimplemented with **torchdistill**, we successfully reproduce the results on the ILSVRC 2012 dataset for the teacher-student pair

---

[10] The configuration is not described in [53], but verified by the authors.

reported in the original papers of AT [52], Tf-KD [51], L_2 and PAD-L_2 [53] methods, and the result of PAD-L_2 was recently reported as the state-of-the-art performance for the teacher-student pair on the ILSVRC 2012 dataset [53]. All the results outperform the baseline performance (S: ResNet-18) which is trained with human-labels only, and the pretrained model is provided by torchvision. Note that FT was validated on ILSVRC 2015 dataset in their original work [16], and we confirm the FT's improvement over a baseline using ILSVRC 2012 dataset as the teacher model (ResNet-34) in torchvision is pretrained on the dataset. The result with the reimplemented CRD is almost comparable to the accuracy reported in the original study [42]. In CRD, both positive and negative samples are leveraged for learning representations, thus turns out to be the most-time consuming method in Table 5. The reimplemented SSKD outperforms the baseline model although the accuracy does not match the reported result [49]. A potential factor may be a different training configuration forced by our limited computing resource (*e.g.*, different batch size per GPU whereas 8 parallel GPUs were used in their work) since we simply refactored and made the authors' published code compatible with the ILSVRC 2012 dataset. As pointed out by Tian *et al.* [42], KD [13] is still a powerful method. Our reimplemented KD outperformed their proposed state-of-the-art method, CRD (71.17%), and achieved the comparable accuracy with their CRD+KD (71.38%) method.

3.3 Reproducing COCO Experiments

To demonstrate that our framework can 1) be applied to different tasks, and 2) collaborate with model architectures that are not implemented in torchvision, we apply the generalized head network distillation (GHND) to bottleneck-injected R-CNN object detectors for split computing [25], using COCO 2017 dataset. Their proposed bottleneck-injected Faster and Mask R-CNNs with ResNet-50 and FPN are designed to be partitioned into head and tail models which will be deployed on mobile device and edge server respectively, for reducing inference speed in resource-constrained edge computing systems. Following the original work on GHND, we apply the method to a pair of the original and bottleneck-injected Faster R-CNNs as teacher and student respectively, and conduct the same experiment for Mask R-CNN as well. As shown in Table 6, the reproduced mean average precision (mAP) match those reported in the original study [25].

Table 6. Validation mAP of bottleneck-injected R-CNN models for split computing (student) trained on COCO 2017 dataset by GHND with original Faster/Mask R-CNN models (teacher). Reproduced results match those reported in the original work [25].

Backbone: ResNet-50 and FPN	mAP		# Epochs	Training time
	BBox	Mask		
Faster R-CNN w/ Bottleneck	0.359	N/A	20	24 hr 13 min
Mask R-CNN w/ Bottleneck	0.369	0.336	20	24 hr 21 min

4   Conclusions

In this work, we presented **torchdistill**, an open-source framework dedicated for knowledge distillation studies, that supports efficient training and configurations systems designed to give users a summary of the experiments. Researchers can build on the framework (*e.g.*, by forking the repository) to conduct their knowledge distillation studies, and their studies can be integrated to the framework by sending a pull request. This will help the research community ensure the reproducibility of the work, and advance the deep learning research while supporting fair method comparison on benchmarks. Specifically, researchers can publish the log, configuration, and pretrained model weights for their champion performance, that will help them ensure the champion performance for specific datasets and teacher-student pairs.

Furthermore, the configuration files for and log files produced by **torchdistill** will help researchers complete the *ML Code Completeness Checklist* (See footnote 6), and we provide the full configurations (hyperparameters), log files and checkpoints including model weights for experimental results shown in Tables 5 and 6 in our code repository (See footnote 1). We provide reference code and configurations for image classification and object detection tasks, and plan to extend our framework for different tasks using popular packages *e.g.*, Transformers [48] for NLP tasks. Our framework will be maintained and updated along with the new releases of PyTorch and torchvision so that users can save time for coding and use it as a standard framework for reproducible knowledge distillation studies.

Acknowledgments. We thank the anonymous reviewers for their comments and the authors of related studies for publishing their code and answering our inquiries about their experimental configurations. We also thank Sameer Singh for feedback about naming the framework.

A   Hard-Coded Module and Forward Hook Configurations

For lowering barriers to high-quality knowledge distillation studies, it would be important to enable users to collaborate with models implemented in popular libraries such as torchvision. However, all the models in the existing frameworks described in this study are reimplemented to extract intermediate representations in addition to the models' final outputs. Figure 4 shows an example of original and hard-coded (reimplemented) forward functions in ResNet model for knowledge distillation experiments. As illustrated in the hard-coded example, the authors [42, 49] unpacked an existing implementation of ResNet model and re-designed interfaces of some modules to extract additional representations (*i.e.*, "f0", "f1_pre", "f2", "f2_pre", "f3", "f3_pre", and "f4").

Furthermore, the modified interfaces also require those in the downstream processes to be modified accordingly, that will need extra coding cost. We emphasize that users are required to repeat this procedure every time they introduce

```
def _forward_impl(self, x):              def forward(self, x, is_feat=False, preact=False):
    x = self.conv1(x)                        x = self.conv1(x)
    x = self.bn1(x)                          x = self.bn1(x)
    x = self.relu(x)                         x = self.relu(x)
                                             f0 = x
    x = self.layer1(x)
    x = self.layer2(x)                       x, f1_pre = self.layer1(x)
    x = self.layer3(x)                       f1 = x
                                             x, f2_pre = self.layer2(x)
    x = self.avgpool(x)                      f2 = x
    x = torch.flatten(x, 1)                  x, f3_pre = self.layer3(x)
    x = self.fc(x)                           f3 = x

    return x                                 x = self.avgpool(x)
                                             x = x.view(x.size(0), −1)
def forward(self, x):                        f4 = x
    return self._forward_impl(x)             x = self.fc(x)

                                             if is_feat:
                                                 if preact:
                                                     return [f0, f1_pre, f2_pre, f3_pre, f4], x
                                                 else:
                                                     return [f0, f1, f2, f3, f4], x
                                             else:
                                                 return x
```

Fig. 4. Forward functions in **original** (left, torchvision-style) and **hard-coded** (right, [42, 49]) implementations of ResNet. Only "x" from "self.fc" is used for vanilla training and prediction.

new models for experiments, and the same issues will be found when introducing new schemes implemented as other types of module (*e.g.*, dataset and sampler) required by specific methods such as CRD [42] and SSKD [49]. Using a forward hook manager in our framework, we can extract intermediate representations from the original models (*e.g.*, Fig. 4 (left)) without reimplementation like Fig. 4 (right), and help users introduce such schemes with wrappers of the module types so that they can apply the schemes simply by specifying in a configuration file used to design an experiment.

The following example illustrates how to specify the input to or output from modules we would like to extract from ResNet model whose forward function is shown in Fig. 4 (left). "f0", "f1_pre", "f2_pre", and "f3_pre" in Fig. 4 (right) correspond to the output from the first ReLU module "relu", and preactivation representations in "layer1", "layer2", and "layer3" modules, which are the inputs to their last ReLU modules (*i.e.*, "layer1.1.relu", "layer2.1.relu", and "layer3.1.relu"). "f4" is the flatten output from average pooling module "avgpool". Similarly, we can define a forward hook manager for teacher model, and reuse the module paths such as "layer1.1.relu" to define loss functions in the configuration file.

```
student:
  ...
  forward_hook:
    input: ['layer1.1.relu', 'layer2.1.relu', 'layer3.1.relu', 'fc']
    output: ['relu']
```

B   Example PyYAML Configuration

Figure 5 shows an example PyYAML configuration file (See footnote 5) to instantiate abstracted modules for an experiment with knowledge distillation by Hinton *et al.* [13].

```
datasets:
  ilsvrc2012:
    name: &dataset_name 'ilsvrc2012'
    type: 'ImageFolder'
    root: &root_dir !join ['~/dataset/', *dataset_name]
    splits:
      train:
        dataset_id: &imagenet_train !join [*dataset_name, '/train']
        params:
          root: !join [*root_dir, '/train']
          transform_params:
            - type: 'RandomResizedCrop'
              params:
                size: &input_size [224, 224]
            - type: 'RandomHorizontalFlip'
              params:
                p: 0.5
            - &totensor
              type: 'ToTensor'
              params:
            - &normalize
              type: 'Normalize'
              params:
                mean: [0.485, 0.456, 0.406]
                std: [0.229, 0.224, 0.225]
      val:
        dataset_id: &imagenet_val !join [*dataset_name, '/val']
        params:
          root: !join [*root_dir, '/val']
          transform_params:
            - type: 'Resize'
              params:
                size: 256
            - type: 'CenterCrop'
              params:
                size: *input_size
            - *totensor
            - *normalize

models:
  teacher_model:
    name: 'resnet34'
    params:
      num_classes: 1000
      pretrained: True
    ckpt: '/path/to/your_own_checkpoint_if_you_have'
  student_model:
    name: 'resnet18'
    params:
      num_classes: 1000
      pretrained: False
    ckpt: './imagenet/kd/ilsvrc2012-resnet18_from_resnet34.pt'
```

```
train:
  log_freq: 1000
  num_epochs: 100
  train_data_loader:
    dataset_id: *imagenet_train
    random_sample: True
    batch_size: 256
    num_workers: 16
    cache_output:
  val_data_loader:
    dataset_id: *imagenet_val
    random_sample: False
    batch_size: 128
    num_workers: 16
  teacher:
    sequential: []
    wrapper: 'DistributedDataParallel'
    requires_grad: False
  student:
    sequential: []
    wrapper: 'DistributedDataParallel'
    requires_grad: True
    frozen_modules: []
  apex:
    requires: False
    opt_level: 'O1'
  optimizer:
    type: 'SGD'
    params:
      lr: 0.1
      momentum: 0.9
      weight_decay: 0.0001
  scheduler:
    type: 'MultiStepLR'
    params:
      milestones: [30, 60, 90]
      gamma: 0.1
  criterion:
    type: 'GeneralizedCustomLoss'
    org_term:
      criterion:
        type: 'KDLoss'
        params:
          temperature: 1.0
          alpha: 0.5
          reduction: 'batchmean'
      factor: 1.0
    sub_terms:

test:
  test_data_loader:
    dataset_id: *imagenet_val
    random_sample: False
    batch_size: 1
    num_workers: 16
```

Fig. 5. First (left) and second (right) halves of an example PyYAML configuration to design a knowledge distillation experiment with hyperparameters using **torchdistill**.

References

1. Ahn, S., Hu, S.X., Damianou, A., Lawrence, N.D., Dai, Z.: Variational information distillation for knowledge transfer. In: Proceedings of the IEEE Conference on Computer Vision and Pattern Recognition, pp. 9163–9171 (2019)
2. Ba, J., Caruana, R.: Do deep nets really need to be deep? In: Advances in Neural Information Processing Systems, pp. 2654–2662 (2014)
3. Buciluă, C., Caruana, R., Niculescu-Mizil, A.: Model compression. In: Proceedings of the 12th ACM SIGKDD International Conference on Knowledge Discovery and Data Mining, pp. 535–541 (2006)
4. Carion, N., Massa, F., Synnaeve, G., Usunier, N., Kirillov, A., Zagoruyko, S.: End-to-end object detection with transformers. In: Vedaldi, A., Bischof, H., Brox, T., Frahm, J.M. (eds.) ECCV 2020, vol. 12346. LNCS. Springer, Heidelberg (2020). https://doi.org/10.1007/978-3-030-58452-8_13
5. Fei-Fei, L., Fergus, R., Perona, P.: One-shot learning of object categories. IEEE Trans. Pattern Anal. Mach. Intell. **28**(4), 594–611 (2006)
6. Gardner, M., et al.: AllenNLP: a deep semantic natural language processing platform. ACL **2018**, 1 (2018)
7. Goyal, P., et al.: Accurate, large minibatch SGD: Training imagenet in 1 hour. arXiv preprint arXiv:1706.02677 (2017)
8. Gundersen, O.E., Kjensmo, S.: State of the art: reproducibility in artificial intelligence. In: Proceedings of the AAAI Conference on Artificial Intelligence, vol. 32 (2018)
9. Han, S., Mao, H., Dally, W.J.: Deep compression: Compressing deep neural networks with pruning, trained quantization and Huffman coding. In: Fourth International Conference on Learning Representations (2016)
10. He, K., Gkioxari, G., Dollár, P., Girshick, R.: Mask R-CNN. In: Proceedings of the IEEE International Conference on Computer Vision, pp. 2961–2969 (2017)
11. He, K., Zhang, X., Ren, S., Sun, J.: Deep residual learning for image recognition. In: Proceedings of the IEEE Conference on Computer Vision and Pattern Recognition, pp. 770–778 (2016)
12. Heo, B., Lee, M., Yun, S., Choi, J.Y.: Knowledge transfer via distillation of activation boundaries formed by hidden neurons. In: Proceedings of the AAAI Conference on Artificial Intelligence, vol. 33, pp. 3779–3787 (2019)
13. Hinton, G., Vinyals, O., Dean, J.: Distilling the knowledge in a neural network. In: Deep Learning and Representation Learning Workshop: NIPS 2014 (2014)
14. Howard, A., et al.: Searching for MobileNetV3. In: Proceedings of the IEEE International Conference on Computer Vision, pp. 1314–1324 (2019)
15. Huang, G., Liu, Z., Van Der Maaten, L., Weinberger, K.Q.: Densely connected convolutional networks. In: Proceedings of the IEEE Conference on Computer Vision and Pattern Recognition, pp. 4700–4708 (2017)
16. Kim, J., Park, S., Kwak, N.: Paraphrasing complex network: network compression via factor transfer. In: Advances in Neural Information Processing Systems, pp. 2760–2769 (2018)
17. Kolesnikov, S.: Accelerated DL R&D (2018). https://github.com/catalyst-team/catalyst. Accessed 28 Sept 2020
18. Krause, J., Stark, M., Deng, J., Fei-Fei, L.: 3D object representations for fine-grained categorization. In: Proceedings of the IEEE International Conference on Computer Vision Workshops, pp. 554–561 (2013)
19. Krizhevsky, A.: Learning multiple layers of features from tiny images (2009)

20. Krizhevsky, A., Sutskever, I., Hinton, G.E.: Imagenet classification with deep convolutional neural networks. In: Advances in Neural Information Processing Systems, pp. 1097–1105 (2012)
21. Li, H., Kadav, A., Durdanovic, I., Samet, H., Graf, H.P.: Pruning filters for efficient convnets. In: Fourth International Conference on Learning Representations (2016)
22. Lin, T.Y., et al.: Microsoft COCO: common objects in context. In: Fleet, D., Pajdla, T., Schiele, B., Tuytelaars, T. (eds.) ECCV 2014. LNCS, vol. 8693, pp. 740–755. Springer, Cham (2014). https://doi.org/10.1007/978-3-319-10602-1_48
23. Mahajan, D., et al.: Exploring the limits of weakly supervised pretraining. In: Ferrari, V., Hebert, M., Sminchisescu, C., Weiss, Y. (eds.) ECCV 2018. Exploring the limits of weakly supervised pretraining, vol. 11206, pp. 185–201. Springer, Cham (2018). https://doi.org/10.1007/978-3-030-01216-8_12
24. Matsubara, Y., Baidya, S., Callegaro, D., Levorato, M., Singh, S.: Distilled split deep neural networks for edge-assisted real-time systems. In: Proceedings of the 2019 Workshop on Hot Topics in Video Analytics and Intelligent Edges, pp. 21–26 (2019)
25. Matsubara, Y., Levorato, M.: Neural Compression and Filtering for Edge-assisted Real-time Object Detection in Challenged Networks. arXiv preprint arXiv:2007.15818 (2020)
26. Mirzadeh, S.I., Farajtabar, M., Li, A., Ghasemzadeh, H.: Improved knowledge distillation via teacher assistant. In: Proceedings of the AAAI Conference on Artificial Intelligence, pp. 5191–5198 (2020)
27. Oh Song, H., Xiang, Y., Jegelka, S., Savarese, S.: Deep metric learning via lifted structured feature embedding. In: Proceedings of the IEEE Conference on Computer Vision and Pattern Recognition, pp. 4004–4012 (2016)
28. Park, W., Kim, D., Lu, Y., Cho, M.: Relational knowledge distillation. In: Proceedings of the IEEE Conference on Computer Vision and Pattern Recognition, pp. 3967–3976 (2019)
29. Passalis, N., Tefas, A.: Learning deep representations with probabilistic knowledge transfer. In: Ferrari, V., Hebert, M., Sminchisescu, C., Weiss, Y. (eds.) ECCV 2018. LNCS, vol. 11215, pp. 283–299. Springer, Cham (2018). https://doi.org/10.1007/978-3-030-01252-6_17
30. Paszke, A., et al.: PyTorch: an imperative style, high-performance deep learning library. In: Advances in Neural Information Processing Systems, pp. 8024–8035 (2019)
31. Peng, B., et al.: Correlation congruence for knowledge distillation. In: Proceedings of the IEEE International Conference on Computer Vision, pp. 5007–5016 (2019)
32. Quattoni, A., Torralba, A.: Recognizing indoor scenes. In: 2009 IEEE Conference on Computer Vision and Pattern Recognition, pp. 413–420. IEEE (2009)
33. Redmon, J., Farhadi, A.: YOLO9000: better, faster, stronger. In: Proceedings of the IEEE Conference on Computer Vision and Pattern Recognition, pp. 7263–7271 (2017)
34. Redmon, J., Farhadi, A.: YOLOv3: An incremental improvement. arXiv preprint arXiv:1804.02767 (2018)
35. Ren, S., He, K., Girshick, R., Sun, J.: Faster R-CNN: towards real-time object detection with region proposal networks. In: Advances in Neural Information Processing Systems, pp. 91–99 (2015)
36. Romero, A., Ballas, N., Kahou, S.E., Chassang, A., Gatta, C., Bengio, Y.: FitNets: hints for thin deep nets. In: Third International Conference on Learning Representations (2015)

37. Russakovsky, O., et al.: ImageNet large scale visual recognition challenge. Int. J. Comput. Vis. **115**(3), 211–252 (2015)
38. Sandler, M., Howard, A., Zhu, M., Zhmoginov, A., Chen, L.C.: MobileNetV2: inverted residuals and linear bottlenecks. In: Proceedings of the IEEE Conference on Computer Vision and Pattern Recognition, pp. 4510–4520 (2018)
39. Sanh, V., Debut, L., Chaumond, J., Wolf, T.: Distilbert, a distilled version of BERT: smaller, faster, cheaper and lighter. In: The 5th Workshop on Energy Efficient Machine Learning and Cognitive Computing (2019)
40. Tan, M., et al.: Mnasnet: platform-aware neural architecture search for mobile. In: Proceedings of the IEEE Conference on Computer Vision and Pattern Recognition, pp. 2820–2828 (2019)
41. Tan, M., Le, Q.: EfficientNet: rethinking model scaling for convolutional neural networks. In: International Conference on Machine Learning, pp. 6105–6114 (2019)
42. Tian, Y., Krishnan, D., Isola, P.: Contrastive representation distillation. In: Eighth International Conference on Learning Representations (2020)
43. Touvron, H., Vedaldi, A., Douze, M., Jégou, H.: Fixing the train-test resolution discrepancy. In: Advances in Neural Information Processing Systems, pp. 8250–8260 (2019)
44. Tung, F., Mori, G.: Similarity-preserving knowledge distillation. In: Proceedings of the IEEE International Conference on Computer Vision, pp. 1365–1374 (2019)
45. Wah, C., Branson, S., Welinder, P., Perona, P., Belongie, S.: The Caltech-UCSD Birds-200-2011 Dataset (2011)
46. Wang, T., Yuan, L., Zhang, X., Feng, J.: Distilling object detectors with fine-grained feature imitation. In: Proceedings of the IEEE Conference on Computer Vision and Pattern Recognition, pp. 4933–4942 (2019)
47. Wolf, L., Hassner, T., Maoz, I.: Face recognition in unconstrained videos with matched background similarity. In: CVPR 2011, pp. 529–534. IEEE (2011)
48. Wolf, T., et al.: Transformers: state-of-the-art natural language processing. In: Proceedings of the 2020 Conference on Empirical Methods in Natural Language Processing: System Demonstrations, pp. 38–45 (2020)
49. Xu, G., Liu, Z., Li, X., Loy, C.C.: Knowledge distillation meets self-supervision. In: Vedaldi, A., Bischof, H., Brox, T., Frahm, J.-M. (eds.) ECCV 2020. LNCS, vol. 12354, pp. 588–604. Springer, Cham (2020). https://doi.org/10.1007/978-3-030-58545-7_34
50. Yim, J., Joo, D., Bae, J., Kim, J.: A gift from knowledge distillation: fast optimization, network minimization and transfer learning. In: Proceedings of the IEEE Conference on Computer Vision and Pattern Recognition, pp. 4133–4141 (2017)
51. Yuan, L., Tay, F.E., Li, G., Wang, T., Feng, J.: Revisiting knowledge distillation via label smoothing regularization. In: Proceedings of the IEEE/CVF Conference on Computer Vision and Pattern Recognition, pp. 3903–3911 (2020)
52. Zagoruyko, S., Komodakis, N.: Paying more attention to attention: improving the performance of convolutional neural networks via attention transfer. In: Fifth International Conference on Learning Representations (2017)
53. Zhang, Y., Lan, Z., Dai, Y., Zeng, F., Bai, Y., Chang, J., Wei, Y.: Prime-aware adaptive distillation. In: Vedaldi, A., Bischof, H., Brox, T., Frahm, J.-M. (eds.) ECCV 2020. LNCS, vol. 12364, pp. 658–674. Springer, Cham (2020). https://doi.org/10.1007/978-3-030-58529-7_39
54. Zmora, N., Jacob, G., Zlotnik, L., Elharar, B., Novik, G.: Neural Network Distiller: A Python Package for DNN Compression Research. arXiv preprint arXiv:1910.12232 (2019)

Reproducible Research Results

Spatio-Temporal Convolutional Autoencoders for Perimeter Intrusion Detection

Devashish Lohani[1,2]([✉]), Carlos Crispim-Junior[1], Quentin Barthélemy[2],
Sarah Bertrand[2], Lionel Robinault[1,2], and Laure Tougne[1]

[1] Univ Lyon, Lyon 2, LIRIS, 69676 Lyon, France
{devashish.lohani,carlos.crispim-junior,laure.tougne}@liris.cnrs.fr
[2] FOXSTREAM, Vaulx-En-Velin, France
{d.lohani,q.barthelemy,s.bertrand,l.robinault}@foxstream.fr

Abstract. In the video surveillance context, a perimeter intrusion detection system (PIDS) aims to detect the presence of an intrusion in a secured perimeter. Existing camera based approaches relies on hand crafted rules, image based classification and supervised learning. In a real world intrusion detection system, we need to learn spatio-temporal features unsupervisely (as annotated data are very difficult to obtain) and use these features to detect intrusions. To tackle this problem, we propose to use a 3D convolutional autoencoder. It is inspired from the DeepFall paper where they use it for an unsupervised fall detection task. In this paper, we reproduce their results on the fall detection task and further extend this model to detect intrusions in a perimeter intrusion dataset. We also provide an extended evaluation scheme which helps to draw essential insights from the results. Our results (The source code is available at https://gitlab.liris.cnrs.fr/dlohani/stcae_pids.) show that we correctly reproduce the results of fall detection task and furthermore our model shows competitive performance in perimeter intrusion detection task. To our knowledge, it is the first time when a PIDS is made in a fully unsupervised manner while jointly learning the spatio-temporal features from a video-stream.

Keywords: Perimeter intrusion detection · Spatio-temporal data · 3D convolutions · Convolutional autoencoder · Unsupervised learning

1 Introduction

High security installations may contain a large boundary with the need to be protected from unwanted elements entering in the boundary. A perimeter intrusion detection system (PIDS) is used to serve this purpose and it aims at detecting the presence of an intrusion in a secured perimeter. An intrusion can be defined as a moving object belonging to a category of items like human, car, truck, motorcycle, *etc.*, which is defined as unauthorized for a particular perimeter or area

© Springer Nature Switzerland AG 2021
B. Kerautret et al. (Eds.): RRPR 2021, LNCS 12636, pp. 47–65, 2021.
https://doi.org/10.1007/978-3-030-76423-4_4

at a given time. The same object might not be categorized as an intruder if it is outside the perimeter or if it is being allowed at a different time, *e.g.* moving cars or people that are outside the boundary are not intruders. Similarly, intrusion objects like people/cars might be allowed to move in an area around daytime for example but unauthorized for the rest of the day, hence the importance of temporality. Stationary objects, even if belonging to an unauthorized category should not be classified as an intrusion, *e.g.* cars parked inside the perimeter must not be detected as an intrusion while a moving car entering or leaving the perimeter must be classified as an intrusion. So, we can understand how difficult is to detect intrusion as it is a rare event which is both time and space dependent and further the definition of an intrusion varies according to the installation to protect and cannot be generalized.

There exists PIDS with various highly sensitive sensors like microwave sensors, electric field sensors, active infrared sensors, *etc.*, to detect changes at different wavelengths to detect intrusions [8]. However, these PIDS produce a large number of false alarms and cannot differentiate between intrusion and other objects and thus requires a lot of human resources [7].

In order to overcome the disadvantages of these sensor based PIDS, many camera based PIDS have been proposed [10,14,16,20]. A set of cameras are assigned with user-defined field-of-view of the area to be surveyed and activity is monitored by intrusion detection algorithms. These algorithms detect the movements of an intruder attempting to breach a security wall or region and alert security. The key problem with video analytics based solution is false alarm [14] which is due to inherent complications of understanding of the object detected in the video especially if the object is far from the camera. The object may appear very small in the image that makes recognition of the object more difficult. Existing PIDS algorithms detect intrusion in a supervised manner by annotating small set of intrusion classes [16,20], using hand crafted features [15,16], treating video stream as an image based data (loosing the spatio-temporal features) and thus employing image based object classification [10,20]. Thus, existing models do not learn the real nature of video, which is a spatio-temporal data. They rely on handcrafted features and treat intrusion detection as a supervised learning problem which is not generalizable in reality as intrusions occur rarely and therefore, we cannot have a large annotated database. Furthermore, we cannot train on few object classes as intrusion classes can practically be very high in number.

To learn the spatio-temporal data unsupervisely from a video stream and then detect intrusion, we propose to use a 3D convolutional autoencoder model. The model is inspired from the work of Nogas *et al.* [13] where they use it for an unsupervised fall detection problem [19]. In this paper, we reproduce their results and further extend their model to do perimeter intrusion detection in a challenging dataset. Our model detects intrusions such as moving car, people, motorcycle, truck, *etc.*, in a secure perimeter, after training in a fully unsupervised setting.

This paper is organized as follows. Section 2 presents some related works found in recent literature about camera based PIDS. Section 3 introduces the

3D convolutional autoencoder with different architectures that we tested. It also details the training and evaluation. Section 4 presents the datasets used for both tasks. Section 5 presents the results and discussion. It provides the reproduced results for fall detection task with a new evaluation scheme which provides some key insights. This section also shows competitive results on the intrusion detection task. Finally, Sect. 6 reports the general conclusions drawn, and suggests future research directions.

2   Related Work

Intelligent video surveillance is a well-established commercial technology that allows the users to monitor and secure areas with the security cameras. It uses computer vision algorithms to detect moving objects in an image and filter non-relevant movements. A Gaussian mixture model for RGB background modeling is proposed in [15], allowing to detect moving objects using background subtraction. A surveillance system is introduced in [16], using closed-circuit television (CCTV) to detect and classify vehicles. They applied real-time vehicle detection and classification algorithms. Object detection is performed with a background subtraction method where the background is modeled by using a Gaussian mixture model. In order to classify the detected vehicles, a method combining histogram of oriented gradients and artificial neural networks (ANN) was used. However, both these works extract features using hand-crafted methods and more importantly they tackle object detection/classification/tracking in open areas where there is no concept of a perimeter and thus no intrusion detection.

An on-line intrusion event detection system is proposed in [20], using a model for training an event detection system based on object tracking. They modeled the training as a multiple instance learning problem, which allowed to train the classifier from annotated events despite temporal ambiguities. But their model uses many handcrafted features and further they try to model intrusion detection with supervised learning, while in reality it is an unsupervised learning problem due to the lack of annotated data as intrusions occur rarely.

Recently, an intelligent intrusion detection system with detection, classification, tracking, and action recognition of an intruder is introduced [10]. They proposed an integrated acquisition device combining optical and thermal cameras, a virtual fence to set the boundary between surveillance and external areas in a graphical user interface, a background model designed to detect moving objects and a convolutional neural network (CNN) to classify moving objects as either intruders or wild animals. Their model also relies on the fact that we have annotated data.

All the above models learn spatial and temporal features of a video stream independent of each other. They treat video frames as still images and learn spatial features, then they treat the temporal succession of spatial features. Overall, none of the existing PIDS learns spatio-temporal features from a video jointly and furthermore, they try to solve perimeter intrusion detection with a supervised learning approach.

Our work draws inspiration from the DeepFall paper [13]. This work is focused on detecting human falls from a video stream in an unsupervised manner (without any annotated data). They formulate the fall detection problem as an anomaly detection problem. They present a novel use of deep spatio-temporal convolutional autoencoders to learn spatial and temporal features from normal activities during training, i.e., they first learn "what is normal". Then during testing, they detect the events which have a high reconstruction error, that is to say the falls. They also present a new anomaly scoring method that combines the reconstruction scores of frames across video sequences to detect falls. Furthermore, they show superior results in comparison to traditional autoencoder and convolutional autoencoder methods to identify falls.

In this work, we reproduce the results of the DeepFall paper [13] and draw key insights from them. We further tackle the problem of intrusion detection as an anomaly detection problem. We train a spatio-temporal convolutional autoencoder to understand "what is not an intrusion" and detect intrusions in testing videos by marking frames with high reconstruction error.

3   3D Convolutional Autoencoders

While 2D-CNN learns appropriate representations for image classification, detection and segmentation tasks [11], they are incapable of capturing the temporal information encoded in consecutive frames for video analysis problems [23]. One widely used solution to this is to add convolutional long short-term memory (ConvLSTM) [17] layers on top of 2D-CNN layers [3]. However, these approaches make the implicit hypothesis that spatial and temporal dimensions are independent and can be processed sequentially, missing the existing correlations between these dimensions.

A 3D kernel can be used to extract both spatial and temporal features from a video by convolving it with the volume formed by stacking temporally contiguous frames of the video [1]. This 3D convolution operation captures spatio-temporal information encoded in the video as information from these contiguous frames is cohesively used to form feature maps [9]. 3D-CNN is better suited for spatio-temporal feature learning than 2D-CNN [18] and it has been also used in the form of an autoencoder [21,23]. Such a 3D autoencoder learns representations that are locally invariant to spatio-temporal deformations of the video encoded by the 3D convolutional feature maps. It is sometimes referred as deep spatio-temporal convolutional autoencoder (DSTCAE) [13].

The idea is to learn the regular/normal visual information from video sequences. The intuition is that the trained autoencoder is able to reconstruct the motion features presented in regular videos with low error but unable to accurately reconstruct motions in irregular videos. In other words, the autoencoder can model the complex distribution of the regular dynamics of appearance changes.

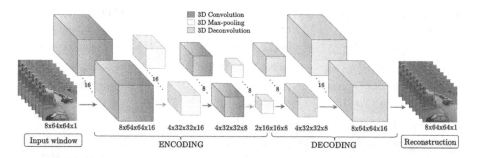

8x64x64x1   8x64x64x16   4x32x32x16   4x32x32x8   2x16x16x8   4x32x32x8   8x64x64x16   8x64x64x1

Input window   ENCODING   DECODING   Reconstruction

Fig. 1. Network architecture of DSTCAE-Deconvolution. The encoder is composed of layers with 3D convolution (red) followed by 3D max-pooling (yellow) and decoder is composed of 3D deconvolution (blue) layers. Each layer has dimensions: time window length × height × width × number of feature maps.

3.1 Input Window Construction

A 3D convolutional autoencoder takes a volume formed by stacking temporally contiguous frames of the video as input and reconstructs it. We refer to these volumes as windows and generate them by applying a temporal sliding window to video frames.

For a video with V frames, window length T, no padding and stride B (in temporal axis), the number of windows (D) generated [13] is given by:

$$D = \left\lfloor \frac{V - T}{B} \right\rfloor + 1. \tag{1}$$

These windows are fed into the network as follows. For an input video, we select first T frames and feed this window to the network. Then we shift by B frames temporally and select next T frames and so on until we cover all the V video frames.

3.2 Architecture Design

We evaluate three variants of the model. In Fig. 1, we illustrate the overall network outline with deconvolution model. Input video is fed as windows to the network where it is encoded by 3D convolution [9] and 3D max-pooling and decoded with a deconvolution operation [5] to obtain the reconstructed window. Encoding and decoding for the three models are illustrated in Fig. 2 and described in detail below.

Encoder: We set the window length $T = 8$, stride $B = 1$ in Eq. (1), resize input video frames to 64×64 and use grayscale image with 1 channel, thus the shape of input hyper-cuboid is 8×64×64×1. This input is encoded with a series of 3D convolution and 3D max-pooling layers. 3D convolutions operate with kernel of 5×3×3, 1×1×1 stride and same padding. The max-pooling layers have

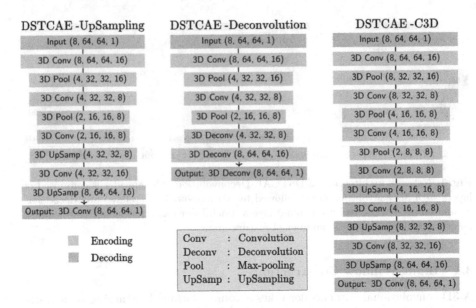

Fig. 2. Encoding and decoding configurations of DSTCAE-UpSampling, DSTCAE-Deconvolution and DSTCAE-C3D networks.

stride and kernel dimensions of $2 \times 2 \times 2$ with same padding. This signify that each max-pooling layer reduce all input dimensions (time window length, height and width) by a factor of 2. Figure 2 shows specifications of encoding and decoding for the three models.

Decoder: We can decode either via upsampling or deconvolution. The upsampling method (DSTCAE-UpSampling) uses a 3D convolution with same parameters as in encoding, followed by a fixed upsampling operation to upscale the input. The upsampling operation uses upsampling factors of $2 \times 2 \times 2$, meaning matrix elements are repeated across each dimension such that the extent of all dimensions is doubled. The DSTCAE-Deconvolution architecture uses 3D deconvolutions [22] with kernel of $5 \times 3 \times 3$, $2 \times 2 \times 2$ stride and same padding [23]. Like upsampling, this results in doubling each dimension of the input. In both methods, the final reconstructed window has exactly the same dimensions as that of the input window.

Finally, the DSTCAE-C3D network is inspired by the work of Tran *et al.* [18], having the same encoding and decoding as DSTCAE-UpSampling, but with an extra 3D convolution + 3D max-pooling layer in encoding, and an extra 3D convolution + 3D upsampling layer in decoding (Fig. 2). These extra max-pooling and upsampling layers have $1 \times 2 \times 2$ kernel dimensions, meaning they result in only spatial dimension change. Thus, it allows to train a deeper network without collapsing the temporal dimension.

A dropout layer with dropout probability of 0.25 is applied after second layer in all three models. We use the ReLU activation function for all hidden layers and tanh activation function at the output layer to constrain the reconstructed pixel values in the range [-1, 1], in order to be comparable to the input. The total training parameters for UpSampling, Deconvolution and C3D models are 15,889, 15,889 and 21,665 respectively.

3.3 Training

All three variants of 3D convolutional autoencoder are trained[1] only on videos with normal behaviour, *i.e.* without any falls or intrusion. All the frames in the videos are resized to 64 × 64, and pixels are rescaled by dividing values by 255 to keep them in the range $[0, 1]$, and then subtracting the per-frame mean from each frame, resulting in pixel values to be in the range $[-1, 1]$.

The training loss of this network is the mean squared error, given by:

$$\mathcal{L}(\theta) = \frac{1}{N} \sum_{i=1}^{N} \|\text{flat}(I_i) - \text{flat}(O_i(\theta))\|_2^2, \tag{2}$$

where $I_i \in \mathbb{R}^{64 \times 64 \times T}$ is the ith window of the input batch of size N, $O_i \in \mathbb{R}^{64 \times 64 \times T}$ is the corresponding reconstructed output window, θ denotes the network parameters, flat(.) is the flattening operator, which flattens the input array into a one dimensional vector and $\| \cdot \|_2$ denotes the Euclidean norm.

The training batch size is set to $N = 32$ for all experiments, where each element I_i of the batch consists of a stack of $T = 8$ frames. The training is performed with Adadelta optimizer for 500 epochs. These parameters were chosen to reproduce the exact results for the fall detection task, and we found no significant reduction in loss after further training.

3.4 Detection of Abnormal Events

Since we train our models only on videos without anomalous events by minimizing the reconstruction error (RE), during testing phase the anomalous (falls or intrusions) frames generally have a higher reconstruction error. We use this reconstruction error for anomaly detection. Given a test video sequence, we apply a sliding window as described in Sect. 3.1. For the ith window I_i, the network outputs a reconstruction of this window O_i. The reconstruction error $r_{i,j}$ between the jth frame of I_i and O_i is calculated as:

$$r_{i,j} = \|\text{flat}(I_{i,j}) - \text{flat}(O_{i,j})\|_2^2. \tag{3}$$

Figure 3 (a) shows the sliding windows and associated reconstruction errors of frames. Since a single frame can be a part of upto $T = 8$ windows, therefore it can have different reconstruction error scores corresponding to each window.

---

[1] All experiments were done on NVIDIA GeForce GTX 1080, with 12 GB of RAM.

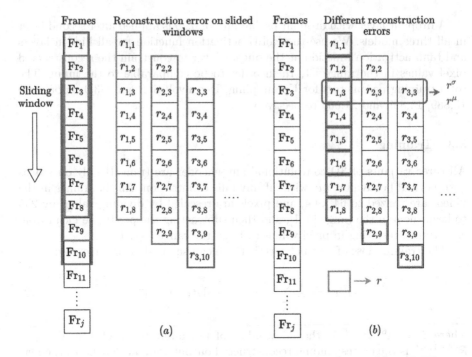

Fig. 3. Illustration of errors: sliding windows on video with j frames (a), and different reconstruction error scores per frame (b).

For example, the frame Fr_3 has three reconstruction errors $r_{1,3}$, $r_{2,3}$ and $r_{3,3}$, in reference to first, second and third window respectively. Since we focus on frame level evaluation, we need one single reconstruction error value for each frame. We propose two ways to obtain the per-frame reconstruction error scores, which are described below.

Reconstruction Error r: A simple way to obtain a per frame reconstruction error is to get the reconstruction error of a frame from the first window it appears in. Since we use a temporal sliding window with window length T and stride $B = 1$, this means that a frame can appear on a maximum of T windows. The reconstruction error r for video frames is obtained as follows. r scores for the first T frames are obtained from the first window, then we slide our window temporally by 1 frame ($B = 1$) and r for the $(T + 1)^{th}$ frame is obtained from the second window and we similarly obtain r scores for next N frames from next N windows.

In Fig. 3 (b), the reconstruction error r is marked with green color. We can observe that for the first 8 frames, r is taken from first window, then from 9th frame onwards, r is taken from last frame of each new window. For the jth frame with $m = \max(1, j - T + 1)$, we obtain r_j as:

$$r_j = r_{m,j}. \tag{4}$$

Cross-Window Reconstruction Errors r^μ and r^σ: Another way to obtain a per frame reconstruction error can be to evaluate the statistics of a frame from the different temporal windows it appears in. Since each window that a frame appears in provides a different temporal context within which this frame can be viewed, we need to consider all the reconstruction errors obtained for a frame across different windows [12].

For the jth frame of the ith window, an anomaly score can be computed based on the mean r_j^μ or standard deviation r_j^σ of the reconstruction errors across temporal contexts with window length T. With $k = \min(j, T)$, we obtain r_j^μ and r_j^σ as follows[2]:

$$
\begin{aligned}
r_j^\mu &= \tfrac{1}{k} \sum_{i=j-k+1}^{j} r_{i,j} \\
r_j^\sigma &= \sqrt{\tfrac{1}{k} \sum_{i=j-k+1}^{j} \left(r_{i,j} - r_j^\mu\right)^2}.
\end{aligned}
\tag{5}
$$

In Fig. 3 (b), the cross-window RE score calculation is depicted with red rectangle. Frame 3 appears in 1st, 2st and 3st window, therefore r_3^μ and r_3^σ are calculated using Eq. (5) with $r_{1,3}$, $r_{2,3}$ and $r_{3,3}$ respectively.

A high value of r_j^μ or r_j^σ means that the jth frame, when appearing at different positions in different windows, is reconstructed with a high average error. For a normal activity or non-intrusion case, the reconstruction error of a frame should not vary a lot with its position in subsequent windows and if it does, then this may indicate anomalous behaviour, such as a fall or an intrusion. Similarly, a high value of r_j for a frame may indicate anomalous behaviour.

3.5   Evaluation Metrics

To check whether these frame level reconstruction error scores are sufficiently high to raise an alarm, we need to choose a threshold. But by choosing a fixed threshold, our evaluation will be biased to this particular dataset and threshold choice. Thus, to be independent from a fixed threshold, we vary the threshold from lowest to highest value of the reconstruction error score and obtain a receiver operating characteristic (ROC) curve [6] and the precision-recall (PR) curve [4]. The area under the curve (AUC) is computed for the ROC and PR curves, *i.e.* AUROC and AUPR respectively with fall or intrusion as the class of interest and this is used as a performance indicator. Higher the value of AUROC or AUPR, better is our model at classifying between anomalous frames and normal activity frames. However, AUPR must be used in case of highly imbalanced classes in the dataset [2,4], that is the case of anomaly detection tasks where normal activity frames (*i.e.* true negatives) are over-represented in the dataset.

For each test video, the RE scores (r, r^μ or r^σ) obtained for each frame are used to calculate AUC of the ROC and PR curve. Following [13], a first metric called "AUROC per video" is computed on each test video, and the average and standard deviation across all test videos are reported. In this metric, the succession of thresholds to separate classes and to estimate the ROC curve is

---

[2] In this paper, r_j^μ and r_j^σ correspond to C_μ^j and C_σ^j defined in [13].

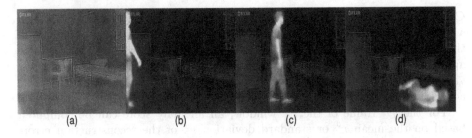

Fig. 4. Some frames drawn from Fall dataset [19]: non-fall frames, like an empty scene (a), a person entering (b), a person in the scene (c); and a fall frame (d).

not common to all test videos. Since the succession of thresholds is adapted to each test video, the ROC curve is in risk to be over-fitted, providing an overly optimistic AUROC score. Consequently, a second metric called "AUC all videos" is computed on ROC and PR curves, but on the whole test set with a threshold common to all test videos, which is the standard way to compute AUC [6]. Using this metric, we obtain AUROC and AUPR scores and they actually measure the generalization power of the detection models.

4 Datasets

Two datasets are used to train and test models: the first one for fall detection, and the second one, which is a private dataset, for perimeter intrusion detection.

4.1 Fall Dataset

This dataset is used for the fall detection task. In this task, we have a video camera which monitors the activity of a person in an area and the aim is to detect and alert as soon as a person falls. The problem here is quite similar to the intrusion detection as it is also an unsupervised task on a video stream [13]. We evaluate the model for detecting falls on the Thermal Fall Detection Activity Recognition dataset [19]. This dataset consists of videos captured by a FLIR ONE thermal camera mounted on an Android phone in a room setting with a single view with either 25 or 15 frames per second (FPS). The dataset contains a total of 44 videos. The training set has 9 videos without any fall event and the testing set contains 35 videos with fall events (828 fall frames out of 36,391 frames). The resolution of the thermal images is 640 × 480. Figure 4 shows some raw frames of the thermal dataset. We pre-process the dataset using Eq. (1) and obtain 22,053 windows to train the studied models.

4.2 Perimeter Intrusion Dataset

This private dataset consists of videos taken from a single thermal camera mounted at a fixed position with a single view in the outdoor uncontrolled setting. The videos are taken at 25 FPS with 400 × 296 frame size resolution and

Fig. 5. Some frames drawn from Perimeter Intrusion dataset without intrusion.

Fig. 6. Some frames drawn from Perimeter Intrusion dataset with intrusions, and intruders like persons or vehicles are labeled in red boxes. (Color figure online)

are then down-sampled at 5 FPS. These videos are intended to monitor the movement of any intruder designated object in the field of view of the camera. A total of 180 videos was collected with 80 videos for training containing only non-intrusion activities and 100 videos for testing. Out of these 100 test videos, 70 test videos contain intrusion and non-intrusion frames and 30 videos contain only non-intrusion frames. This 30% of only non-intrusion videos for testing is important in order to verify if the model is capable to distinguish between intrusion and non-intrusion activities. Each training video is converted into windows using Eq. (1) and we had a total of 47,998 windows for training.

The complexity of the dataset can be seen in Fig. 5 and 6 with some sample snapshots of the videos. Since video is taken outside, we have different daylight timing of the day/night and different weather conditions. Very often the strong wind wobbles the camera, or an electric wire in front of it and herbs nearby. The camera covers an intersection of the road with a long deep view of one road. Unlike the Fall dataset, here abnormality can be of any type like some person, a bike, car, truck, other vehicle or even a group of them. As discussed in the Introduction, an object belonging to an intruder class (like car, person, other vehicles) is considered an intrusion only if it shows movement in the monitored area, regardless of time of the day. They can come and go to any of the three entry/exit points of roads. Sometimes human intruder appears or disappears into the herbs seen on the right side of the video frames. Multiple intrusions are often present at some given instant. This makes intrusion detection very difficult. Furthermore, some cars are frequently parked and should not be detected as an intrusion. Since the camera captures a long view of one road, objects appear very small as they go far away, and their detection becomes even more complicated.

5   Results and Discussion

We evaluate the models on two different tasks, namely fall detection [19] and intrusion detection. With fall detection, we try to reproduce the results of the paper [13]. All three variants of 3D convolutional autoencoder were trained and tested on both tasks.

5.1   Reproducibility on the Fall Detection Task

The results of all three models are presented in Table 1. The training time is the total time taken in minutes to train a particular model with all the training set. Similarly, testing time is the total time taken to test all the test set with a particular model. In column "AUROC per video", we evaluate AUROC score for each test video separately and report average value with associated standard deviation (in brackets) for all the test videos in order to compare our reproduced results with the paper [13].

We can observe that we were able to reproduce the paper results correctly, some slight differences are possibly due to different model weight initialization. We can also observe that all three models perform equivalently well with r and

Table 1. Reproducibility of results of DeepFall [13] for different models with different reconstruction errors (RE) to evaluate: (i) computational times, (ii) AUROC per video, average +/- standard deviation across all videos of the test set, and (iii) AUC (ROC and PR) for all test videos.

Models	RE	Time		AUROC per video		AUC all videos	
		Training	Testing	[13]	Ours	ROC	PR
DSTCAE UpSampling	r^σ	309.52 min	49.88 s	0.96(0.03)	0.96(0.02)	0.96	**0.29**
	r^μ		48.61 s	0.95(0.04)	0.94(0.04)	0.88	0.23
	r		47.11 s	–	0.94(0.04)	0.89	0.24
DSTCAE Deconvolution	r^σ	311.01 min	56.31 s	0.96(0.02)	0.96(0.02)	0.96	**0.27**
	r^μ		55.94 s	0.94(0.04)	0.94(0.04)	0.88	0.23
	r		54.92 s	–	0.94(0.04)	0.89	0.21
DSTCAE C3D	r^σ	310.50 min	55.98 s	0.97(0.02)	0.96(0.03)	0.95	**0.25**
	r^μ		54.52 s	0.93(0.07)	0.90(0.07)	0.85	0.19
	r		54.23 s	–	0.91(0.06)	0.87	0.21

r^μ. Even though we do not observe a high difference in testing times for models with r, r^μ and r^σ but still models with r takes the least time. This is because calculating cross-window RE score induces latency in the system (need to wait for scores of next 7 frames to calculate score for current frame) while for r we can get the frame score at current window without any delay. In our experiments, C3D model did not outperform the other two models contrary to the claim in DeepFall [13]. We can observe that all models have similar performance for r^σ, however for r^μ and r, DSTCAE-UpSampling and DSTCAE-Deconvolution have performed slightly better than C3D model. The training time is observed as approximately the same for all models. UpSampling models are the fastest during testing and with the best performance.

To qualitatively understand the difference between ROC and PR curves computed on the whole test set, as explained in Sect. 3.5, Fig. 7 plots these two curves for the different models and RE scores. The ROC curve shows overall good performance for all the models, but we can remark that models with r^σ perform superior to others. However, all models have very poor performances in the PR curve, showing that the fall class is not well separated from the non-fall class.

In order to quantitatively assess these results, we can refer to the column "AUC all videos" of Table 1. The AUROC values show that the models with r^σ do not degrade their performance in comparison to AUROC per video, indicating that this RE score is able to capture inter-video variabilities well. The models with r^μ and r show an approximately 6% degradation in performance. But AUROC score is not preferred for a highly imbalanced dataset because ROC curves may provide an excessively optimistic view of the performance [2]. Instead, when dealing with highly skewed datasets, PR curves give a more informative picture of an algorithm's performance [4]. This is the case in fall detection because fall frames are rare in the videos, hence the fall test set has highly

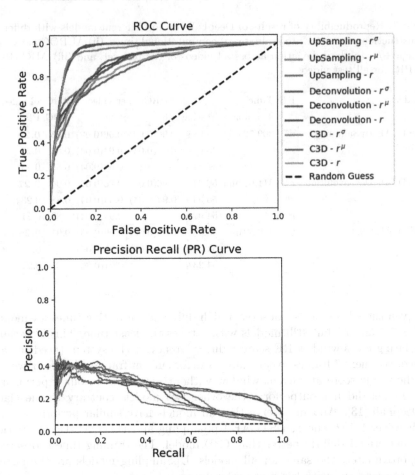

Fig. 7. ROC (top) and PR (bottom) curves (of type "all videos") for the fall detection task, for different models and RE scores.

imbalanced class proportion. In other words, AUPR is more sensitive to misclassification of fall classes. Contrary to the AUROC scores, we can observe that we have poor AUPR scores for all the models. This indicates that these models are not able to correctly detect falls in videos.

5.2 Application to the Perimeter Intrusion Detection Task

Figure 8 shows the evolution of reconstruction error r for a test video from Perimeter Intrusion dataset when tested with DSTCAE-UpSampling. The normal activity (no intrusion) has a low r score. When an intrusion enters the video, the r score starts increasing and reaches a peak when the intruder is closest to the camera. This r score decreases as the intrusion goes far away from the camera and gradually disappears. We can also observe that there are three peaks and they correspond to intrusion activities.

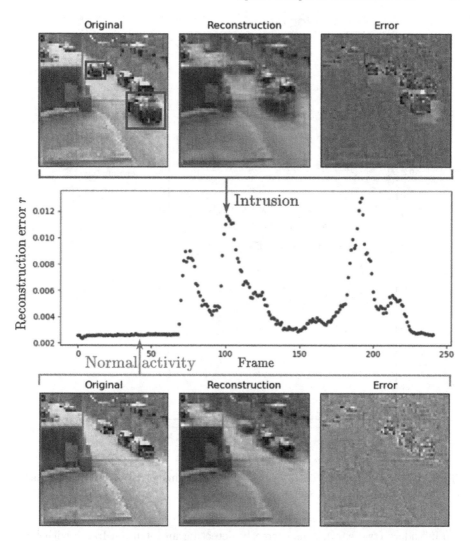

Fig. 8. Evolution of reconstruction error r for a test video from Perimeter Intrusion dataset. The original (64×64 resized), reconstructed and error frames are shown for an intrusion (top) and a normal activity (bottom). The three peaks correspond to intrusion activities with high r score.

The three images below the curve show the original frame at the point, its reconstructed frame, and the associated error map. We can observe that for normal activity, the error map correctly reveals no movement activity of the parked cars and thus no intrusion. In the images above the curve, we can see the image associated with a high reconstruction error score. We can observe that the reconstructed frame and error map shows the movement information of

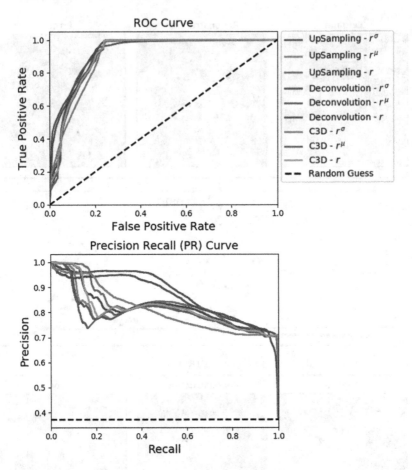

Fig. 9. ROC (top) and PR (bottom) curves for the perimeter intrusion detection task, for different models and RE scores.

two intruders (two cars), thus correctly detecting an intrusion frame with high reconstruction error score.

Figure 9 shows the ROC and PR curves for the perimeter intrusion detection task tested over all the videos of the test set, for different models and RE scores. We can observe that in ROC curve, it is difficult to assess which model has better performance. The PR curve however highlights the differences among models. We observe that UpSampling r^σ (in blue) and C3D r^σ (in pink) have similar ROC curves but their PR curves clearly show that UpSampling r^σ has better performance (larger area).

To quantitatively analyze these curves, AUC are listed in Table 2. We report the AUROC and AUPR scores over all the videos of the test set. We observe that the training and testing time is almost similar for all the models. Even though all models have approximately the same performance in terms of AUROC score, we

Table 2. Results on perimeter intrusion detection task for different models with different reconstruction errors (RE) to evaluate: (i) computational times, and (ii) AUC (ROC and PR) for all test videos of the Perimeter Intrusion dataset.

Models	RE	Time		AUC all videos	
		Training	Testing	ROC	PR
DSTCAE UpSampling	r^σ	590.25 min	55.19 s	0.93	**0.88**
	r^μ		52.05 s	0.91	0.81
	r		51.24 s	0.92	0.83
DSTCAE Deconvolution	r^σ	594.95 min	61.15 s	0.93	**0.86**
	r^μ		59.57 s	0.91	0.80
	r		58.55 s	0.91	0.82
DSTCAE C3D	r^σ	591.10 min	60.38 s	0.90	0.81
	r^μ		59.46 s	0.91	0.80
	r		57.98 s	0.91	0.82

observe that DSTCAE-UpSampling r^σ has highest performance of 0.88 in terms of AUPR score. Furthermore, it can be observed that upsampling models have lowest computational times. Unlike for Fall detection task, C3D models rank last among other evaluated models. Here, the gap between AUROC and AUPR scores is smaller than in the case of the fall detection (Table 1). This indicates that our models perform well regardless of the evaluation measure. The results without cross-window scores, *i.e.* with r models, are close to models with r^σ and r^μ. Furthermore, since the r score of the current frame is obtained only from the current window (inducing zero latency), it is compatible to be used in a real-time setting. Results indicate that the 3D convolutional autoencoder can successfully model intrusion events unsupervisedly.

5.3   Discussion

Since both perimeter intrusion detection and fall detection have highly imbalanced classes, thus AUPR is more suitable metric than AUROC. We observe that evaluated architectures have a better performance in perimeter intrusion detection as compared to fall detection in terms of AUPR scores. Furthermore, the gap between AUROC and AUPR scores is lower in intrusion detection in comparison to fall detection. This can be attributed to the fact that in intrusion detection we are trying to detect movement of an intruder in a designated space: the results show that the 3D convolutional autoencoder is able to capture any movement well with the 3D spatio-temporal convolutions. However, in fall detection, we have a more difficult problem: the model needs to detect a particular type of movement, *i.e.* fall of a person, but not the other movements like walking, running, gesticulating, *etc.*. As results demonstrate, the 3D convolutional autoencoder classifies the two classes with lower performances in this case.

In convolutional autoencoders, there are two methods to apply a deconvolution operation [5]: (i) a convolution (filtering step) followed by an upsampling (interpolation step), and (ii) a deconvolution, also called a transposed convolution, which learns the weights in a single step. Concerning 3D networks, there is no evidence about the best method to deconvoluate 3D data. On both tasks, the UpSampling based method seems to be faster along with better detection scores than the Deconvolution one, although these improvements are quite marginal.

6   Conclusion

In this paper, we evaluated different forms of a 3D convolutional autoencoder for two unsupervised tasks. We also provided an extended evaluation using the metric "AUROC/AUPR for all videos" which evaluates capability of a model to capture inter-video variabilities. On the task of reproducibility of fall detection, we successfully reproduced the results of the Deepfall paper. We conclude that models with r^σ as reconstruction error have highest performance both in terms of AUROC per video and AUC for all videos. We observe a degradation in performance of models with r and r^μ when evaluated for AUROC all videos. This shows that r^σ captures inter-video variabilities better than other two metrics. The high gap between AUROC and AUPR values shows the limitation of current models for the fall detection task.

We further evaluated these models for perimeter intrusion detection in a challenging thermal video dataset. We can conclude that we have approximately similar performance for all the models. The models with upsampling were the fastest during testing and provided best results with r^σ. We observe that we have a smaller gap between AUROC and AUPR scores as compared to the fall detection results. This shows that these models capture inter-video variabilities better for the task of perimeter intrusion detection. Our results indicate that the 3D convolutional autoencoder models intrusion detection very well. To our knowledge, it is the first time that intrusion detection was carried out in a completely automatic and unsupervised manner.

For future works on the intrusion detection task, robustness of the model on different lighting conditions, sudden changes of luminosity and very slow intruder displacement needs to be further examined. We will also explore ways on how to choose a fixed threshold for the RE score, in order to allow a practical implementation of this PIDS.

References

1. Baccouche, M., Mamalet, F., Wolf, C., Garcia, C., Baskurt, A.: Spatio-temporal convolutional sparse auto-encoder for sequence classification. In: BMVC, pp. 124.1–124.12 (2012)
2. Branco, P.O., Torgo, L., Ribeiro, R.P.: A survey of predictive modelling under imbalanced distributions. arXiv preprint arXiv:1505.01658 (2015)
3. Chong, Y.S., Tay, Y.H.: Abnormal event detection in videos using spatiotemporal autoencoder. In: ISNN, pp. 189–196 (2017)

4. Davis, J., Goadrich, M.: The relationship between Precision-Recall and ROC curves. In: ICML, pp. 233–240 (2006)
5. Dumoulin, V., Visin, F.: A guide to convolution arithmetic for deep learning. arXiv preprint arXiv:1603.07285 (2016)
6. Fawcett, T.: An introduction to ROC analysis. Pattern Recognit. Lett. **27**, 861–874 (2006)
7. Fennelly, L.J., Perry, M.: Physical security: 150 things you should know. Butterworth-Heinemann (2016)
8. Garcia, M.L.: Vulnerability assessment of physical protection systems. Elsevier (2005)
9. Ji, S., Xu, W., Yang, M., Yu, K.: 3D convolutional neural networks for human action recognition. IEEE Trans. Pattern Anal. Mach. Intell. **35**, 221–231 (2012)
10. Kim, S.H., Lim, S.C., et al.: Intelligent intrusion detection system featuring a virtual fence, active intruder detection, classification, tracking, and action recognition. Ann. Nucl. Energy **112**, 845–855 (2018)
11. Liu, L., et al.: Deep learning for generic object detection: a survey. Int. J. Comput. Vis. **128**, 261–318 (2020)
12. Nogas, J., Khan, S.S., Mihailidis, A.: Fall detection from thermal camera using convolutional LSTM autoencoder. In: ARIAL Workshop, IJCAI (2018)
13. Nogas, J., Khan, S.S., Mihailidis, A.: Deepfall: non-invasive fall detection with deep spatio-temporal convolutional autoencoders. J. Healthc Inform. Res. **4**, 50–70 (2020)
14. Norman, B.C.: Assessment of video analytics for exterior intrusion detection applications. In: ICCST, pp. 359–362 (2012)
15. Prakash, U., Thamaraiselvi, V.: Detecting and tracking of multiple moving objects for intelligent video surveillance systems. In: ICCTET, pp. 253–257 (2014)
16. Saran, K., Sreelekha, G.: Traffic video surveillance: vehicle detection and classification. In: ICCC, pp. 516–521 (2015)
17. Shi, X., Chen, Z., Wang, H., Yeung, D.Y., Wong, W.K., Woo, W.C.: Convolutional LSTM network: a machine learning approach for precipitation nowcasting. In: NIPS, pp. 802–810 (2015)
18. Tran, D., Bourdev, L., Fergus, R., Torresani, L., Paluri, M.: Learning spatiotemporal features with 3D convolutional networks. In: ICCV, pp. 4489–4497 (2015)
19. Vadivelu, S., Ganesan, S., Murthy, O.V.R., Dhall, A.: Thermal imaging based elderly fall detection. In: Chen, C.-S., Lu, J., Ma, K.-K. (eds.) ACCV 2016. LNCS, vol. 10118, pp. 541–553. Springer, Cham (2017). https://doi.org/10.1007/978-3-319-54526-4_40
20. Vijverberg, J.A., Janssen, R.T., de Zwart, R., de With, P.H.: Perimeter-intrusion event classification for on-line detection using multiple instance learning solving temporal ambiguities. In: ICIP, pp. 2408–2412 (2014)
21. Wang, X., Xie, W., Song, J.: Learning spatiotemporal features with 3DCNN and ConvGRU for video anomaly detection. In: ICSP, pp. 474–479 (2018)
22. Zeiler, M.D., Krishnan, D., Taylor, G.W., Fergus, R.: Deconvolutional networks. In: CVPR, pp. 2528–2535 (2010)
23. Zhao, Y., Deng, B., Shen, C., Liu, Y., Lu, H., Hua, X.S.: Spatio-temporal autoencoder for video anomaly detection. In: ACM MM, pp. 1933–1941 (2017)

Creating Emotion Recognition Algorithms Based on a Convolutional Neural Network for Sentiment Analysis

Vera Ivanyuk[1,2(✉)] ⓘ and Ekaterina Tsapina[2]

[1] Financial University under the Government of the Russian Federation, Moscow, Russia
[2] Bauman Moscow State Technical University, Moscow, Russia

Abstract. The objective of the research is the development and evaluation testing of a speed-optimized «Dual-trained Lazy CNN» neural network model for language-dependent sentiment analysis in Slavic languages in specific cultural context, as well as the software implementation of the resulting network. Convolutional neural networks are easy to train and implement. To train them, a standard error back propagation algorithm is used, and because the filter weights are evenly distributed the number of parameters in the convolutional neural network is small. From the viewpoint of computational linguistics, convolutional neural networks are a powerful tool for classification, that, however, does not have any language intuition, which significantly complicates the analysis of algorithm errors. However, it is convolutional networks that are widely used in text data analysis tasks. Neural networks always work with big data and often require a lot of processing power. Therefore, to simplify computations, it makes sense to use «lazy» NNs. A «lazy» neural network is a network, which, if it receives input data that repeats the patterns that were previously processed by it, returns a result that was obtained earlier.

Keywords: Emotion recognition · Convolutional neural network · Sentiment analysis · Slavic languages · Russian language

1 Introduction

In 1980, American psychologist Dr Robert Plutchik developed a concept in which he established the distinction of 8 basic emotions [16]. The result of the work was the «wheel of emotions» – visualization of the human emotional spectrum.

Intuitively, basic emotions can be divided into three groups: positive (joy, trust), negative (anger, disgust, fear), and neutral (anticipation, surprise, and sadness).

Implementations of the emotion wheel include modern voice assistants: Alice (Yandex), Siri (Apple), Google Assistant (Google), Alexa (Amazon Echo), Cortana (Microsoft), and Marusya (Mail.ru Group). In addition to various useful technical functions, all of them can imitate emotions depending on the user's mood.

The basis for creating emotion recognition algorithms was the work of Martin Porter [17]. The most famous is his stemming algorithm, which allows identifying the semantic basis of the entered words to further analyze their emotional connotation.

© Springer Nature Switzerland AG 2021
B. Kerautret et al. (Eds.): RRPR 2021, LNCS 12636, pp. 66–79, 2021.
https://doi.org/10.1007/978-3-030-76423-4_5

Stemming is the process of finding the stem for a given source word. The word stem does not necessarily match the morphological root of the word. Porter's stemmer is a stemming algorithm published by Martin Porter in 1980. The original version of stemmer was intended for English and was written in BCPL. Martin later created the Snowball project and, using the main idea of the algorithm, wrote stemmers for common Slavic languages, including Russian [17].

The main idea behind the Porter stemmer is that there is a limited number of word-formation suffixes, and the stemming occurs without using any stem bases: only a set of existing suffixes and manually set rules.

The advantage of the Porter stemming algorithm is that it does not use any dictionaries or databases, which increases processing speed and expands the range of application.

The objective of the study is the development of a convolutional neural network model for sentiment analysis. For preparing this paper, we used the methods and approaches described in the following works:

The authors Tripathi, Suraj, et al. [25] proposed a self-designed emotion recognition model based on convolutional neural network. Tripathi, Suraj, et al. achieved an almost 7% increase in overall accuracy. Kant, Neel, et al. [8] analyzed tweets using an LSTM model and suggested a formalized sentiment score for a tweet. Calefato, Fabio, et al. [4] presented their own emotion recognition model based on binary classifiers to detect six basic emotions. The authors Majumder, Navonil, et al. [13] conducted a comparative analysis of the state-of-the-art emotion detection methods using convolutional neural networks. Ghosal, Deepanway, et al. [7] empirically showed that the performance of the neural network directly depends on the quality of the dataset used. The authors Lopez, Marc Moreno, and Jugal Kalita [12] suggested a neural network architecture for emotion recognition. As the experiment showed, the proposed architecture was also suitable for a limited Russian-language cultural context, which will be proved further in the present paper. Perikos, Isidoros, and Ioannis Hatzilygeroudis [15] present an emotion detection system used to automatically recognize emotions in text. Alswaidan, Nourah, and Mohamed El Bachir Menai [2] detect emotions by analyzing the text without using neural networks. Qadir, Ashequl, and Ellen Riloff [18] research general emotional background of short messages on Twitter using convolutional neural networks. They showed that the method they were using outperformed classical methods by 5 to 18%. The authors Acheampong F. A. et al. [1] suggest applying correlation analysis to emotion detection tasks and not using neural networks. The study by Kratzwald, Bernhard, et al. [10] shows that neural network ensembles perform much better than individual methods. The authors Batbaatar, Erdenebileg, et al. [3] proposed a novel neural network architecture, called SENN (Semantic-Emotion Neural Network) which can utilize both semantic/syntactic and emotional information by adopting pre-trained word representations.

2   Spectral, Frequency-, and Paradigm-Based Speech Evaluation

Spectral Analysis. Since a speech signal is a time-varying process, its spectral description is based on the concept of short-term analysis. To this end, the speech signal $s(t)$ is divided into equal overlapping segments, called frames, within which the signal properties change little, so the signal can be considered quasi-stationary. Usually, the frame duration is chosen to be 10–30 ms, and it is formed by multiplying the signal $s(t)$ by the window $w(t - n\Delta T)$ where $n = 0, 1, 2 \ldots$ – the frame number index, ΔT – the 5–10 ms interval between neighbouring frames, which provides the necessary level of detail of the spectral description in time. Next, spectral analysis is performed for each frame, resulting in a sequence of amplitude spectra $S(f, n)$, where f – frequency, n – frame number. A sequence of spectra $S(f, n)$ representing the speech signal is typically called a spectrogram of speech or visible speech. The found spectrum $S(f, n)$ differs from the current spectrum $S(f, t)$ in that it represents the latter at discrete times $n\Delta T$.

Usually, to obtain spectra $S(f, n)$ different modifications of the discrete Fourier transform for spectral analysis with a linear frequency scale are used. In this case, the spectrum is located at a number of discrete, equidistant frequencies. Recently, there has been considerable interest in spectrum analyzers based on a bank of bandpass filters that generally take into account the features of frequency analysis of sound in the auditory system.

In the practice of spectral analysis of speech, a logarithmic intensity scale is often used. Its application is justified by the fact that intensity coding in receptors obeys the Weber-Fechner law, according to which the just noticeable difference ΔI in external stimulus affecting the receptor is proportional to the initial stimulus I i.e. $\Delta I \sim \Delta \beta I$ where $\Delta \beta$ – the increase in the receptor response. Hence $\beta \sim lgI$, and therefore, the receptor response is proportional to the logarithm of the external stimulus.

In the following, we present a survey of papers showing practical implementation of spectral analysis. In the study by Chauhan, Rahul, et al. [6] it is shown that the spectral analysis of speech can be used to identify emotions that do not depend on the text. In the paper by Xie, Baijun, et al. [26] the analysis of the general emotional background of a song is conducted. The authors propose a system for classification of songs ranging from depressing to positive using method for extracting novel spectral features based on a sinusoidal model. The paper by Thiangtham, Chaidiaw, and Jakkree Srinonchat [24] addresses the problem of speech analysis using FFT Spectrum Analysis.

Frequency analysis is one of the cryptanalysis methods based on the assumption that there is a nontrivial statistical distribution of individual characters and their regular sequences in both open and encrypted types of text, which, up to the replacement of individual characters, will also be preserved in the encryption and decryption processes.

Frequency analysis assumes that the number of occurrences of the same character of the alphabet in texts of sufficient length is the same in different texts written in the same language. In the case of monoalphabetic encryption, if in a ciphertext area there is a symbol with such a similar probability of occurrence, then it is realistic to assume that it is this encrypted letter. The same reasoning applies to bigrams (sequences of two letters) and trigrams in cases of polyalphabetic ciphers.

This type of analysis is based on the fact that the test consists of words, and those, in turn, of letters. The number of different letters in each language is limited, so the letters can be simply listed. The most important characteristics of such a text will be the repeatability of letters, different diagrams, trigrams and n-grams, the compatibility of different letters with each other, the alternation of consonants/vowels and some others.

The idea is to calculate the occurrences possible m-grams (denoted by n^m) in open text long enough for analysis (denoted by $T = t_1, t_2 \ldots t_l$) composed of letters of the national alphabet (denoted by $\{a_1, a_2, \ldots a_n\}$. In the process, successive m-grams of text are viewed: $t_1 t_2 \ldots t_m, t_2 t_3 \ldots t_{m+1}, \ldots, t_{i-m+1} t_{l-m+2} \ldots t_l$.

If $L(a_{i1} a_{i2} \ldots a_{im})$ – the number of occurrences of the m-gram $a_{i1} a_{i2} \ldots a_{im}$ in the text T, and L – the total number of m-grams analyzed, then it is possible to establish experimentally that at sufficiently large L, frequencies $L(a_{i1} a_{i2} \ldots a_{im})/L$ for such m-grams will differ little from each other.

Because of this, the relative frequency is considered an approximation of the probability $P(a_{i1} a_{i2} \ldots a_{im})$ of occurrence of the given m-gram at a randomly selected position in the text (this approach is used for statistical determination of probability).

The following contributions contain findings of practical implementation of the frequency analysis. The paper by Canales, Lea et al. [5] demonstrates the efficiency of the frequency text analysis in emotion detection. In the study by Kim, Evgeny, and Roman Klinger [9] a comparative analysis of all emotion recognition methods is performed.

In the research by Shivhare, Shiv Naresh, and Saritha Khethawat [22] an algorithm for emotion detection from text is proposed. The authors Sim, Kwee-Bo, et al. [23] identify such emotions as happiness, anger, and surprise using the frequency analysis of speech signal.

Latent Semantic Analysis (LSA). Latent semantic analysis (LSA) is a natural language information processing method that analyzes the relationship between a library of documents and the terms found in them and identifies the characteristic factors (concepts) inherent in all documents and terms.

The method of latent semantic analysis is based on the principles of factor analysis, in particular, the identification of latent relationships of the studied phenomena or objects. When classifying/clustering documents, this method is used to extract context-sensitive values of lexical units using statistical processing of large text bodies.

LSA can be compared to a simple type of neural network consisting of three layers: the first layer contains a set of words (terms), the second – a certain set of documents corresponding to certain situations, and the third, hidden layer (middle layer) is a set of nodes with different weight coefficients connecting the first and second layers.

As the input information, the LSA uses a term-document matrix describing the dataset used for training the system. The elements of this matrix typically contain weights that take into account the frequency of use of each term in each document and the participation of the term in all documents (tf-idf). The most common variant of LSA is based on the matrix decomposition by singular values (SVD – Singular Value Decomposition). Using SVD decomposition, any matrix is decomposed into a set of orthogonal matrices, the linear combination of which is a fairly accurate approximation to the original matrix.

Text Convolution. Let us consider a sequence of words $w_{1:n} = w_1, \ldots, w_n$, each with their corresponding d_{emb} - dimensional word embedding $E_{[w_i]} = w_i$. A one-dimensional convolution of width k is computed by shifting a sliding window of size k along the sentence and applying the same «filter» to each window in the sequence, where the filter is a dot product with a weight vector u, often followed by a nonlinear activation function. We define the operator $\oplus(w_{i:i+k-1})$ as a concatenation of vectors $w_i, \ldots, w_{i+k-1}$. Concatenation (lat. concatenatio «chaining; coupling») is the operation of glueing linear structure objects. Then the concatenated vector of the $i - th$ window is $x_i = \left[w_i; w_{i+1}; \ldots; w_{i+k-1} \right], x_i \in \mathbb{R}^{k \times d_{emb}}$.

The filter is then applied to each window - vector, which gives scalar values p_i:

$$p_i = g(x_i \cdot u) \tag{1}$$

$$x_i = \oplus(w_{i:i+k-1}) \tag{2}$$

$$p_i \in \mathbb{R}, \; x_i \in \mathbb{R}^{k \times d_{emb}}, \; u \in \mathbb{R}^{k \times d_{emb}}$$

where g is the nonlinear activation function.

It is common to use l different filters $u_1, \ldots, u_l$ that can be assembled into a matrix U, and a bias vector g is often added:

$$p_i = g(x_i \cdot U + b) \tag{3}$$

$$p_i \in R^l, \; x_i \in \mathbb{R}^{k \times d_{emb}}$$

$$U \in \mathbb{R}^{k \times d_{emb} \times l}, \; b \in R^l.$$

Each vector p_i is a set of values that represent (or generalize) the $i - th$ window. Ideally, each measurement captures an independent type of indicative information.

There are narrow and wide convolutions. In a sentence of length n with a window of size k, there are $n-k+1$ positions to start a sequence, so we get $n-k+1$ vectors $p_{1:n-k+1}$. This is called a narrow convolution. An alternative is to supplement the sentence with $k - 1$ padding-words to each side, then we will get $n + k + 1$ vectors $p_{1:n+k+1}$. This is called a wide convolution. The number of resulting vectors will be denoted by the letter m.

3   Dataset Selection and Correction

Slavic languages have their own unique cultural and emotional context, which developed in the language paradigm of emotional socialism and accordingly distorted the sentiment of not only idiomatic and synecdochic expressions but also individual words and phrases. Thus, many words, phrases, synecdoches that have become traditional despite the negative semantic charge have a positive emotional connotation and vice versa.

For training and cross-validation of the network, we used the RuTweetCorp dataset [https://study.mokoron.com/#download] compiled by Yuliya Rubtsova [19–21] which in most cases is a reference for training and testing neural networks designed to work with the Russian language.

This dataset actually contains a significant number of erroneous elements, such as statements in Kazakh and Ukrainian, as well as a large number of context-sensitive synecdoches and idioms. In order to improve the quality of the dataset, it was automatically and manually corrected by excluding foreign-language phrases, context-dependent idioms, and expressions with an undetectable emotional component. After the above processing, only 18484 records out of 334836 were left.

The resulting dataset was divided into two equal parts intended for training the network and its cross-validation (Table 1).

Table 1. Model training and cross-validation dataset.

Class label	Number of training objects	Number of validation objects
0 (hate/disgust)	2288	2288
1 (sad)	2297	2297
2 (happy)	2283	2283
3 (fear/surprise)	2374	2374

4 Topology of the Neural Network Output Part

The neural network architecture uses filters with height $h = (2, 3, 4, 5)$, which are designed for parallel processing of bigrams, trigrams, 4-g, and 5-g, respectively (see Fig. 1).

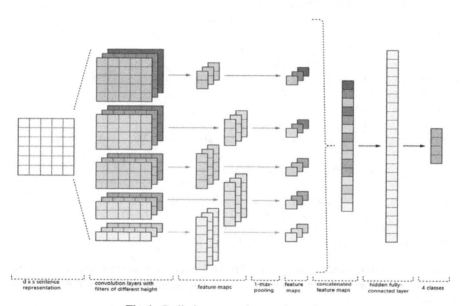

| d x s sentence representation | convolution layers with filters of different height | feature maps | 1-max-pooling | feature maps | concatenated feature maps | hidden fully-connected layer | 4 classes |

Fig. 1. Preliminary neural network topology.

The neural network was complemented with 10 convolution layers for each filter height, the activation function being ReLU.

```
w2v_model = Word2Vec.load('/content/drive/My Drive/Colab
Notebooks/W2V PSW/model.w2v')
DIM = w2v_model.vector_size
embedding_matrix = np.zeros((NUM, DIM))
for word, i in tokenizer.word_index.items():
    if i >= NUM:
        break
    if word in w2v_model.wv.vocab.keys():
        embedding_matrix[i] = w2v_model.wv[word]
from keras.layers import Input
from keras.layers.embeddings import Embedding
tweet_input = Input(shape=(SENTENCE_LENGTH,),
dtype='int32')
tweet_encoder = Embedding(NUM, DIM, in-
put_length=SENTENCE_LENGTH,
weights=[embedding_matrix], trainable=False)(tweet_input)
from keras import optimizers
from keras.layers import Dense, concatenate, Activation,
Dropout
from keras.models import Model
from keras.layers.convolutional import Conv1D
from keras.layers.pooling import GlobalMaxPooling1D
import tensorflow as tf
branches = []
x = Dropout(0.2)(tweet_encoder)
for size, filters_count in [(2, 10), (3, 10), (4, 10),
(5, 10)]:
    for i in range(filters_count):
                branch = Conv1D(filters=1, ker-
nel_size=size, padding='valid', activation='relu')(x)
        branch = GlobalMaxPooling1D()(branch)
        branches.append(branch)
x = concatenate(branches, axis=1)
```

After being processed by convolution layers, feature maps are fed into subsampling layers for the $1 - max$-pooling operation, extracting the most significant n-grams from the text.

```
        branch = GlobalMaxPooling1D()(branch)
        branches.append(branch)
    x = concatenate(branches, axis=1)
```

At the next stage, they are combined into a common feature vector (at the pooling layer), which is fed into a hidden fully-connected layer with 30 neurons. At the last stage, the final feature map is fed into the softmax output layer of the neural network.

Since neural networks are prone to overfitting, dropout regularization is added after the embedding layer and before the hidden fully-connected layer with the vertex dropping probability $p = 0.2$.

```
x = Dropout(0.2)(x)
x = Dense(30, activation='relu')(x)
x = Dense(1)(x)
output = Dense(4, activation='softmax')(x)
adam = optimizers.Adam(lr=0.01)
#'sparse_categorical_accuracy', 'accuracy'
model = Model(inputs=[tweet_input], outputs=[output])
model.compile(loss='sparse_categorical_crossentropy', op-
timizer='adam', met-rics=['sparse_categorical_accuracy'])
model.summary()
from keras.callbacks import ModelCheckpoint
```

5 Learning Outcomes

The study examined the neural network architecture shown in Fig. 2. Categorical cross-entropy was used as the empirical risk function, and categorical accuracy was used as the metric.

To build quality metrics for this model, we introduce the concept of an error matrix (Table 2). This is a way to divide objects into four categories depending on the combination of the true response and the algorithm response.

Table 2. Error matrix.

	$y = 1$	$y = 0$
$a(x) = 1$	True Positive (TP)	False Positive (FP)
$a(x) = 0$	False Negative (FN)	True Negative (TN)

From here we get two quality metrics: precision and recall:

$$precision = \frac{TP}{TP + FP} \tag{4}$$

$$recall = \frac{TP}{TP + FN} \tag{5}$$

Precision reflects what percentage of objects assigned to a particular class by the classifier actually belong to that class. Recall shows the fraction of the total amount of the class that was actually retrieved by the classifier. The key factor in choosing these metrics is independence from the ratio of classes.

But keep in mind that the metrics described above are suitable for solving binary problems, whereas the problem of sentiment analysis is based on a 4-state model, which means that it is a multiclass problem.

In multiclass classification cases, metrics are usually reduced to binary form. There are 2 approaches – micro- and macro-averaging.

Let the sample consist of k classes. In micro-averaging, characteristics are averaged across all classes, and then the final two-class metric is calculated. For example, precision will be calculated using the formula:

$$precision(a, X) = \frac{\overline{TP}}{\overline{TP} + \overline{FP}} \tag{6}$$

Where $\overline{TP} = \frac{1}{k} \sum_{i=1}^{k} TP$, $\overline{FP}$ is calculated similarly.

In macro-averaging, the final metric for each class is calculated first, and then the results are averaged across the classes. In this case, precision will look as follows:

$$precision(a, X) = \frac{1}{k} \sum_{i=1}^{k} precision_i(a, X) \tag{7}$$

$$precision_i(a, X) = \frac{TP_i}{TP_i + FP_i} \tag{8}$$

The micro-averaging technique is less sensitive to the ratio of class sizes, as opposed to macro-averaging.

Let us define the $f1\_score$ metric as the harmonic mean of precision and recall:

$$f1\_score = 2 \frac{precision \; recall}{precision + recall} \tag{9}$$

The model was trained in two stages. At the first stage of training, we froze the embedding layer which is a trained Word2Vec model. All other layers were trained for 15 epochs (17610000 back propagation cycles at 712844 unique words each epoch). The results are shown in Table 3.

Table 3. Model training.

Class label	Precision	Recall	F1-score
0 (hate/disgust)	0.9493	0.7448	0.8347
1 (sad)	0.7271	0.8167	0.7693
2 (happy)	0.6857	0.8765	0.7695
3 (fear/surprise)	0.9666	0.7936	0.8716

Achieved accuracy metric value as a result of the experiment: 0.8077.

At the second stage, the embedding layer was unfrozen, and the model was trained for another 5 epochs. The results are shown in Table 4.

Table 4. Results.

Class label	Precision	Recall	F1-score
0 (hate/disgust)	0.9781	0.7605	0.8557
1 (sad)	0.7682	0.8785	0.8197
2 (happy)	0.7379	0.8953	0.8090
3 (fear/surprise)	0.9647	0.8395	0.8977

As a result of the experiment, the final value of the accuracy metric reached 0.8434.

Indirect SOTA analysis. As shown above, standard measures such as precision and F1 were used as the main criteria. Direct SOTA-analysis was not performed due to the lack of data on the training results of other networks on the corrected dataset. The studies presented in Table 4 indicate directly that they used RuTweetCorp in its original version, which contains a large number of ambiguous and foreign-language expressions, while most of the studies do not indicate which emotion classification was used. Despite the above, the SOTA characteristic common to this type of research, such as the accuracy of emotion detection, can be used as a comparative criterion for Russian-specific neural networks and datasets (Table 5).

Table 5. Indirect SOTA analysis.

Language specific algorithm	SOTA average accuracy	Dataset	Paper
M-BERT BaseFiT (Russian)	0.874	RuTweetCorp (full version)	https://github.com/sis metanin/sentiment-ana lysis-in-russian
Dual-trained Lazy CNN	0.843	RuTweetCorp (clean version)	–
nb-blinov (Russian)	0.816	ROMIP-2012	https://arxiv.org/ftp/ arxiv/papers/1808/1808. 07851.pdf [14]
Naive-Bayes + Thesaurus (Russian)	0.697	RuTweetCorp (full version)	https://www.fruct.org/ publications/fruct23/ files/Lag.pdf [11]

To test the network, a software was developed to «deconvolve» the neural network and interpret the results. The algorithm is presented below (see Fig. 2)

```
from tensorflow.keras.models import load_model
from google.colab import files
from IPython.display import Image
from tensorflow.keras.preprocessing import image
import numpy as np
classes = ['anger / disgust', 'sadness', 'happiness',
'surprise / fear']
r=0
model = load_model('/content/drive/My Drive/Colab Note-
books/check4_6_2/cnn-trainable-05-0.84.hdf5')
leniv=0
model.summary()
======================================================
import pandas as pd
import tensorflow as tf
from keras.preprocessing.text import Tokenizer
from keras.preprocessing.sequence import pad_sequences
n2 = ['text', 'sent']
data_leniv = pd.read_csv('/content/drive/My Drive/Colab
Notebooks/leniv.csv', sep=';',encoding = "cp1251", er-
ror_bad_lines=False, names=n2)
columns = ['text', 'sent']
df = pd.DataFrame(data_leniv, columns=columns)
phrase = 'I'm so glad it ended well'
phrase2=preprocess(phrase)
#print(phrase2)
kz=data_leniv[data_leniv.text == phrase2]
bul = any(df.text == phrase2)
if bul==True:
  a=int(kz.sent)
  leniv=1
if leniv ==0:
================================
```

.

We also implemented the reputation system which has the following form:

- from $-\infty$ to 0 – «hostile»;
- 0 – «neutral»;
- from 0 to $+\infty$ – «friendly»;

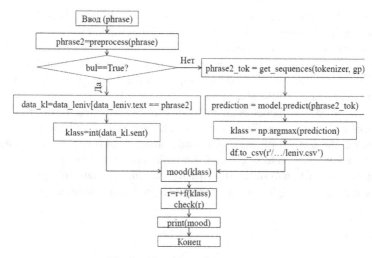

Fig. 2. Algorithm of the program.

Figure 3 shows an example of one communication session with the emotion recognition algorithm. The initial reputation value is neutral.

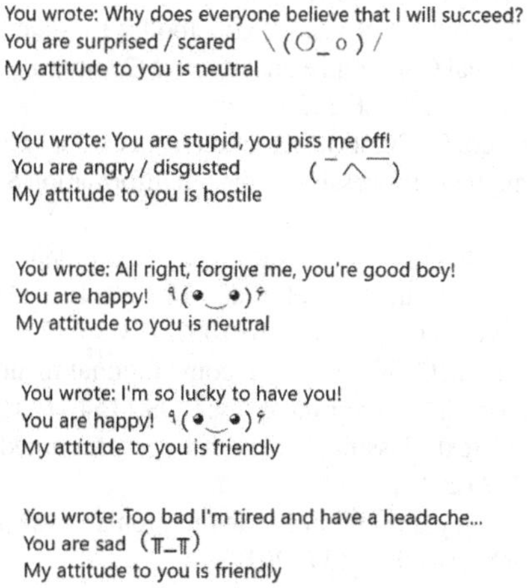

You wrote: Why does everyone believe that I will succeed?
You are surprised / scared   \ (O_ o) /
My attitude to you is neutral

You wrote: You are stupid, you piss me off!
You are angry / disgusted   (ˉ ∧ ˉ)
My attitude to you is hostile

You wrote: All right, forgive me, you're good boy!
You are happy! ٩(● _ ●)۶
My attitude to you is neutral

You wrote: I'm so lucky to have you!
You are happy! ٩(● _ ●)۶
My attitude to you is friendly

You wrote: Too bad I'm tired and have a headache...
You are sad (╥_╥)
My attitude to you is friendly

Fig. 3. An example of communication with an emotion recognition algorithm that recognizes the interlocutor's mood.

6 Conclusion

In the paper, we set and solved the task of developing methods and software for sentiment analysis and construction of emotion recognition algorithm.

The method of sentiment analysis using a neural network showed good results when actually testing the software. In the future, it will be possible to teach the network to detect more emotions – trust, vigilance, etc.

The procedure for selecting data using root search allowed us to get high-quality training datasets. Removing the modified stop word list during preprocessing allowed in-creasing the accuracy of the algorithm.

Using the Word2Vec model as an embedding layer simplified the discretization of word vectors and made it possible to create a large dictionary for the network.

In general, the method of text classification using a convolutional neural network performed well and proved to be effective for multiclass classification.

Comparative SOTA analysis has shown that even with small but high-quality datasets, one can achieve a fairly high level of emotion recognition in natural language.

References

1. Acheampong, F.A., Wenyu, C., Nunoo-Mensah, H.: Text-based emotion detection: advances, challenges, and opportunities. Eng. Rep.-C **2**(7), e12189 (2020)
2. Alswaidan, N., El Bachir Menai, M.: A survey of state-of-the-art approaches for emotion recognition in text. Knowl. Inf. Syst. **62**(8), 2937–2987 (2020). https://doi.org/10.1007/s10 115-020-01449-0
3. Batbaatar, E., Li, M., Ryu, K.H.: Semantic-emotion neural network for emotion recognition from text. IEEE Access **7**, 111866–111878 (2019)
4. Calefato, F., Lanubile, F., Novielli, N.: EmoTxt: a toolkit for emotion recognition from text. In: 2017 Seventh International Conference on Affective Computing and Intelligent Interaction Workshops and Demos (ACIIW). IEEE (2017)
5. Canales, L., Martínez-Barco, P.: Emotion detection from text: a survey. In: Proceedings of the Workshop on Natural Language Processing in the 5th Information Systems Research Working Days, JISIC (2014)
6. Chauhan, R., Yadav, J., Koolagudi, S.G., Rao, K.S.: Text independent emotion recognition using spectral features. In: Aluru, S., et al. (eds.) IC3 2011. CCIS, vol. 168, pp. 359–370. Springer, Heidelberg (2011). https://doi.org/10.1007/978-3-642-22606-9_37
7. Ghosal, D., et al.: DialogueGCN: a graph convolutional neural network for emotion recognition in conversation. arXiv preprint arXiv:1908.11540 (2019)
8. Kant, N., et al.: Practical text classification with large pretrained language models. arXiv preprint arXiv:1812.01207 (2018)
9. Kim, E., Klinger, R.: A survey on sentiment and emotion analysis for computational literary studies. arXiv preprint arXiv:1808.03137 (2018)
10. Kratzwald, B., et al.: Deep learning for affective computing: text-based emotion recognition in decision support. Decis. Supp. Syst. **115**, 24–35 (2018)
11. Lagutina, K., et al.: Sentiment classification of Russian texts using automatically generated thesaurus. In: Proceedings of the 2018 23rd Conference of Open Innovations Association (FRUCT). IEEE (2018)
12. Lopez, M.M., Kalita, J.: Deep learning applied to NLP. arXiv preprint arXiv:1703.03091 (2017)
13. Majumder, N., et al.: DialogueRNN: an attentive RNN for emotion detection in conversations. In: Proceedings of the AAAI Conference on Artificial Intelligence, vol. 33, pp. 6818–6825 (2019)

14. Panchenko, A.: Sentiment index of the Russian speaking Facebook. arXiv preprint arXiv: 1808.07851 (2018)
15. Perikos, I., Hatzilygeroudis, I.: Recognizing emotion presence in natural language sentences. In: Iliadis, L., Papadopoulos, H., Jayne, C. (eds.) International Conference on Engineering Applications of Neural Networks, vol. 384. Springer, Berlin, Heidelberg (2013). https://doi. org/10.1007/978-3-642-41016-1_4
16. Plutchik, R., Kellerman, H. (eds.): Theories of Emotion, vol. 1. Academic Press, Cambridge (2013)
17. Porter, M.F.: Snowball: a language for stemming algorithms (2001)
18. Qadir, A., Riloff, E.: Learning emotion indicators from tweets: hashtags, hashtag patterns, and phrases. In: Proceedings of the 2014 Conference on Empirical Methods in Natural Language Processing EMNLP (2014)
19. Rubtsova, Y.V.: A method for development and analysis of short text corpus for the review classification task. In: Trudy XV Vserossiiskoy naychnoy konferencii RCDL 2013, pp. 269–275 (2013)
20. Rubtsova, Y.: Reducing the degradation of sentiment analysis for text collections spread over a period of time. In: Różewski, P., Lange, C. (eds.) Knowledge Engineering and Semantic Web, pp. 3–13. Springer International Publishing, Cham (2017). https://doi.org/10.1007/978-3-319-69548-8_1
21. Rubtsova, Y.: Reducing the deterioration of sentiment analysis results due to the time impact. Information 9(8), 184 (2018)
22. Shivhare, S.N., Khethawat, S.: Emotion detection from text. arXiv preprint arXiv:1205.4944 (2012)
23. Sim, K.-B., et al.: Emotion recognition based on frequency analysis of speech signal. Int. J. Fuzzy Log. Intell. Syst. 2(2), 122–126 (2002)
24. Thiangtham, C., Srinonchat, J.: Speech emotion feature extraction using FFT spectrum analysis. In: Applied Mechanics and Materials, vol. 781. Trans Tech Publications Ltd. (2015)
25. Tripathi, S., et al.: Deep learning based emotion recognition system using speech features and transcriptions. arXiv preprint arXiv:1906.05681 (2019)
26. Xie, B., Kim, J.C., Park, C.H.: Musical emotion recognition with spectral feature extraction based on a sinusoidal model with model-based and deep-learning approaches. Appl. Sci. 10(3), 902 (2020)

Tree Defect Segmentation Using Geometric Features and CNN

Florian Delconte[1]([✉]), Phuc Ngo[1], Isabelle Debled-Rennesson[1],
Bertrand Kerautret[2], Van-Tho Nguyen[3], and Thiery Constant[4]

[1] Université de Lorraine, LORIA, ADAGIo, 54000 Nancy, France
`florian.delconte@loria.fr`
[2] Université Lumière Lyon 2, LIRIS, Imagine, 69365 Lyon, France
[3] Department of Applied Geomatics, Centre d'applications et de recherche
en télédétection, Université de Sherbrooke, 2500 boul.de l'université,
Sherbrooke, QC J1K2R1, Canada
[4] Université de Lorraine, AgroParisTech, INRAE, SILVA, 54000 Nancy, France

Abstract. Estimating the quality of standing trees or roundwood after felling is a crucial step in forest production trading. The on-going revolution in the forest sector resulting from the use of 3D sensors can also contribute to this step. Among them the terrestrial lidar scanning is a reference descriptive method offering the possibility to segment defects. In this paper, we propose a new reproducible method allowing to automatically segment the defects. It is based on the construction of a *relief map* inspired from a previous strategy and combining with a convolutional neural network to improve the resulting segmentation quality. The proposed method outperforms the previous results and the source code is publicly available with an online demonstration allowing to test the defect detection without any software installation.

Keywords: Wood surface defects · Defect segmentation · Relief map · LIDAR · Centerline · U-Net

1 Introduction

In the domain of biological image processing, the wood structures are often exploited to address various objectives, for instance, species identification [2], wood quality estimation [7], tree microhabitats identification [21], tracability [23], or plant growing analysis [6]. These various applications rely on different image acquisition modalities such as classical 2D bitmap images (including hyperspectral images), 3D point cloud (from multi-view stereo 3D or LiDAR scan) or 3D volumetric images (medical X-Ray CT scanner [14] or ultra sound [5]).

This research was made possible by support from the French National Research Agency, in the framework of the project WoodSeer, ANR-19-CE10-011.

B. Kerautret et al. (Eds.): RRPR 2021, LNCS 12636, pp. 80–100, 2021.
https://doi.org/10.1007/978-3-030-76423-4_6

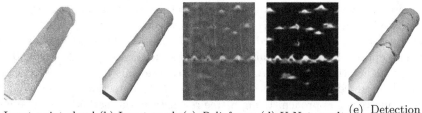

(a) Input point cloud (b) Input mesh (c) *Relief map* (d) U-Net result (e) Detection & comparison

Fig. 1. Overview of the proposed method: input LiDAR 3d points (a) and its reconstructed mesh (b) are used to construct the *relief map* (c) which is exploited in U-Net (d). The defects are segmented and compared to ground truth (e).

The aim of this work is to detect defects located on the trunk surface of living tree (see teasing Fig. 1). Various types of defects are identified by biology experts (also called *singularity*) depending on their origins and their development stages (burls, branch scar, picot, . . .). Figure 2 illustrates samples of defects on beech and oak species. The detection of such a structure is a key point for the value determination and the optimization of the transformation taking knotiness or aesthetics into consideration. The defect detection on living tree is not an easy task in the image processing domains, since each type of singularities presents numerous geometric variations both inter or intra species. Figure 2 (a, b) illustrates a same defect type on a same species but presenting a very different geometric shape.

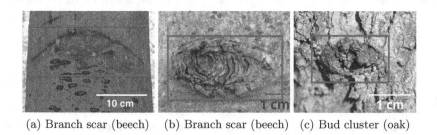

(a) Branch scar (beech)   (b) Branch scar (beech)   (c) Bud cluster (oak)

Fig. 2. Examples of defects: scar and picot. Defect areas are highlighted in red. (Color figure online)

In this work, the defect detection is addressed by using 3D scan of trunk (as illustrated in Fig. 1). Schütt *et al.* can be considered as the pioneers to exploit the terrestrial LiDAR data for tree defect detection [24]. The authors proposed to localise singularity by combining 3D terrestrial LiDAR with 2D images. After using a cylindrical coordinate transformation, a neural network is trained and used to extract the singularity areas. The method was promising, however the extraction process needs a potential interactive correction and no details are given to reproduce the method nor the result quality measures. Thomas *et al.*

proposed later an automatic method to detect severe surface defects by using a 2D circle fitting algorithm [27]. The method was then improved with a parallel implementation in order to reduce execution time [28]. One of the limitation of such an approach, was the minimum detectable defect size was 12.7 cm and with a relief higher than 1.27 cm. Answering to the previous limitation, Kretschmer *et al.* [13] added more geometry in the singularity detection by using a cylinder fitting based approach. Using a tree reconstruction method [19], a series of cylinders is fitted according to the wood main axis and each 3D point is associated to its cylinder part. Such an association allows to generate a distance map that is used to extract manually the defects. The proposed strategy is not automatic, however it allows to detect smaller defects with near 4.3 cm for the minimal size and 2 cm for the relief height. Observing that the wood trunk does not always fit perfectly a cylinder, Nguyen *et al.* [18] proposed an automatic patch-based method that allows to better follow the trunk geometry. The main algorithm relies on the recovering of the trunk centerline [10] allowing to avoid the cylinder fitting step of previous works.

The methods described in the previous part are designed specifically for the wood defect estimation but it could be interesting to mention other general approaches that are exploited for surface-crack detection in an industrial context. For instance, Tabernik *et al.* [25] proposed a segmentation-based deep-learning method to detect surface anomaly. Even if the considered images differ from the tree defect context, their strategy could be interesting to adapt since the proposed architecture does not request training with numerous images. In other context of the train industry, the defect on rail surface were analysed through [4]. Like the previous works, their approach was based on the deep learning and can detect various defects like weld, squat or joint. Finally, we can refer to another application of micro cup surface inspection from a confocal laser microscopy images that exploits neural network to detect defects on very textured images [30].

Following the previous strategy introduced by Nguyen *et al.* [18], we propose a new method based on the construction of a new *relief map* image combined with a convolutional neural network (CNN) to precisely segment tree defects. The main overview of the method is given on Fig. 3. The *relief map* is constructed from the input mesh (upper part of Fig. 3) and the convolutional neural network is exploited to segment defect area (lower part of Fig. 3) that can be visualized on the original input mesh. The first step of the new approach is described in the following section (Sect. 2) with the overview of the centerline detection, followed by *relief map* image construction. Associated to this representation, the segmentation process based on the U-Net architecture is introduced in Sect. 3. The experiment part presenting the main results and reproducibility links are addressed in Sect. 4 before concluding.

2   Geometric Tools

The proposed method relies on three geometric tools: (i) the *centerline of the wood log*, (ii) the *reference and delta distances* and (iii) the *relief map*. The first

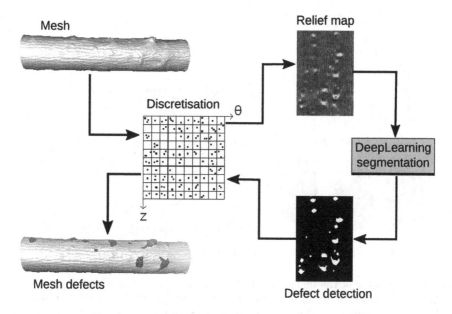

Fig. 3. Pipeline of the proposed method.

two tools are introduced in [10,18] and summarized in following sections. The third tool, the *relief map*, is defined in Sect. 2.3. It permits to represent the input 3D points with a 2D map characterising the relief of the points, relatively to the centerline of the wood log and from a fitted tangent plane.

2.1   Centerline of the Wood Log

In [10] a method is presented to extract the centerline of 3D shapes using solely partial mesh scans of the shapes. The centerline is a polyline with several small segments (see Fig. 4 (b, c)). It is obtained by constructing an accumulation map from input faces and normal vectors (see Fig. 4 (a)) and by filtering it with a confidence vote. Since the method inputs are only a set of faces, the centerline can also be recovered both from full and partial mesh (see Fig. 4 (b, c)). The details of the algorithm are available in the associated reference [11] and on the *GitHub* repository:

https://github.com/kerautret/CDCVAM

Due to the non constant diameter of wood logs, a process of optimization must be done to obtain a smooth centerline of the wood logs. In [18], the authors used a smoothing process based on cubic spline. Note that the implementation details and reproductive evaluation can be found in the complementary work [17] with the *GitHub* repository:

https://github.com/vanthonguyen/treelogdefectsegmentation

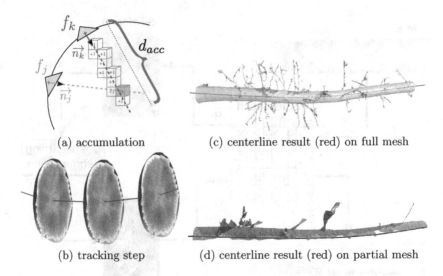

(a) accumulation   (c) centerline result (red) on full mesh

(b) tracking step   (d) centerline result (red) on partial mesh

Fig. 4. Illustration of the main idea of the centerline extraction algorithm: (a) accumulation step from surface faces f_k and f_j in the direction of their normal vectors ($\overrightarrow{n_j}$ and $\overrightarrow{n_k}$); (b) example of tracking step from the 3D accumulation values. Images (c) and (d) show the centerline extraction respectively on full and partial mesh. (Color figure online)

2.2   Reference and Delta Distances

In order to easily access the neighborhood of each point on the wood log surface, we work in cylindrical coordinates. A local coordinate system (C_i, u_i, v_i, w_i) is defined for each segment S_i of the centerline. A point $P(x, y, z)$ in Cartesian coordinates corresponds to the cylindrical coordinates (r_P, θ_P, z_P) with:

- r_P is the distance between P and P', the projection of P on the segment S_i of the centerline.
- z_P is the height of P along the centerline.
- θ_P is the angle formed between the segment PP' and the axis v_i of local coordinate system associated to S_i.

For more details of transformation in cylindrical coordinate, we refer the readers to [18]. To correctly detect the local relief variation around each point P of the wood log, a rectangular neighborhood is studied, named *patch* $\mathcal{P}_P$, it is proportional to the size and circumference of the wood log (see Fig. 5 (a) and [18] for details). $\mathcal{P}_P$ characterizes the shape of the log around the point P. The central straight line fitting the points of $\mathcal{P}_P$ is calculated by a RANSAC based linear regression. The delta distance, noted by $delta_P$, is defined as the distance from P to the fitting line. It represents the relief of the tree at P (see Fig. 5 (b)). We use the delta distance in the next section to generate the relief maps.

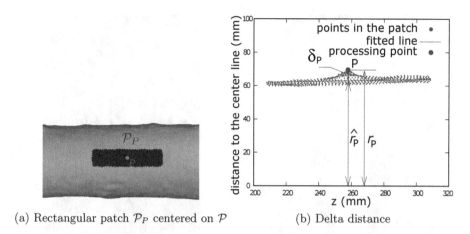

(a) Rectangular patch $\mathcal{P}_P$ centered on $\mathcal{P}$ (b) Delta distance

Fig. 5. (a) A patch in blue, associated to the red point, is used to compute the reference distance of this point. (b) Computation of the reference distance for the red point. See [18] for more details. (Color figure online)

2.3 Relief Map

A *relief map* is a 2D representation of the tree mesh. It is obtained by firstly discretizing the cylindrical point space and by secondly, completing the missing information with a multi-resolution analysis. This map is used to segment the defects. It must also allow a reverse operation, *i.e.*, compute from pixels of the map the corresponding 3D points of the mesh.

Cylindrical Space Discretisation. The relief map represents the *unfolding of the wood log*. The width of the map is the circumference of the trunk, *i.e.*, $2\pi * r_m$ with r_m the average radius of the trunk. The height of the map is the height of the trunk, obtained by subtracting the z component of the point having the maximum height and the one of minimum height. Each point of the tree mesh is associated to a cell of the relief map. We then calculate a value to represent all the points of a cell. The chosen value is the **maximum value of the delta distances** of the points associated to the cell. An illustration is given in Fig. 6. The two maps are generated from the same input mesh. On the left, intensity of the pixels is calculated from the distance to the centerline. On the right, intensity of the pixels is calculated from the delta distances. With the map obtained by the distance to the centerline, we can observe the artefacts, the yellow and red traces, due to the non-cylindrical tree, while using the delta distance, these traces disappear and the defects become more visible. Figure 7, on the first line, provides several relief maps deduced from this process.

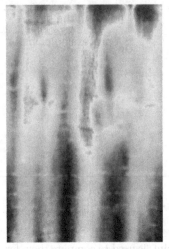 

(a) Distances to the centerline   (b) Relief map

Fig. 6. Difference between the distance map (a) and the relief map (b).

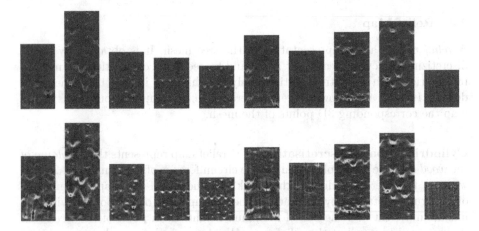

Fig. 7. Examples of relief maps. Red color for the stronger reliefs. Blue color for the lower reliefs. The upper row is not improved with a multi-resolution analysis. (Color figure online)

Multi-resolution Analysis. It is possible that some cells of the relief map do not contain a value because no point is associated with them. To handle this, we propose a multi-resolution analysis to improve the obtained relief map. In the proposed process, for every empty cell, we reduce the resolutions by a factor $\frac{1}{2^n}$, with $n \in \mathbb{N}$, until the cell contains at least one point. It should be noticed that if n is too high, we may lost information of delta distance for the defect detection. Therefore, during the multi-resolution analysis, we fix the limite of n to four. Figure 8 illustrates the multi-resolution analysis to obtain a value in an empty cell. We consider in this example an array T with a resolution of 10×10. Some cells contain black dots, corresponding to the points previously discretized. In others, there is none, like the cell located in $(2, 2)$. The multi-resolution analysis is illustrated by the colors of the borders of the table. Respectively, the black, red and blue borders correspond to resolutions reduced by a factor of $\frac{1}{1}$, $\frac{1}{2^1}$, $\frac{1}{2^2}$. We look for the information in the cell $(2, 2)$, then $(1, 1)$ of the red discretization, then $(0, 0)$ of the blue discretization, etc. ... The value in the $(2, 2)$ cell is then the maximum of the delta distances of the points in the $(0, 0)$ cell of the blue discretization. To represent the discretization in the form of an image we associate a gray intensity to the delta distance. This intensity is distributed on a fixed scale: 1cm equals ten gray levels starting from -5. The colored relief maps in this article are obtained by applying a color scheme from blue to red. The bottom row in Fig. 7 shows the improvement brought to the relief maps with the multi-resolution analysis. We can see in Fig. 9, results of the multi-resolution analysis centered on a branch scar type defect.

3 Segmentation with U-Net Architecture

Hereafter, we process the detection of defects on tree barks using the previously obtained relief map. Note that the 3D problem of defect detection on tree bark surfaces becomes a 2D problem of relief map segmentation. More precisely, it is a binary-image-classification in which each pixel of the relief map will be classified as defect or not. We can observe in Fig. 7, that the defects on tree barks may have arbitrary size, shape and orientation. Furthermore, the roughness of the tree bark, the variability of the defects on the same species and between the different species make the detection task difficult to automate by conventional segmentation algorithms.

Over the past few years, the deep-learning methods are becoming common and successful for the segmentation task with remarkable performance improvements. Indeed, they often achieve the highest accuracy rates on popular segmentation benchmarks comparing to the classical computer-vision approaches. Furthermore, the deep-learning algorithms can be adapted to different problems as they can learn the hidden high-level features from the image directly, and have capacity to represent and recognize the complex structures.

In this paper, we use a deep learning-based segmentation method, namely U-Net [22], to detect tree bark defects with the relief maps as input. It should be mentioned that in the context of surface-singularity detection, several neural network architectures have been proposed (see Sect. 1). As stated in [22], U-Net enables the model to be trained using a small number of samples, and to create a precise pixel-wise mask of interest objects in the images. Thus, it is a well-suited architecture for our segmentation problem. In the following, we describe a modified version of the original U-Net [22] for detecting tree bark defects, and the generation of training data from the relief maps.

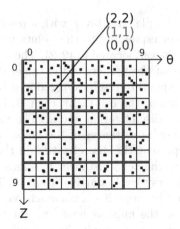

Fig. 8. Illustration of the multi-resolution analysis on an example of size 10×10. Ajouter description

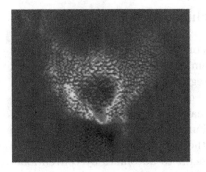

Fig. 9. Effect of multi-resolution analysis. Left: Without multi-resolution processing, we can see the missing pixels. Right: A relief map completed with multi-resolution analysis.

3.1 Segmentation Network

The U-Net was first introduced in [22] as a fully convolutional network (FCN) architecture for biomedical image segmentation, and it was designed for a precise pixel-wise segmentation. Recently, many variants of U-Net architecture have been proposed to address the segmentation of medical images, satellite images such as U-Net++ [31], KU-Net [29], TernausNet [8], ... U-Net is well-known for its performance to be trained with very few training images.

U-Net is an auto-encoder architecture. The encoder stage takes the input images and extracts features from objects in the image, then condenses them into smaller layers. These features are propagated in the decoder stage to produce a segmentation.

The original U-Net proposes to use convolution layers followed by max pooling for down-sampling in encoding part, while the decoding part consists of up-

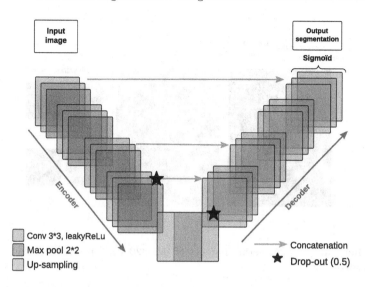

Fig. 10. The architecture for tree bark defect detection based on U-Net [22].

sampling followed by concatenation with the corresponding layer of the encoding part. Each layer is followed by the rectify linear unit (ReLu) activation function, except the last one. This final layer is a 1×1 convolution followed by a pixel-wise soft-max over the final feature map. The cross entropy loss function is used to update weights of the network. The soft-max function redistributes the weights of the final layer of the network in the interval of $[0, 1]$ modeling a probability distribution over predicted output classes. In total the network has 23 convolutional layers. More details of U-Net can be found in [22].

In this paper, to address our problem of detecting tree bark defects which is defined as two-class segmentation, we made several changes to the original U-Net. In order to reduce the over-fitting of the considered neural network, we apply a regularization technique, called *drop-out*. More precisely, we add two dropout layers in the encoder and decoder, with probability 0.5, to randomly drop some of the connections between layers. In addition, due to the dying ReLU problem [16] –*i.e.,* the ReLU neurons become inactive and only output 0 for any input– the Leaky ReLu activation function is employed instead of ReLU from the original architecture. Finally, in the last layer, we use a Sigmoid activation function instead of soft-max function to ensure the output pixel values range between 0 and 1. For the training, we use input image of size 320×320 pixels. The proposed network architecture is illustrated in Fig. 10.

3.2   Training Data

The training dataset for U-Net framework is built from the relief maps generated from tree bark surfaces by the process described in Sect. 2. It should be mentioned that we only have 25 annotated meshes –*i.e.,* 25 relief maps with

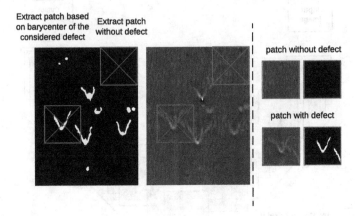

Fig. 11. Illustration of extracting patches of size 320×320 pixels from the relief and the annotated maps.

ground-truths– of tree bark surfaces for the learning process (for more details, see Sect. 4.1). Due to this limited number of samples, two strategies have been adopted to augment the existing data while keeping the significant characteristics of learning objects which are tree bark defects. First and foremost, we split each relief map into patches of same size. For this, we carry out two types of cutting (see Fig. 11). The first one aims to obtain samples centered on defects. More precisely, we perform the splitting of relief map according to the barycenter of the connected component associated to the defect in the annotated image. Note that if a defect is close to the border, a translation is applied to obtain a patch containing the defect and being included in the map. The second one collects samples that do not contain any defect so that the network can learn tree bark without defect. Some samples of extracted patches with and without defects are given in Fig. 12. It should be mentioned that the size of the generated patches is limited by the width and height of our relief maps. As observed in Fig. 7, the relief maps may have different sizes because of the discretization being made with respect to the circumference and height of the tree bark (see Sect. 2). For our framework, the patches are of size 320×320 pixels which is the largest size that could be extracted from the relief maps. The obtained images are then randomly separated into two subsets with a ratio of 7:3 for the training and validation of the network.

After this splitting process, different transformation techniques have also been used on the obtained patches for data augmentation. In particular, we consider the operations: rotation, vertical and horizontal flip, zoom and deletion of rectangular area randomly [3]. Note that this data augmentation is performed on the fly, *i.e.*, during the training time.

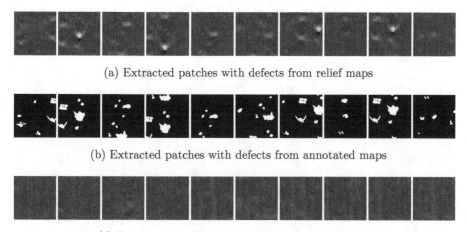

(a) Extracted patches with defects from relief maps

(b) Extracted patches with defects from annotated maps

(c) Extracted patches without defect from relief maps

Fig. 12. Some samples from training data.

4 Experiments

4.1 Dataset

We have two datasets for our experiments: **INRAE1a** and **INRAE1b**. INRAE1a contains 10 trunks of different species: beech (1), birch (1), elm (1), fir (2), red oak (2), wild cherry (2) and service wood (1). INRAE1b contains 15 meshes including alder (4), aspen (4), beech (1), birch (2), horn beam (1), lime (1), red oak (2). The first dataset was used in [18], experiments were carried out on INRAE1a to compare performance and robustness of our method with [13] and [18] on different tree species. The relief maps of INRAE1a are given in Fig. 14. The second dataset is used for the training and illustrated in Fig. 13.

Both datasets have the ground-truths being made by hand-labeling defects. The ground-truth is given as a set of point indices associated to the defect. These indices are then used to generate the annotated maps for training the network.

4.2 Network Training

The training process was first performed on the relief maps generated from 15 meshes of INRAE1b. We used the parameters recommended in [17] for computing these maps. After splitting the obtained relief maps into patches (see Sect. 3.2), we divide the patches of each map into two subsets: 70% for training and 30% for validation. This subdivision allows to have the same bark variability on training and validation. To summarize, the whole dataset has 265 images of size 320×320 pixels, it is partitioned into 204 images for training and 61 images for validation.

The training process is done on GPU (geforce RTX 2080Ti with 12Go RAM). The modified U-Net is implemented using *Tensorflow 2.2* [26] and *Keras* [9]. During the training, data augmentation was applied randomly to the input images,

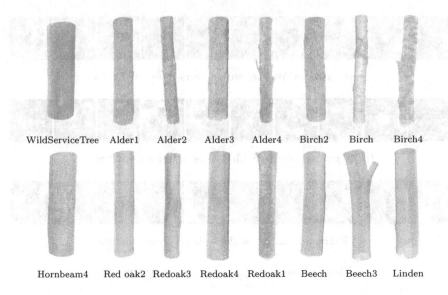

WildServiceTree Alder1   Alder2   Alder3   Alder4   Birch2   Birch   Birch4

Hornbeam4   Red oak2 Redoak3   Redoak4   Redoak1   Beech   Beech3   Linden

Fig. 13. Illustration of input 3D points of the mixed test.

including rotation, vertical and horizontal flip, zoom and deletion of rectangular area randomly [3]. We used the Adam optimiser [12], and set the learning rate at 0.0001, the two parameters $\beta_1 = 0.9$ and $\beta_2 = 0.99$ (default values in *Tensorflow 2.2*). We trained our network for 40 epochs, each epoch comprised 63 steps with 10 images per batch. About the parameters of dropout rate δ and Leaky ReLu activation α, several values have been tested, and we come out with $\delta = 0.5$ and $\alpha = 0.01$ for the smallest loss function (binary cross entropy) on the validation. It should be mentioned that our training is quite fast, it takes about 14 s per epoch. In other words, the proposed architecture allows a high-quality segmentation and very fast training –about **10 min** for the whole training process– with very small dataset. In particular, the prediction takes, on average, 451 ms per map.

4.3   Experimental Results

The first experiments were performed on INRAE1a. More precisely, the relief maps were generated for the 10 meshes of the dataset, then predicted by our network which is previously trained on INRAE1b. The output prediction is a gray-level image. We threshold this image at 0.5 to obtain a binary image in which the white pixels indicate the tree defect and black is not. The results are given in Fig. 14.

To evaluate and compare the methods, we used the classic metrics: precision, recall and F measure (F1). For a fair comparison, we performed the evaluation measures on the mesh points, as done in [18], but not the predicted maps. As described in Sect. 2.3, from pixel positions, we can easily retrieve the mesh point indices associated to the pixel, and identify those points for localizing the defects on the mesh.

Fig. 14. Results on INRAE1a. First row: relief maps, second row: ground-truths, Third row: predictions by our network.

Table 1 shows the obtained results. Generally, the proposed method outperforms both cylindrical-based [13] and patch-based [18] methods. We improve the detection performance, about 41% and 8% better in F1 measure comparing to [13] and [18], respectively. Figure 15 shows a visual comparison on meshes of the results obtained by the proposed method and the patch-based method [18]. We can see in Fig. 15 (a) that our method tends to produce fewer false positives, but sometimes miss small defects. This may due to the fact that the network has not been trained with samples containing small defects. Figure 15 (b) is an example where the detection by our method covers better the form of defects than patch-based method [18].

We carried out a second experiment to demonstrate the generalization of the network. Using the same parameters, we trained our CNN on mixed data of INRAE1a and INRAE1b, i.e., 25 meshes in total. We generated 5 different folds, each of which contains 20 meshes for training and 5 for validation. Table 2 summarizes the distribution of data and the results obtained. For each fold in Table 2, the meshes indicated in *Mesh id* correspond to test data, and the others

Table 1. Comparison results: Overall row is computed from the sum of TP, TN, FP and FN on all the tested meshes.

INRAE1a	Patch method [18]			Cylinder method [13]			Our method		
	Prec	Recall	F1	Prec	Recall	F1	Prec	Recall	F1
Fir1	**0.747**	0.769	0.757	0.137	**0.937**	0.238	0.746	0.857	**0.797**
Fir2	0.673	0.775	0.719	0.353	0.452	0.395	**0.792**	**0.801**	**0.795**
WildCherry1	0.696	0.765	0.728	0.683	0.512	0.584	**0.757**	**0.881**	**0.813**
WildCherry2	**0.846**	0.711	0.771	0.661	0.822	0.732	0.799	**0.955**	**0.870**
Redoak1	0.749	**0.742**	0.744	0.479	0.444	0.459	**0.866**	0.696	**0.770**
Redoak2	0.428	**0.833**	**0.564**	0.061	0.400	0.104	**0.730**	0.428	0.538
Beech	0.670	**0.604**	0.634	0.360	0.289	0.320	**0.863**	0.591	**0.701**
Birch	0.733	**0.756**	0.744	0.607	0.421	0.496	**0.774**	0.726	**0.748**
Elm	0.694	**0.755**	0.721	0.494	0.309	0.378	**0.881**	0.642	**0.741**
WildServiceTree	0.247	**0.741**	0.370	0.057	0.463	0.100	**0.856**	0.504	**0.633**
Overall	0.685	0.740	0.710	0.289	0.563	0.380	**0.793**	**0.789**	**0.790**

are used for training. In this way, we ensure to test and compare our method with the others on all available data. It can be observed that, over the 5 folds, we generally obtain the best F1 measure, and almost better on the precision comparing to [13] and [18]. The worst scoring result by the proposed method is *Beech3* in the *fold 5*, we are at 0.336 for F1. Though, this score is comparable to the best score of 0.493 obtained by [18].

Note that the measured results of the methods [18] and [13] for the dataset INRAE1a (see Table 2) are from [18], while the results on the new dataset in Table 2 are obtained by using the source code from the *GitHub* repository with the recommended parameters described in [17,18].

An online demonstration for testing the proposed method is available at:
https://kerautret.github.io/TLDDC/

5   Source Code to Reproduce Results

5.1   Global View

The source code to reproduce the results presented in the article, including *relief map* and segmentation, is available at the *GitHub* repository:
https://github.com/FlorianDelconte/TLDDC
The repository is composed of different files and directories:

- The directory **Centerline** contains the centerline code.
- The directory **examples** contains INRAE1e and INRAE1b meshes, each mesh is accompanied by two files indicating the ground-truth location of

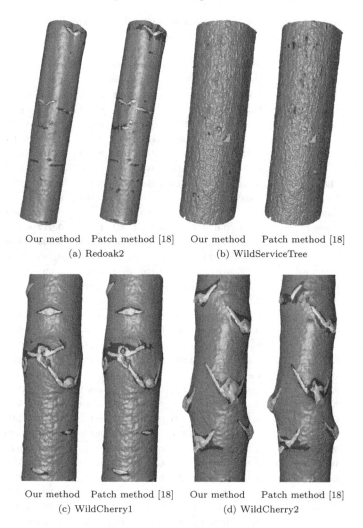

Our method   Patch method [18]   Our method   Patch method [18]
(a) Redoak2   (b) WildServiceTree

Our method   Patch method [18]   Our method   Patch method [18]
(c) WildCherry1   (d) WildCherry2

Fig. 15. Comparison on mesh. Yellow is true positive, red is false negative and green is false positive compared to the ground-truth. (Color figure online)

defects using mesh faces and mesh points, suffixed by *-groundtruth.id* and *-groundtruth-points.id* respectively.

- The directory **models** contains the trained models in the paper: five files of *.hdf5* extension for the corresponding k-fold, and one named *KFoldAssociation* for a relation file between mesh example and the k-fold.
- The directories **mesures** and **run** contain python and bash scripts to directly reproduce the results of this article.
- The code for generating the relief maps is found in *UnrolledMap.h*, *UnrolledMap.cpp*, *DefectSegmentationUnroll.h* and *DefectSegmentationUnroll.cpp*.

Table 2. Comparison results on mixed dataset. Overall row is computed from the sum of TP,TN,FP and FN on all the tested meshes.

Fold number	Mesh id	Patch method [18]			Cylinder method [13]			Our method		
		Prec	Recall	F1	Prec	Recall	F1	Prec	Recall	F1
1	Beech	**0.872**	0.511	0.643	0.325	0.316	0.318	0.853	**0.655**	**0.740**
	Birch	0.647	**0.843**	0.731	0.577	0.445	0.500	**0.818**	0.692	**0.749**
	Alder1	0.089	**0.746**	0.158	0.044	0.380	0.075	**0.798**	0.391	**0.524**
	Aspen1	0.462	0.721	0.562	0.174	0.671	0.274	**0.831**	**0.794**	**0.811**
	Hornbeam4	0.308	0.802	0.445	0.016	**0.954**	0.030	**0.779**	0.589	**0.669**
Overall		0.480	**0.687**	0.563	0.089	0.484	0.150	**0.831**	**0.687**	**0.750**
2	Elm	0.771	0.669	**0.715**	0.158	**0.670**	0.253	**0.889**	0.578	0.699
	Fir1	0.600	**0.824**	0.693	0.107	0.758	0.187	**0.831**	0.819	**0.824**
	Alder2	0.446	0.796	0.571	0.283	0.530	0.366	**0.612**	**0.843**	**0.707**
	Aspen2	0.666	**0.619**	**0.641**	0.352	0.303	0.323	**0.917**	0.419	0.574
	Birch4	0.673	0.572	0.616	0.509	0.532	0.518	**0.694**	**0.819**	**0.750**
Overall		0.618	**0.674**	0.643	0.199	0.527	0.286	**0.759**	0.673	**0.712**
3	Fir2	0.656	0.814	0.725	0.279	0.514	0.360	**0.820**	**0.822**	**0.820**
	Redoak1	0.706	**0.743**	0.723	0.487	0.373	0.420	**0.834**	0.681	**0.748**
	Alder3	0.414	**0.556**	0.474	0.352	0.431	0.385	**0.775**	0.381	**0.510**
	Aspen3	0.544	0.523	0.532	0.116	0.386	0.175	**0.892**	**0.579**	**0.701**
	Linden	0.791	0.600	0.681	0.154	**0.950**	0.264	**0.874**	0.644	**0.740**
Overall		0.624	**0.648**	0.635	0.189	0.565	0.281	**0.845**	0.635	**0.724**
4	Redoak2	0.428	**0.827**	**0.562**	0.062	0.474	0.108	**0.802**	0.350	0.486
	WildCherry1	0.680	0.772	0.721	0.679	0.593	0.632	**0.826**	**0.805**	**0.814**
	Alder4	0.901	0.625	0.737	0.782	0.489	0.601	**0.952**	**0.756**	**0.841**
	Aspen4	0.897	0.454	0.602	0.341	**0.729**	0.463	**0.953**	0.632	**0.759**
	Redoak4	0.479	**0.760**	**0.587**	0.086	0.271	0.12	**0.815**	0.431	0.563
Overall		0.749	0.617	0.676	0.379	0.589	0.460	**0.904**	**0.699**	**0.787**
5	WildCherry2	0.788	0.744	0.765	0.807	0.674	0.733	**0.852**	**0.943**	**0.894**
	WildServiceTree	0.262	**0.732**	0.384	0.051	0.479	0.090	**0.856**	0.559	**0.675**
	Beech3	0.497	**0.491**	**0.493**	0.143	0.192	0.16	**0.867**	0.231	0.364
	Birch2	0.395	**0.595**	0.474	0.083	0.175	0.108	**0.804**	0.454	**0.580**
	Redoak3	0.563	0.618	0.587	0.143	**0.656**	0.232	**0.862**	0.622	**0.722**
Overall		0.564	**0.638**	0.597	0.222	0.480	0.301	**0.851**	0.627	**0.721**

5.2   Installation

For compilation process, the program requires this libraries to be installed:

- DGtal 1_1_0 or later: https://github.com/DGtal-team/DGtal
- Eigen3: https://eigen.tuxfamily.org/dox/GettingStarted.html
- GNU GSL: https://www.gnu.org/software/gsl/
- PCL: https://pointclouds.org/downloads/

To use the segmentation models, these following dependencies are necessary:

- Tensorflow2.2: https://www.tensorflow.org/install/pip
- tensorflow-addons: https://www.tensorflow.org/addons/overview

– openCV: https://pypi.org/project/opencv-python/

Instructions for installing on ubuntu 20.04 and debian 10 have been tested and are detailed on *GitHub*. Once the dependencies are installed and the sources downloaded, the code is built by using the following commands:

```
cd TLDDC
mkdir build
cd build
cmake .. -DDGtal_DIR=/path/to/DGtalSourceBuild
make
```

Two executable files are generated in the **build** directory:

– *segunroll* allows to generate relief maps from meshes.
– *segToMesh* allows to project the segmentation of the defects of the relief map towards the mesh.

5.3   Usage

To generate the relief map, run the following command from **build**:

```
./segunroll -i InputMesh [-h] [-n] [CenterlineParameters] [ReliefMapParameters]
```

With

– *InputMesh* is the path to a trunk mesh.
– *-h* is the option for the command line helper.
– *-n* is the option allows to invert the normals of the faces of the meshes[1].
– *CenterlineParameters* contains the parameters of centerline computation (--*accRadius*, --*trackStep*, --*binWidth*, --*patchWidth*, --*patchHeight*, --*voxelSize*). They are set by default with the recommended values in [17].
– *ReliefMapParameters* contains the parameters for the relief map (--*decreaseFactor*, --*grayscaleOrigin*, --*intensityPerCm*). They are also set with default values.

The following files are created after executing the command:

– *centerline.off*: the generated centerline.
– *discretisation.txt*: the discretization map.
– *output.pgm*: the generated relief map.

To segment the bark tree defects, run the following command from **build**:

```
python3 ../run/predict.py InputReliefMap PathToModel Threshold
```

With

– *InputReliefMap* contains the path to the relief map.

---

[1] The normals must be directed towards the interior of the tree.

– *PathToModel* contains the model file, one of the five in the **models** directory.
– *Treshold* contains the threshold ($[0; 255]$) to apply on the network prediction.

The following files are created after executing the command:

– *outputSEG.pgm*: the prediction result by the network.
– *outputSEGTRESH.pgm*: the segmented image after thresholding.

To project the segmented result on the input mesh, run the following command from **build**:

```
./segToMesh -i InputMesh
```

With *InputMesh* contains the path to the same mesh used to generate the relief map. The following files are created after executing the command:

– *output-defect.id*: the file containing the id of the points of the mesh belonging to a defect (to compare with groundTruth).
– *Poutputdefect.off*: the output mesh with the segmented defects in green.

To execute these three scripts in succession, run the command from **run**:

```
./deep-segmentation.sh PathToModel InputMesh Treshold
```

To reproduce the measurements in Table 1, run the following command from **mesures**:

```
./testINRAE1A.sh
```

This command fill the *results.tex* file which contains the performance measure presented in this article.
To reproduce the Table 2 table, run the following command from **mesures**:

```
./testK_folds.sh
```

After executing this command, five files are created: *resultsN.tex* (with $N = 1...5$) containing the performance measure corresponding to the lines in Table 2.

6   Conclusion

From the difficult problem of tree defect detection, new contributions is proposed in this work with first a new relief map able to locally adapt itself on global shape of the trunk. Such an adaption is important since the trunk geometry may appear with significant variations which make wrong the segmentation of the defect. The second contribution, is to propose a segmentation process based on the U-Net architecture allowing to outperform the previous works. The results, source code and dataset are all available on a git repository allowing the reproduction of the results together with an online demonstration.

In future works, we plan to address the defect classification. Such features will be interesting to get a finer estimation of the wood quality. Other perspectives consist in investigating the 3D point cloud semantic segmentation such as PointNet [20], ConvPoint [1], PointCNN [15], ...

References

1. Boulch, A.: ConvPoint: continuous convolutions for point cloud processing. Comput. Graph. **88**, 24–34 (2020)
2. Carpentier, M., Giguère, P., Gaudreault, J.: Tree species identification from bark images using convolutional neural networks. In: 2018 IEEE/RSJ International Conference on Intelligent Robots and Systems (IROS), pp. 1075–1081 (2018)
3. Devries, T., Taylor, G.W.: Improved regularization of convolutional neural networks with cutout. CoRR abs/1708.04552 (2017)
4. Faghih-Roohi, S., Hajizadeh, S., Núñez, A., Babuska, R., De Schutter, B.: Deep convolutional neural networks for detection of rail surface defects. In: International Joint Conference on Neural Networks (IJCNN), pp. 2584–2589 (2016)
5. Gilbert, G.S., Ballesteros, J.O., Barrios-Rodriguez, C.A., Bonadies, E.F., et al.: Use of sonic tomography to detect and quantify wood decay in living trees. Appl. Plant Sci. **4**(12), 1600060 (2016)
6. G'elard, W., Herbulot, A., Devy, M., Casadebaig, P.: 3D leaf tracking for plant growth monitoring. In: 2018 25th IEEE International Conference on Image Processing (ICIP), pp. 3663–3667. IEEE (2018)
7. He, T., Liu, Y., Yu, Y., Zhao, Q., Hu, Z.: Application of deep convolutional neural network on feature extraction and detection of wood defects. Measurement **152**, 107357 (2020)
8. Iglovikov, V., Shvets, A.: TernausNet: U-Net with VGG11 encoder pre-trained on ImageNet for image segmentation. CoRR abs/1801.05746 (2018)
9. Keras. https://keras.io/guides/functional_api/
10. Kerautret, B., Krähenbühl, A., Debled-Rennesson, I., Lachaud, J.O.: Centerline detection on partial mesh scans by confidence vote in accumulation map. In: 2016 23rd International Conference on Pattern Recognition (ICPR), pp. 1376–1381 (2016)
11. Kerautret, B., Krähenbühl, A., Debled-Rennesson, I., Lachaud, J.-O.: On the implementation of centerline extraction based on confidence vote in accumulation map. In: Kerautret, B., Colom, M., Monasse, P. (eds.) RRPR 2016. LNCS, vol. 10214, pp. 116–130. Springer, Cham (2017). https://doi.org/10.1007/978-3-319-56414-2_9
12. Kingma, D., Ba, J.: Adam: a method for stochastic optimization. In: International Conference on Learning Representations (2014)
13. Kretschmer, U., Kirchner, N., Morhart, C., Spiecker, H.: A new approach to assessing tree stem quality characteristics using terrestrial laser scans. Silva Fennica **47**, 1071 (2013)
14. Krähenbühl, A., Kerautret, B., Debled-Rennesson, I., Mothe, F., Longuetaud, F.: Knot segmentation in 3D CT images of wet wood. Pattern Recogn. **47**(12), 3852–3869 (2014)
15. Li, Y., Bu, R., Sun, M., Wu, W., Di, X., Chen, B.: PointCNN: convolution on x-transformed points. In: Advances in Neural Information Processing Systems, pp. 820–830 (2018)
16. Lu, L., Shin, Y., Su, Y., Karniadakis, G.E.: Dying ReLU and initialization: theory and numerical examples (2019)
17. Nguyen, V.-T., Kerautret, B., Debled-Rennesson, I., Colin, F., Piboule, A., Constant, T.: Algorithms and implementation for segmenting tree log surface defects. In: Kerautret, B., Colom, M., Monasse, P. (eds.) RRPR 2016. LNCS, vol. 10214, pp. 150–166. Springer, Cham (2017). https://doi.org/10.1007/978-3-319-56414-2_11

18. Nguyen, V.T., Kerautret, B., Debled-Rennesson, I., Colin, F., Piboule, A., Constant, T.: Segmentation of defects on log surface from terrestrial lidar data. In: 2016 23rd International Conference on Pattern Recognition (ICPR), pp. 3168–3173. IEEE (2016)
19. Pfeifer, N., Gorte, B., Winterhalder, D.: Automatic reconstruction of single trees from terrestrial laser scanner data. In: International Archives of the Photogrammetry Remote Sensing & Spatial Information Sciences, vol. 35 (2004)
20. Qi, C.R., Su, H., Mo, K., Guibas, L.J.: PointNet: deep learning on point sets for 3D classification and segmentation. In: Proceedings of the IEEE Conference on Computer Vision and Pattern Recognition, pp. 652–660 (2017)
21. Rehush, N., Abegg, M., Waser, L.T., Brändli, U.B.: Identifying tree-related microhabitats in TLS point clouds using machine learning. Remote Sens. **10**(11), 1735 (2018)
22. Ronneberger, O., Fischer, P., Brox, T.: U-Net: convolutional networks for biomedical image segmentation. CoRR abs/1505.04597 (2015)
23. Schraml, R., Entacher, K., Petutschnigg, A., Young, T., Uhl, A.: Matching score models for hyperspectral range analysis to improve wood log traceability by fingerprint methods. Mathematics **8**(7), 1071 (2020)
24. Schütt, C., Aschoff, T., Winterhalder, D., Thies, M., Kretschmer, U., Spiecker, H.: Approaches for recognition of wood quality of standing trees based on terrestrial laser-scanner data. Laser-scanners for forest and landscape assessment. Int. Arch. Photogram. Remote Sens. Spatial Inf. Sci. **36**, 179–182 (2004)
25. Tabernik, D., Sela, S., Skvarc, J., Skocaj, D.: Segmentation-based deep-learning approach for surface-defect detection. J. Intell. Manuf. **31**, 759–776 (2020). https://doi.org/10.1007/s10845-019-01476-x
26. Tensorflow. https://www.tensorflow.org/api_docs
27. Thomas, L., Shaffer, C.A., Mili, L., Thomas, E.: Automated detection of severe surface defects on barked hardwood logs. Forest (10171) (2006)
28. Thomas, R.E., Thomas, L.: Using parallel computing methods to improve log surface defect detection methods. In: 18th International Nondestructive Testing and Evaluation of Wood Symposium; 24–27 September 2013, Madison, WI. General Technical Report, FPL-226. US Department of Agriculture, Forest Service, Forest Products Laboratory, Madison, WI, pp. 196–205 (2013)
29. Wagner, F., et al.: Using the U-net convolutional network to map forest types and disturbance in the Atlantic rainforest with very high resolution images. Remote Sens. Ecol. Conserv. **5**, 360–375 (2019)
30. Weimer, D., Thamer, H., Scholz-Reiter, B.: Learning defect classifiers for textured surfaces using neural networks and statistical feature representations. Procedia CIRP **7**, 347–352 (2013)
31. Zhou, Z., Rahman Siddiquee, M.M., Tajbakhsh, N., Liang, J.: UNet++: a nested U-Net architecture for medical image segmentation. In: Stoyanov, D., et al. (eds.) DLMIA/ML-CDS -2018. LNCS, vol. 11045, pp. 3–11. Springer, Cham (2018). https://doi.org/10.1007/978-3-030-00889-5_1

Pith Estimation on Tree Log End Images

Rémi Decelle[1]([✉]), Phuc Ngo[1], Isabelle Debled-Rennesson[1], Frédéric Mothe[2], and Fleur Longuetaud[2]

[1] Université de Lorraine, CNRS, LORIA, UMR 7503,
54506 Vandoeuvre-lès-Nancy, France
`remi.decelle@loria.fr`
[2] Université de Lorraine, AgroParisTech, INRAE, SILVA, 54000 Nancy, France

Abstract. In this paper, we present an algorithm for pith estimation from digital images of wood cross-sections. The method is based on a probabilistic approach, namely *ant colony optimization* (ACO). After introducing the approach, we describe the implementation and the reproduction of the method linking to an online demonstration. Results show that the approach performs as well as state-of-the-art methods. The estimated pith is below 5mm from the ground truth. It is a fast method that could be used in real-time environment. This paper also gives the details about the intern parameter choice and shows how to use the C++ source code for testing, as well as provides limit cases of the proposed method and future improvements.

Keywords: Agent-based method · Local orientation · Hough transform

1 Introduction

The centre of the annual rings, also called *pith*, is one of the most important feature to be detected since it can be related to wood quality [1,8,20] and it allows to extract other features on log-end image [6,7,10,17] such as annual rings, ring widths, knots, heartwood and sapwood. In the literature, several methods have been proposed for pith detection on log cross-sections. Most of them [2,3,9,14,15,24] have been developed for X-ray computed tomographic (CT) images. The techniques based on CT images allow an efficient and robust detection of external and internal characteristics of tree logs, including the pith. However, the CT scanners are very expensive, and not every laboratory or wood-industry sites (*e.g.,* sawmills) can acquire such a device.

Recently, there have been some efforts to develop pith detection methods on RGB images of cross sections from tree logs [12,13,19,21]. Contrary to CT images, RGB images exhibit disturbances like sawing marks, dirt or ambient light variations, which make the detection more challenging (see Fig. 1). On the other side, the acquisition of such images can be done with low-cost and more accessible devices (*e.g.,* smartphone camera, industrial camera, ...) and could be

© Springer Nature Switzerland AG 2021
B. Kerautret et al. (Eds.): RRPR 2021, LNCS 12636, pp. 101–120, 2021.
https://doi.org/10.1007/978-3-030-76423-4_7

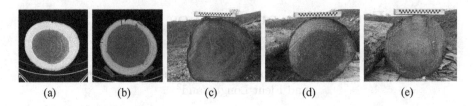

(a)   (b)   (c)   (d)   (e)

Fig. 1. Examples of image for pith detection: (a–b) CT images, (c–e) digital images captured in log-yard. Digital images taken in realistic environments may contain disturbances: (c) light condition, (d) soiling and dirt, (e) sawing marks.

used everywhere, from the forest on the harvester, to the sawmill stocking area, or at the road side for wood sells. Furthermore, the current camera technologies provide images of quality and high resolution, and this allows us to extract the wood quality features, including pith, on such images using the image processing methods.

To the best of our knowledge, four works [12,13,19,21] have been published in the context of pith detection on digital images of rough, untreated log ends. Except in [12] which uses a deep neural network (DNN), the others rely on tree ring analysis and use image processing tools for the detection. More precisely, it is assumed that most tree rings close to the pith approximate a circular shape, and thus the normal directions of these rings would point towards the pith. Based on this idea, the pith detection is generally processed in three steps:

1. Estimate normal directions from tree ring local orientations.
2. Accumulate the normals in an accumulation space.
3. Extract the pith from the accumulation space.

Generally, Hough transform [5] is used as accumulator of normal directions, then the pith is identified at the point with maximum accumulation, or the barycenter of points above a given accumulation threshold. In other words, the pith detection methods differ at the local orientation estimation step. In [19], Norell and Borgefors presented two detection methods using two different techniques to estimate the normal directions: the quadrature filters and the Laplacian pyramids. The proposed methods are robust to disturbances; *e.g.,* rot, dirt or snow. However, a prior segmentation of the log end is needed before the detection. Later, Schraml and Uhl [21] proposed to compute the local orientations with Fourier spectrum analysis. The approach was fast, robust, and accurate in estimating the pith position. It, however, requires some preconditions about the cross-section size and its location in the image for initializing the computation. Recently, Kurdthongmee *et al.* [13] used histogram of oriented gradient (HOG) to estimate normals of the tree rings. As stated in the paper, the algorithm provides only an approximation of the pith location, and needs more treatments to identify it exactly.

In this paper, we propose a general method to estimate pith location on digital images taken in realistic environments; *e.g.,* in the sawmill, forest, log-yard, or on the road. The raw images are directly processed without any prior segmentation nor knowledge of log end visual appearance, shape or location. In particular, the proposed method must not only provide accurate pith estimation, but also be efficient in computation time to be used in real-time applications. To this end, we consider a smooth gradient based method to compute local orientations; this method was originally used for fingerprint images [11]. Then, a probabilistic approach, based on Ant Colony Optimization (ACO) [4], is performed to accumulate the normals of tree rings in a robust way. Finally, the pith is located at the barycenter of points above a given accumulation threshold.

The proposed method is described in the following section (Sect. 2), with the details of the local orientation computation and the ACO algorithm. Section 3 gives the description of the source code and its usage. The experimental results and parameter discussions are addressed in Sect. 4, followed by the conclusion.

2   Algorithm for Pith Detection

The proposed algorithm to estimate pith location on digital images is composed of four steps. Firstly, a pre-processing is applied on input image to remove sawing marks visible on log ends. In case of high-resolution images, a resizing step can be applied to reduce the computation time. Secondly, we compute local orientations for pixels of the pre-processed image. Then, the ACO algorithm is used to accumulate the normals, and finally extract the pith from this accumulator. For an accurate pith estimation, the ACO algorithm and the pith extraction are performed twice: the first to coarsely estimate the pith region, and the second for the precise pith location.

2.1   Pre-processing Image

Pith estimation methods based on ring analysis strongly depend on local orientation estimations. In this paper, we work with raw images in which there might be sawing marks on rough log ends. The presence of sawing marks perturbs the orientation estimations. To reduce errors induced by sawing marks and also computation time, we perform this pre-processing step. Firstly, the input image is converted into gray-scale, then down-sampled with a factor s using bi-linear interpolation. Secondly, we remove sawing marks using the method proposed in [18] which is based on Fast Fourier Transform (FFT).

Typically, sawing marks are straight lines being parallel or in fan-shape and not always evenly spaced. This repetitive pattern suggests that filtering in the Fourier domain is suitable to reduce them. Indeed, in the Fourier spectrum, they correspond to the line passing through the centre with a direction perpendicular to them. In other words, the energy level will be high along this line. Therefore, by reducing this energy and converting filtered spectrum back to spatial domain, sawing marks can be removed or at least reduced. More precisely, we first compute a Fast Fourier Transform (FFT) and filter the Fourier spectrum with a band-pass filter, also remove both horizontal and vertical lines. Then, we threshold it with a value λ to filter high value energy points corresponding

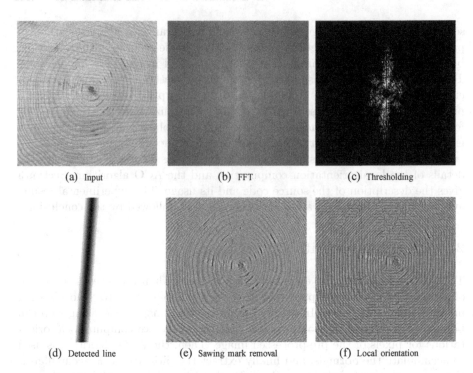

(a) Input   (b) FFT   (c) Thresholding

(d) Detected line   (e) Sawing mark removal   (f) Local orientation

Fig. 2. Removing sawing marks and estimation of local orientations: (a) input gray-scale image, (b) FFT of (a), (c) threshold (b) with $\lambda = 0.875$, (d) detected line after convoluted with a Gaussian of $\sigma = 6$, (e) image after removing sawing marks, and (f) estimated local orientations (red lines) on (e). (Color figure online)

to sawing marks. A line fitting, using principal component analysis (PCA), is applied on the obtained points to find the direction of the line. This line is further convoluted with a Gaussian filter of standard deviation σ, and pixel-wise multiplied with the original Fourier spectrum to reduce energy along the line. The result is transformed back into a spatial image using the inverse FFT. The process is illustrated in Fig. 2 (a–e).

2.2   Local Orientation

After removing sawing marks, we now compute normal directions for blocks of pixels in the image using a smooth gradient based method. The method was used in [11] to assess the local orientation in fingerprint images. It is a least mean square orientation estimation in a local area, namely a window of size w. More precisely, the gradient $\nabla(u, v) = [\nabla_x(u, v), \nabla_y(u, v)]^t$ is estimated for each block centered at pixel (u, v) as follows.

$$\nabla_x(u, v) = \sum_{i=u-\frac{w}{2}}^{i=v+\frac{w}{2}} \sum_{j=u-\frac{w}{2}}^{j=v+\frac{w}{2}} 2\delta_x(i, j)\delta_y(i, j) \tag{1}$$

$$\nabla_y(u, v) = \sum_{i=u-\frac{w}{2}}^{i=v+\frac{w}{2}} \sum_{j=u-\frac{w}{2}}^{j=v+\frac{w}{2}} \delta_x^2(i, j)\delta_y^2(i, j) \tag{2}$$

where $\delta_x(i, j)$ and $\delta_y(i, j)$ are the derivatives with respect to x and y of the pixel (i, j). The derivatives are estimated by a Sobel operator [22]. Then, the local orientation of the block centered at (u, v) is computed as:

$$\theta(u, v) = \frac{1}{2} \tan^{-1} \left(\frac{\nabla_y(u, v)}{\nabla_x(u, v)} \right) \tag{3}$$

Figure 2 (f) shows an example of local orientations estimated by this method.

2.3 Ant Colony Optimization

We now describe the process of accumulating normals using ACO which is an algorithm inspired by the behavior of ant species. Ants deposit pheromones that help other ants of the colony to make the best choice in their goal. *Ant system* [4] was the first ACO algorithm, it is applied for solving different combinatorial optimization problems; *e.g.,* traveling salesman problem (TSP), quadratic assignment problem (QAP) and the job-shop scheduling problem (JSP). Since then, a large number of ACO algorithms have been developed to address various problems like edge detection [16,23]. It has, to our knowledge, never been used as accumulator of local orientations.

The main idea of the proposed method is that a certain number of ants are uniformly placed on the rough log-end image. They can freely move on the image and use normal values as pheromones. Their final goal is the pith. Each ant iteratively lays down pheromones as it moves towards the pith, and they all move towards the pith area where there is a high quantity of pheromones. The process is summarized in Algorithm 1. Hereafter, we describe in details the different steps of the proposed ACO algorithm.

Initialization. (Line 1 and 2 in Algorithm 1) Let $K \times K$ be the number of ants and $\pi^{(t)}$ be the pheromone matrix at iteration t. At the beginning, K ants are placed in an uniform grid on the pre-processed image, and the pheromone matrix $\pi^{(0)}$ is initialized with random values drawn from a normal distribution.

Computation of Probabilistic Transition Matrix. (Line 5 to 9 in Algorithm 1) An ant can move randomly with a probability that evolves during the

---

Algorithm 1: Ant colony optimization for normal accumulation

Input: The estimated local orientations I_θ
          The number of ants $K \times K$
          The maximum number of iterations N
          The number of block clusters around an ant $n \times n$
          The size of each block cluster $\omega \times \omega$ pixels

Output: The pheromone matrix π

Variables : η_k^t: The desirability matrix of the kth ant at iteration t
                 τ_k^t: The probabilistic transition matrix of the kth ant at iteration t
                 ρ_k^t: The deposited pheromone matrix of the kth ant at iteration t
                 π^t: The pheromone matrix at iteration t

1 Initialize the positions of the K ants

2 Initialize the pheromone matrix π^0

3 for $t = 1 \ldots N$ **do**

4   **for** $k = 1 \ldots K^2$ **do**

5   Let (a, b) be the position of the kth ant

        /* Compute the deposited pheromone matrix ρ^t of the kth ant */

6   Let B be the $n \times n$ block clusters of size $\omega \times \omega$ centered at (u, v) in I_θ

7   **foreach** $h \in B$ **do**

8   Let (o_x, o_y) be the median value of local orientations of h

9   Let l be the line of orientation (o_x, o_y) passing through (u, v)

10   Increase ρ_k^t by 1 along l

        /* Compute the desirability matrix η of the ant to move
           towards a position (u, v) */

11   **foreach** $(u, v) \in \eta_k^t$ **do**

12 $\eta_k^t(u, v) = \dfrac{1}{\sqrt{(u-a)^2 + (v-b)^2 + 1}}$

        /* Compute the probabilistic transition matrix ρ of the ant to
           move towards a position (u, v) */

13   **foreach** $(u, v) \in \tau_k^t$ **do**

14 $\tau_k^t(u, v) = \dfrac{(\pi^t(u,v))^\alpha (\eta_k^t(u,v))^\beta}{\sum_{i,j} (\pi^t(i,j))^\alpha (\eta_k^t(i,j))^\beta}$

        /* Move the ant according to the probabilistic transition
           matrix τ_k^t */

15   Let (x, y) be the position of the maximum probability in τ_k^t

16   Move the ant to the position (x, y)

    /* Update the pheromone matrix π^t after all K ants moved */

17 $\pi^{t+1} = (1 - \gamma)\pi^t + \sum_{k=1}^{K} \rho_k^t$

    /* Early-stopping criteria */
    /* Compute the new pith position */

18   The current pith position $\mathbf{p}_{t+1}$ is estimated according to π^{t+1}

    /* Compute the distance between the current and the last pith
       position */

19 $d_{t+1} = \|\mathbf{p}_{t+1} - \mathbf{p}_t\|_2$

    /* Compute the average of the last five distances */

20 $a_d = \frac{1}{5} \sum_{k=t-3}^{t+1} d_k$

21   **if** $a_d < \varepsilon$ **then**

22   Break

23 Return $\pi^{(N)}$

---

optimization. At iteration t, the probability for an ant k, currently at position (a, b), to move to the position (u, v) is defined by:

$$\tau_k^t(u, v) = \frac{\left(\pi^t(u, v)\right)^\alpha \left(\eta_k^t(u, v)\right)^\beta}{\sum_{i,j} \left(\pi^t(i, j)\right)^\alpha \left(\eta_k^t(i, j)\right)^\beta} \tag{4}$$

where $\tau^t(u, v)$ is the amount of pheromone at (u, v), $\eta_k^t(u, v)$ is the desirability of the kth ant to move towards (u, v), and equal to the inverse distance from (u, v) to (a, b):

$$\eta_k^t(u, v) = \frac{1}{\sqrt{(u - a)^2 + (v - b)^2 + 1}} \tag{5}$$

The desirability can be seen as a weighting of pheromone matrix. It aims to ensure ants having a higher probability to move towards local maxima and not towards the global one. α and β are respectively parameters to control the influence of $\tau_k^t(u, v)$ and $\eta_k^t(u, v)$. The ratio $\frac{\alpha}{\beta}$ allows to modify the behavior of ants; a high ratio value leads ants to move more quickly to the pheromone peaks, while a low value leads ants to continue to explore areas in image.

Pheromone Deposit. (Line 12 to 16 in Algorithm 1) Each ant is the centre of an image block cluster. The cluster consists of $n \times n$ blocks, and each block has a size of $\omega \times \omega$ pixels. For each block cluster, the median value of local orientations (see Sect. 2.2) is considered as the block orientation. Then a line is drawn according to the orientation and passing through (u, v). All elements of the deposited pheromone matrix ρ_k^t along the line are incremented by 1. Indeed, depositing pheromones along the whole line allows to include lines intersections which could not happened if pheromone deposit is locally done. Figure 3 illustrates this step of pheromone deposit of an ant.

Updating the Pheromone Matrix. (Line 17 in Algorithm 1) The pheromone matrix is updated once all ants have moved:

$$\pi^{t+1} = (1 - \gamma)\pi^t + \sum_{k=1}^{K} \rho_k^t \tag{6}$$

where ρ_k^t is the deposited pheromone matrix of the kth ant at iteration t, and γ is the rate of pheromone evaporation; the higher γ is, the faster pheromones are removed.

The process is repeated maximum N times (Line 3 in Algorithm 1). In order to reduce computational time, the pheromone matrix π^t is resized by a factor m comparing to the pre-processed image I. In other words, if I is of size $H \times W$, then π^t is of size $\frac{H}{m} \times \frac{W}{m}$.

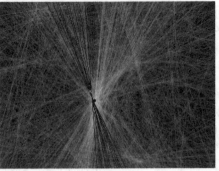

Fig. 3. Left: Image with the ants in yellow crosses, the pith in red, a cluster of 3×3 blocks of size 8×8 pixels and normals (according to the cluster) in green lines. Right: Normal accumulation by pheromone matrix with the considered ant in yellow cross, the 9 green lines corresponding to the normal directions of the block clusters and the pith estimation in red. (Color figure online)

2.4 Pith Extraction

To extract the pith position from the pheromone matrix π, we take the barycentre of all the pixels above $\kappa * \max(\tau)$ in π. Indeed, taking the maximum value of accumulation is less robust than the barycentre of the highest values. Note that the higher κ is, the more sensitive to small variations the pith estimation is.

Furthermore, we introduce an early stopping criterion in Algorithm 1. At each iteration t, we estimate the pith location and compute the distance between the current and the last estimation. Instead of running for N iterations, the algorithm could stop as soon as the average of the last five distances falls below a threshold ε.

3 Code Sources

3.1 Download and Installation

The proposed method is implemented in Matlab 2019b and C++ using the open source library OpenCV[1] (OPEN Computer Vision). Both implementations are available at the github repository:

https://gitlab.com/Ryukhaan/treetrace/-/tree/master/pith

The installation is done with a cmake[2] procedure (see *README.md*[3]). In the following, we focus on the C++ implementation.

---

[1] https://opencv.org/.

[2] http://www.cmake.org.

[3] https://gitlab.com/Ryukhaan/treetrace/-/blob/master/README.md.

3.2   Description and Usage

The repository has four packages:

- **aco** computes the Ant Colony Optimization algorithm for one image;
- **normals** computes normal accumulations using Bresenham lines;
- **orientation** computes local orientations for one image;
- **ui** manages the display (pheromones, ants position on image, and so on).

Once the installation is done, the executable file is in the **build** directory and named **AntColonyPith**.

- **Input:** The image to be processed;
- **Command Line:** To run the program from the CODESOURCES/build

```
./AntColonyPith --input=path_to_image [list_of_parameters]
```

```
./AntColonyPith --input path_to_image --parameters path_to_parameters.json
```

For instance, to run the program on **harvest.jpeg** with default parameters

```
./AntColonyPith --input ../../samples/harvest.jpeg
```

To run the program on **harvest.jpeg** with 10×10 ants, $\alpha = 1.0$ and without animation

```
./AntColonyPith --input ../../samples/harvest.jpeg --ant=10 --alpha=1.0
                --animated=false
```

or

```
./AntColonyPith --input ../../samples/harvest.jpeg -n 10 -a 1.0 --animated=false
```

To run the program on **harvest.jpeg** with parameters in **parameters.json**

```
./AntColonyPith --input ../../samples/harvest.jpeg
                --parameters ../AntColonyPith/parameters.json
```

More details about the options are given in the command line helper.

```
./AntColonyPith --help
```

The options can be provided in two ways:
- using command line with usual options,
- providing a JSON file with all parameters (an example of JSON file, namely *parameters.json*[4], is provided within the repository).
- **Output:** Two files are created. The first one consists of the detected pith position in CSV format. The second one is an image of the input image with the detected pith denoted by a cross.

---

[4] https://gitlab.com/Ryukhaan/treetrace/-/blob/master/pith/c++/AntColonyPith/parameters.json.

Fig. 4. Examples from **Besle** (the first two rows) and **BBF** (the last row) datasets.

4   Experimental Results

4.1   Experiments on Real Images

We experiment our algorithm on two datasets obtained from Douglas fir trees: **Besle** consists of 65 images and **BBF** consists of 40 images (see Fig. 4 for some examples). RGB images are converting into grayscale using the usual weighted method. Both datasets include the raw log ends taken in the forest or log yard, the images contain different disturbances such as sawing marks, dirt and light variations. Some visual results are shown in Fig. 5 by running the proposed method with the default parameters. The values of default parameters are given in the file *parameters.json* (see Footnote 4). Further experiments about computation time and algorithm convergence are presented in the next sections. Note that we take the average value overall experiments on images in both datasets.

4.2   Accuracy of the Method

For our implementation, we process twice the described method Sect. 2. RBG image are converted into grayscale (with the function *imread* and the option *IMREAD_GRAYSCALE* from Opencv). The first run is to coarsely estimate the pith while the second run is for a precise pith estimation. For the first run, we split the image into 4×4 sub-images to manage the sawing marks removal (see Sect. 2.1). After retrieving the first pith estimation, this latter is converted back to coordinate of the original image. We select a sub-image of size 512×512 pixels centered on it and process again the algorithm (including the preprocessing without subdivision).

Ground truths were done by two operators. Each operator independently, for each image, pointed the pith. The truth is the average of these two measures.

To determine the parameters' values, we manually minimized over the whole **BBF** dataset the sum of distances between ground truths and results. Then, we

Fig. 5. Pith position (black cross) detected by the proposed method on raw log-end images using default parameters.

Table 1. Pre-processing parameters for both steps. H is the height of the Fourier spectrum.

	λ	δ	σ	Band-pass
For the both stages	0.875	0.4	6	$\frac{H}{3} < f < \frac{H}{64}$

validated those values on **Besle** dataset. Tables 1 shows the parameters obtained for the preprocessing. Parameters for the ACO-based algorithms are set as follows (the values are the same for both phase unless otherwise indicated):

- $K = 16$: the number of ants $K \times K$;
- $\alpha = 2.0$: the control of the pheromone influence in (4);
- $\beta = 1.0$: the control of the heuristic influence in (4);
- $\gamma = 0.07$: the evaporation rate in (6);
- $m = 5$ for the first run then $m = 2$ for the second one: how many pixels an element in the matrix τ stands for;
- $n = 3$: the size of the blocks cluster (see Sect. 2.3);
- $\omega = 8$: the size in pixels of a block (see Sect. 2.3);
- $\kappa = 0.8$: threshold to the barycentre (see Sect. 2.4)
- $\varepsilon = 2$ for the first run then $\varepsilon = 0.5$: the thresh to early stop the algorithm.
- $N = 50$: the maximum number of iterations;

We have compared our results with [12,13] and [21] on our datasets. For the algorithm of Kurdthongmee et al.,[13], we get optimized parameters with a

Table 2. Average, standard deviation, minimum and maximum between ground truths and estimated piths by our method and methods of [12,13,21] methods (in mm) and average time to proceed one image (in ms).

Besle	Mean	StDev	Min	Max	Time (ms)
[21]	**2.29**	**0.98**	**0.39**	**4.96**	8344
[13]	25.06	21.23	2.15	92.44	667
[12]	2.88	1.67	0.87	7.61	**138**
Our method	2.34	1.02	0.46	5.04	1611

BBF	Mean	StDev	Min	Max	Time (ms)
[21]	2.39	1.48	0.49	7.59	8660
[13]	38.38	38.91	3.14	232.74	721
[12]	12.69	53.55	0.50	341.92	**186**
Our method	**2.26**	**1.32**	**0.44**	**4.63**	1745

subregion of size 24 × 24 pixels and a quantization factor of 12. We also used optimized parameters of our dataset for Schraml and Uhl algorithm [21]. For the comparison with the DNN [12], we have done a twofold cross-validation. For each imageset, half of images have been used for the training and the other half for the validation. Two models were trained for each imageset by inverting the training and the validation sets. Ground truths consist of a square of 300 × 300 with the pith position at the center. A data augmentation have been processed on-the-flight (i.e. each time each image was transformed before passing through the DNN). The DNN hyperparameters were the same as [12], only input size have been modified which is 576 × 432 for both imageset (the ground truth is resized according to that). The DNN returns a box with a probability of finding a pith in it. The predicted pith is the center of the box with the highest probability. To compare each method, we have aggregated all predictions from trained models (which gives us predictions for all images).

Table 2 presents a statistical analysis of the three algorithms on our datasets. The deep learning method is the fastest but drawbacks are the learning time and the creation of dataset with ground truths. Our method is, in average, 5 times faster than [21] and can be easily parallelized. We can observe that both our method and [21] are more accurate than [12,13]. The results [12] are worse on **BBF** imageset, this may be due to the small number of images in it.

Figure 6 presents boxplots for our method, [21] and [12] to better illustrate the differences between them. We excluded [13] since the results are less accurate than the three others. For **Besle** imageset, our method is a little less accurate than [21]. [12] is even a little less accurate and presents one outlier (7.61 mm). Its first and third quartiles are higher than our method and [21]. For **BBF** imageset, [21] has one outlier (7.6 mm) and [12] has four outliers above 10 mm.

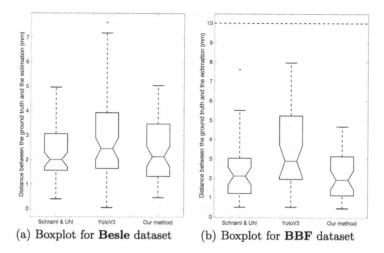

(a) Boxplot for **Besle** dataset   (b) Boxplot for **BBF** dataset

Fig. 6. Boxplots of distance between ground truths and pith estimation (in mm) for [12, 21] and our method.

4.3   Effect of Parameter Changes on Computation Time

Hereafter, the experiments are carried out to analyse the effects of parameter changes. First, we focus on computation time then on precision and convergence.

Let estimate the time complexity for one iteration in Algorithm 1. Let I be the input image of size $H \times W$. According to Algorithm 1, there are K^2 ants, and they can freely move on I. Let now estimate the time complexity for an ant, namely the kth ant. Firstly, the desirability matrix η and the probabilistic transition matrix ρ associated to the kth ant are computed in $\mathcal{O}(\frac{HW}{m^2})$. Secondly, for the pheromone deposit, we must recall that each ant is the centre of an image block cluster which consists of $n \times n$ blocks and each block is of size $\omega \times \omega$. Therefore, to estimate the block orientation, we compute n^2 times the median of an array of ω^2 pixels. This operation is done by sorting the array and costs $\mathcal{O}(n^2 \omega^2 \log \omega)$. We also compute n^2 times the deposited pheromone matrix ρ_k^t along the directional line l. In the worst case, the length of l is equal to $\sqrt{(\frac{H}{m})^2 + (\frac{W}{m})^2}$. In other words, the pheromone matrix update is done in $\mathcal{O}(\frac{n^2}{m}\sqrt{H^2 + W^2})$. Finally, the ant's position is updated in $\mathcal{O}(1)$. Once each ant has moved, the pheromones matrix π^t is updated in $\mathcal{O}(\frac{HW}{m^2})$. Therefore, the total time complexity for one iteration is:

$$\mathcal{O}\left(K^2\left[n^2\omega^2 \log \omega + \frac{n^2}{m}\sqrt{H^2 + W^2} + \frac{1}{m^2}HW + 1\right] + \frac{1}{m^2}HW\right) \quad (7)$$

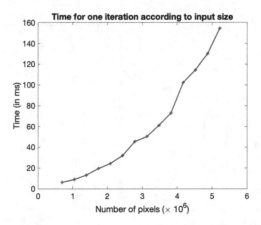

Fig. 7. Computation time for one iteration according to the size of input image (in ms).

We can simplify this equation by keeping only the main input parameters, which are K, H and W. The total time complexity is therefore:

$$\mathcal{O}\left(K^2 \left[\sqrt{H^2 + W^2} + HW + 1 \right] \right) \tag{8}$$

We now validate this theoretical time complexity by the experiments. Firstly, it can be seen in $Eq.$ (7) that the method is quadratic with respect to the size of the input image I. This is confirmed by Fig. 7, we have the computation time for one iteration according to I.

From $Eq.$ (7), the method has a linear time complexity with respect to the number of ants K^2. Indeed, Fig. 8 (a) shows the computation time according to K. The number of ants quadratically increases, and thus the computation time.

Still in $Eq.$ (7), the computation time decreases as m increases. Figure 8 (b) shows the computation time according to m. It can be seen that having a value of m higher than 1 is really computationally helpful. Indeed, the matrix π is widely used during the process, from the pheromones deposit to the pheromones updates (reducing the size of η, τ and π). Let now look at two parameters: the block size $\omega \times \omega$ and the number of clusters $n \times n$ around the ant. First, the computation time according to the block size is shown in Fig. 8 (c). As the number of block is at least one, the computation time does not start at 0. For a block size of 3×3 it takes in average 243 ms, while for a block size of 11×11 it is 259 ms. Note that the computation time depends on the length of the line l used to update ρ (which depends on local orientations). For n, it should be quadratic. As n should be at least one, the computation time does not start at 0. Figure 8 (d) shows the computation time according to n, and it is nearly quadratic. Again, this is due to the length of l.

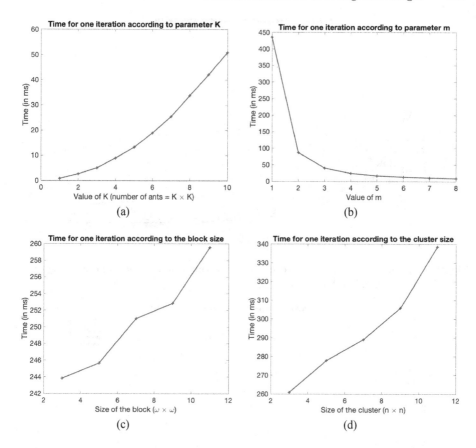

Fig. 8. Computation time for one iteration according to (a) the number of ants K, (b) the size of τ, (c) the block size ω and (d) the cluster size n.

4.4   Effects of Parameter Changes on the Convergence

We now analyse the influence of parameters regarding the convergence of the algorithm. More precisely, the algorithm converges if the Euclidean distance between two successive estimations does not vary more than one pixel. We compute the average variations at each iteration over the whole set of images. We also fit a curve $ae^{bx} + c$ for each change in the value of parameters. It is done by using non linear least squares with trust-region algorithm and for initial value $a = \frac{\max - \min}{2}, b = 0$ and $c = 0$.

First, we focus on the number of ants $K \times K$. Figure 9 shows the convergence speed according to K. One can see that the more ants are, the fastest the algorithm converges. With only four ants, the algorithm fluctuates between some positions. However, a high number of ants does not speed up convergence but makes the convergence point more stable (the parameter c is lower with a high value of K).

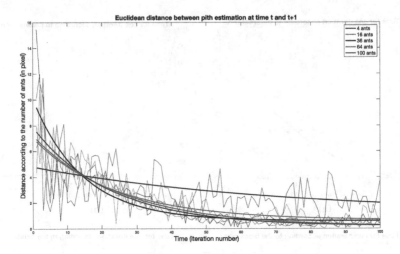

Fig. 9. Variation in both axis between the pith estimation at time t and at time $t+1$ according to the number $K \times K$ of ants.

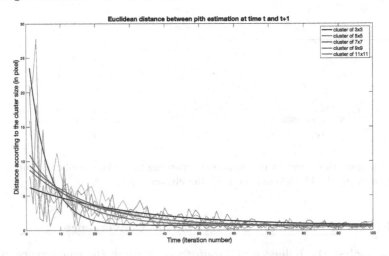

Fig. 10. Variation in both axis between the pith estimation at time t and at time $t+1$ according to the cluster size ω.

Let us now focus on the block's size ω. Figure 11 shows the convergence speed according to ω. It seems that large block speeds up convergence but not as sharply as K. It is observed that an increasing in ω seems to slow down the convergence. This is due to an increase in the deposited pheromones. Indeed, the higher ω is, there more pheromones in the *wrong* places are. Therefore, it requires more iterations to remove those pheromones.

Let us now consider the number of blocks n. Figure 10 shows the convergence speed according to n. Contrary to intuition, a large number of blocks does not

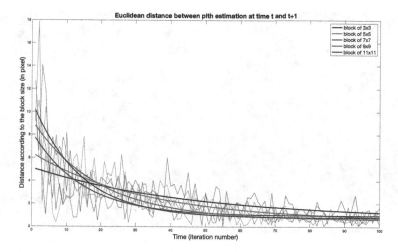

Fig. 11. Variation for both axis between the pith estimation at time t and at time $t+1$ according to the block size n.

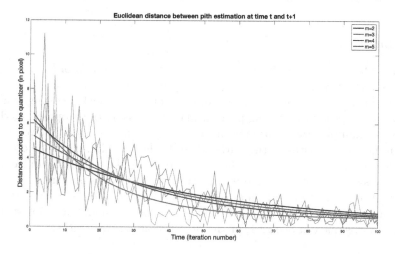

Fig. 12. Variation in both axis between the pith estimation at time t and at time $t+1$ according to the parameter m.

lead to an important acceleration of convergence, but it slows the algorithm down. This could be due to a less accurate local orientation with larger blocks.

Finally, we look at m. As a reminder, the higher m is, the smaller τ is. Figure 12 shows the convergence speed according to m. It appears that m slightly speeds up the convergence. Raising the value of m causes a slightly decelera-tion the convergence. It could be explained by the fact that with a small τ the small variations in the local orientation are not considered when ants deposits pheromones.

Fig. 13. Examples of wrong pith estimation. Left: The tree rings are in low resolution and the sawing marks are not straight lines. Right: the sawing marks are straight lines but tree rings are in low resolution and really small.

4.5   Limit Cases

Our algorithm relies mainly on tree ring analysis. In other words, if the tree rings are not well presented in the input log-end image, then the detection result could be inaccurate. Figure 13 shows some examples in which tree ring analysis is difficult and leads to a wrong pith estimation by using the proposed method. These two examples are not from both datasets. Indeed, our algorithm works very well on introduced datasets (no outliers). In both examples, it can be observed that tree rings are barely visible that makes difficult their analysis. Indeed, the pre-processing step may remove information about tree rings, which leads our algorithm to an inaccurate pith estimation. Furthermore, there are many other disturbances on such images; for instance, the sawing marks are not straight lines as we assumed in Sect. 2.1, or the presence of log-tree cracks.

4.6   Image Credits

All images used in this paper are from the French National Research Agency, in the framework of the project TreeTrace, ANR-17-CE10-0016. Some samples (images in Fig. 5 and Fig. 13) are available for testing on the github repository[5].

5   Conclusion

In this paper, we presented a probabilistic method for detecting pith position on digital images of rough, untreated log ends. More precisely, the proposed method

---

[5] https://gitlab.com/Ryukhaan/treetrace/-/tree/master/pith/samples.

is based on ant colony optimization (ACO) to robustly accumulate the normals of ring tree, then the pith location is extracted from this accumulation space as barycenter of points above a threshold. The experiments demonstrated that the proposed method provides not only an accuracy pith estimation (a distance of less than 5 mm from the ground truths), but also is efficient in computation time and it could be used in real-time applications. In addition to the implementation of the method, an online demonstration is available for testing at:

https://ngophuc.github.io/ACO_PithDetection_IPOLDemo

It could be noticed that the algorithm has many parameters. Though, they are set with default values and allow a good performance on tested images. Generally, the algorithm provides a very accurate pith estimation. A study on the role and effect of the different parameters is addressed in the paper for a better understanding of the parameters on the presented method. Based on this study, a perspective is to reduce the number of parameters and further provide an automatic approach to determine the best parameters adapted to a given image or a set of images of same characteristic. Furthermore, for reducing computation time of the algorithm, parallelism should be considered in future work.

Acknowledgment. This research was made possible by support from the French National Research Agency, in the framework of the project TreeTrace, ANR-17-CE10-0016.

References

1. Akachuku, A., Abolarin, D.: Variations in pith eccentricity and ring width in teak (Tectona grandis lf). Trees **3**(2), 111–116 (1989)
2. Bhandarkar, S.M., Faust, T.D., Tang, M.: A system for detection of internal log defects by computer analysis of axial CT images. In: Proceedings of the 3rd IEEE Workshop on Applications of Computer Vision (WACV 1996), USA, p. 258. IEEE Computer Society (1996)
3. Boukadida, H., et al.: PithExtract: a robust algorithm for pith detection in computer tomography images of wood-application to 125 logs from 17 tree species. Comput. Electron. Agric. **85**, 90–98 (2012)
4. Dorigo, M., Maniezzo, V., Colorni, A., et al.: Ant system: optimization by a colony of cooperating agents. IEEE Trans. Syst. Man Cybern. B Cybern. **26**(1), 29–41 (1996)
5. Duda, R.O., Hart, P.E.: Use of the hough transformation to detect lines and curves in pictures. Commun. ACM **15**(1), 11–15 (1972)
6. Entacher, K., Planitzer, D., Uhl, A.: Towards an automated generation of tree ring profiles from CT-images. In: 5th International Symposium on Image and Signal Processing and Analysis (ISPA), pp. 174–179. IEEE (2007)
7. Fabijanska, A., Danek, M., Barniak, J., Piórkowski, A.: Towards automatic tree rings detection in images of scanned wood samples. Comput. Electron. Agric. **140**, 279–289 (2017)
8. Fallah, A., Riahifar, N., Barari, K., Parsakhoo, A.: Investigating the out-of-roundness and pith-off-centre in stems of three broadleaved species in hyrcanian forests. J. Forensic Sci. **58**, 513–518 (2012). https://doi.org/10.17221/13/2012-JFS

9. Gazo, R., Vanek, J., Abdul-Massih, M., Benes, B.: A fast pith detection for computed tomography scanned hardwood logs. Comput. Electron. Agric. **170**, 105–107 (2020)

10. Hanning, T., Kickingereder, R., Casasent, D.: Determining the average annual ring width on the front side of lumber. In: Optical Measurement Systems for Industrial Inspection III, vol. 5144, pp. 707–717 (2003)

11. Hong, L., Wan, Y., Jain, A.: Fingerprint image enhancement: algorithm and performance evaluation. IEEE Trans. Pattern Anal. Mach. Intell. **20**(8), 777–789 (1998)

12. Kurdthongmee, W.: A comparative study of the effectiveness of using popular DNN object detection algorithms for pith detection in cross-sectional images of parawood. Heliyon **6**(2), e03480 (2020)

13. Kurdthongmee, W., Suwannarat, K., Panyuen, P., Sae-Ma, N.: A fast algorithm to approximate the pith location of rubberwood timber from a normal camera image. In: 15th International Joint Conference on Computer Science and Software Engineering (JCSSE), pp. 1–6. IEEE (2018)

14. Longuetaud, F., et al.: Automatic knot detection and measurements from X-ray CT images of wood: a review and validation of an improved algorithm on softwood samples. Comput. Electron. Agric. **85**, 77–89 (2012)

15. Longuetaud, F., Leban, J.M., Mothe, F., Kerrien, E., Berger, M.O.: Automatic detection of pith on CT images of spruce logs. Comput. Electron. Agric. **44**(2), 107–119 (2004)

16. Nezamabadi-Pour, H., Saryazdi, S., Rashedi, E.: Edge detection using ant algorithms. Soft. Comput. **10**(7), 623–628 (2006)

17. Nordmark, U.: Models of knots and log geometry of young Pinus sylvestris sawlogs extracted from computed tomographic images. Scand. J. For. Res. **18**(2), 168–175 (2003). https://doi.org/10.1080/02827580310003740

18. Norell, K.: Automatic counting of annual rings on Pinus sylvestris end faces in sawmill industry. Comput. Electron. Agric. **75**(2), 231–237 (2011)

19. Norell, K., Borgefors, G.: Estimation of pith position in untreated log ends in sawmill environments. Comput. Electron. Agric. **63**(2), 155–167 (2008)

20. Rune, G., Warensjo, M.: Basal sweep and compression wood in young scots pine trees. Scand. J. For. Res. **17**(6), 529–537 (2002). https://doi.org/10.1080/02827580260417189

21. Schraml, R., Uhl, A.: Pith estimation on rough log end images using local fourier spectrum analysis. In: Proceedings of the 14th Conference on Computer Graphics and Imaging (CGIM 2013), Innsbruck, AUT (2013)

22. Sobel, I., Feldman, G.: An isotropic 3x3 image gradient operator. In: History and Definition of the So-Called "Sobel Operator" (1990)

23. Tian, J., Yu, W., Xie, S.: An ant colony optimization algorithm for image edge detection. In: 2008 IEEE Congress on Evolutionary Computation (IEEE World Congress on Computational Intelligence), pp. 751–756. IEEE (2008)

24. Wei, Q., Leblon, B., La Rocque, A.: On the use of X-ray computed tomography for determining wood properties: a review. Can. J. For. Res. **41**(11), 2120–2140 (2011)

Structure, Concept and Result Reproducibility of the Benchmark on Vesselness Filters

Jonas Lamy[1]([✉])[iD], Bertrand Kerautret[1][iD], Odyssée Merveille[2][iD], and Nicolas Passat[3][iD]

[1] Université Lyon 2, LIRIS (UMR 5205), Lyon, France
jonas.lamy@univ-lyon2.fr
[2] Univ Lyon, INSA-Lyon, Université Claude Bernard Lyon 1, UJM-Saint Etienne, CNRS, Inserm, CREATIS UMR 5220, U1206, F-69100 Lyon, France
[3] Université de Reims Champagne Ardenne, CReSTIC, EA 3804, 51097 Reims, France

Abstract. This paper focuses on the structure and the concept of the framework used in the vesselness filters benchmark that was recently introduced. Vesselness filters are used to detect the presence of vessels in an image. There exists a wide variety of such filters and comparing their respective strengths and weaknesses is a non-trivial task, especially given the different contexts in which they are published. This benchmark was designed to ease such comparison process whereas remaining easy to customize. More specifically, this paper presents the benchmark structure and architecture. It also shows how to integrate new vesselness filters and/or new metrics in the benchmark with the requirements for future comparisons and online demonstrations.

Keywords: Benchmark · Vesselness filtering · CT Images · Reproducibility

1 Introduction

Vessel enhancement is an important step of the vessel segmentation process. Many vessel enhancement algorithms have been proposed over the last twenty years. However, the enhancement step is often overlooked, and very few filters are actually used in medical applications. Having a deeper look at these algorithms, one quickly realizes that it is hard to evaluate and compare them by relying on the associated literature. Indeed, most of them are tested on different (often private) datasets, which blurs the meaning of the filter scores across different papers. Based on these considerations, we decided to design a benchmark framework that allows for a comparison between vessel enhancement filters for 3D images.

This work was funded by the French *Agence Nationale de la Recherche* (R-Vessel-X, grant ANR-18-CE45-0018).

B. Kerautret et al. (Eds.): RRPR 2021, LNCS 12636, pp. 121–135, 2021.
https://doi.org/10.1007/978-3-030-76423-4_8

In this paper, we first briefly recall the benchmark [7] (Sect. 2). Then, we propose a detailed description of the benchmark conception with a focus on how to add new algorithms that fit the benchmark framework and how to add new metrics (Sect. 3). We also describe how to reproduce the results obtained in [7] (Sect. 4). Finally, an online demonstration is highlighted in Sect. 5 before conclusion.

Table 1. List of the methods currently available in the benchmark framework with their characteristics.

Method	Base	Main ideas	Date
Sato *et al.* [13]	Hessian	Vessel reconnection, noise control	1997
Frangi *et al.* [4]	Hessian	Blobs and plates removal with noise control	1998
Meijering *et al.* [11]	Hessian	Neurite detection	2004
OOF [8]	Hessian	Analysis restricted by a sphere	2010
Jerman [5]	Hessian	Volume ratio of tubular structures	2016
Zhang [14]	Hessian	K-mean with sigmoid using Jerman base	2018
RORPO [12]	Morphology	Vote on path opening	2018

2   Overview of the Benchmark of Vesselness Filters

The different algorithms used in the benchmark [7] are summarized in Table 1. The aim is to cover the main reference approaches starting from the pioneering ones with Sato [13] and Frangi [4] that exploit the Hessian matrix in a scale space analysis. These two approaches are able to take into account a certain amount of noise level and can carry out reconnection between vessel parts. Based on Hessian analysis, four more recent algorithms were considered in the benchmark: (i) the Meijering approach initially designed for neurite detection [11]; (ii) OOF which prevents response overflow from the scale space using a spherical framework equivalent to the Hessian matrix [8]; (iii) Jerman, that uses a volume ratio of tubular structures to better exploit the eigen values, producing a more consistent response; and (iv) Zhang that improves Jerman solution with a specialized preprocessing using a K-means classification combined with a sigmoid filter [14]. Finally, to cover other types of approaches, we integrated in the framework a method based on morphological filters that uses path opening and path-based structuring elements [12].

Main Measures and Metrics. To evaluate the impact of the different algorithms, the responses of the filters are segmented by thresholding and compared with ground-truth. Then, the amounts of true positives, true negatives, false positives and false negatives are computed to define other metrics. In particular, we consider the Dice score that accounts for the overlap between the thresholded volume and the ground-truth, and the Matthew's Correlation Coefficients

(MCC). The latter one has a similar purpose but also takes into account the true negatives, leveraging the metric for highly imbalanced datasets.

Evolutive Structure. As it will be described in the following sections, the proposed framework is generic enough to handle different types of images and filters. It can also be used to integrate other algorithms. We benchmarked the enhancement of liver vessels but any other kinds of structures and images can be considered. The only parts that need to be swapped in that case are the mask and reference images. The addition of new metrics is also possible in order to focus on other types of quality features.

Open Framework with Online Demonstration. The source code of the benchmark is available on a *GitHub* repository:

https://github.com/JonasLamy/LiverVesselness

The main organization of the benchmark is described hereafter and a direct access allows to test the different algorithms from an online demonstration that allows to upload specific data:

https://kerautret.github.io/LiverVesselnessIPOLDemo

From this work, the aim is to gather existing and future new algorithms in order to cover state of the art algorithms. In the sequel, we first show how to replicate the results and apply each filter using different data.

3 Filter Design and Integration

Since vessel segmentation is generally the final target application, the benchmark compares the thresholded output of a vesselness filter with a binary ground-truth. For each threshold value, several metrics are computed and aggregated in a CSV format. In medical applications, the area of interest is often an organ, for instance the liver in a CT scan of the torso. Our benchmark thus supports the use of masks to compute the metrics only in chosen/relevant areas.

The benchmark is implemented in C++ and the ITK library [6], which handles multiple medical images formats such as nifti, mhd, dicom series, etc.

3.1 Design of Base Usage

A vessel enhancement filter is designed to highlight the vessels in a 3D volume. This is often performed by improving the contrast of tubular structures whereas removing or decreasing the signal of the other structures and the background. In our benchmark framework, we wanted the filter implementations to be standalone programs so that they could be reused in other applications. Thus, a candidate filter should satisfy the following rules for a proper inclusion into the benchmark pool of vesselness filters:

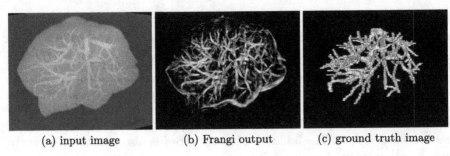

(a) input image   (b) Frangi output   (c) ground truth image

Fig. 1. Illustration of the Frangi algorithm (Antiga implementation) (b) applied in the masked liver (a), and compared to the ground-truth (c).

- parameters should have `--input` for input option;
- parameters should have `--output` for output option;
- a mask option `--mask` should be available where the filtered pixel values are set to zero where mask is zero and unaltered otherwise. We recommend to implement the masking as the final step of the filter, so that the masking does not generate phantom structures with high responses;
- the output of the enhancement filter should be normalized between $[0, 1]$;
- finally if *dicom* series are likely to be used, a `--inputIsDicom` option should also be available.

The CodeList 1 illustrates a commande line example defined to apply the algorithm Antiga on a sample image of the **Data** directory that contains the Ircad database (see links on the *GitHub* repository). The input sample, ground-truth and results are visible on Fig. 1.

```
./Antiga --input ../../data/3Dircadb1.10/patientIso.nii --output antiga.nii
--mask ../../data/3Dircadb1.10/liverMaskIso.nii --sigmaMin 2.0 --sigmaMax
3.0. --nbSigmaSteps 3 --alpha 0.5 --beta 0.5 --gamma 5
```

Code List. 1. Command line example to apply Antiga algorithm (Fig. 1) from the build directory.

Providing a mask or a region of interest greatly modifies the results of some filters. For instance, Zhang filter uses a K-means-based enhancement specifically designed for the hepatic vessels; then it performs very well on images of the liver alone, but using a whole CT scan, it will shift the K-means intensity classes resulting in poor results, see Fig. 2.

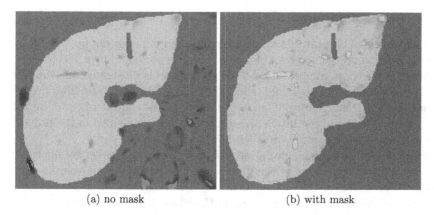

(a) no mask   (b) with mask

Fig. 2. Zhang filtering results using same parameters with (b) and without masks (a). Color scale spreads from blue (low response) to yellow (high response). (Color figure online)

```
{
    "Antiga" :
    [
        {
            "Output":"antiga1.nii",
            "Arguments":[
                {"sigmaMin":"2.0"},
                {"sigmaMax":"2.5"},
                {"nbSigmaSteps":"3"},
                {"alpha":"0.7"},
                {"beta":"0.1"},
                {"gamma":"5"}
                ]
        },
        {
            "Output":"antiga2.nii",
            "Arguments":[
                {"sigmaMin":"2.6"},
                {"sigmaMax":"2.3"},
                {"nbSigmaSteps":"3"},
                {"alpha":"0.5"},
                {"beta":"0.5"},
                {"gamma":"5"}
                ]
        },
    ],
    "Meijering" :
    {
        "Output":"meijering.nii",
        "Arguments":[
            {"alpha":"0.4"},
            {"sigmaMin":"1.6"},
            {"sigmaMax":"1.8"},
            {"nbSigmaSteps":"5"}
            ]
    }
}
```

Code List. 2. Examples of two parameter sets defined to run several instances of two different algorithms: two executions for the Antiga algorithm and another for the Meijering algorithm.

3.2   Design of a Parameter Set

The effectiveness of a filter in an experiment often depends on its parameterization. In our framework, each set of parameters is represented by a json object. An example of file containing several sets of parameters is illustrated on CodeList 2. A parameter object name should reflect the name of the vesselness filter program. It has two attributes: "output" (i.e. the name of the output of the filter), and "arguments" (a list of the filters arguments as they are defined in the program). The output naming convention is left to the user's choice.

Here are some naming conventions we used. If the parameter set file is a mix of several filters, the name of the filter should be in the output volume naming scheme. For instance, the output filenames defined in the three parameter sets are prefixed with the algorithm name in CodeList 2. If the parameter set file is composed of the same filter with several variants of parameters, then the values of the moving parameters should be in the name for easier post-analysis.

The parameters are then used by the benchmark to call the corresponding command line to run the enhancement filter, so that the first parameter set will produce the following command line given in CodeList 3.

```
./Antiga --input inputVolume.nii --output antiga1.nii --sigmaMin 2.0
--sigmaMax 3.0 --alpha 0.7 --beta 0.1 --gamma 5
```

Code List. 3. First command line generated from the parameter set file of CodeList 2.

3.3   Database Listing

The benchmark uses a database described by a listing text file. The listing file format should follow this pattern: name of the image instance (a.k.a. volume name/patient Id), path to the input volume, path to the binary ground-truth, path to the mask volume (ROI). At least one mask is required, but any arbitrary number of masks can be added.

```
3Dircadb1.10 // Name
PathToFolder/patientIso.nii //input image
PathToFolder/vesselsIso.nii  // groundtruth
PathToFolder/liverMaskIso.nii // first mask
PathToFolder/dilatedVesselsMaskIso.nii // second mask
```

Code List. 4. Example of database listing file.

CodeList 4 shows an example of database listing file. In this example, all the filters and their associated parameters are applied to `patientIso.nii` and compared to the ground-truth `vesselsIso.nii`. Metrics are computed in two areas: the mask of the liver, and the mask formed by the dilated vessels. All the associated resulting vesselness output volumes and csv files are stored in a folder named 3Dircad1.10.

3.4 Benchmark Parameters

Once the filter parameters and the database file are ready, the last step is to configure the benchmark. Once again, we chose a json file so that the tracking of carried out experiments is easier (see CodeList 5).

```
{
    "Settings":{
        "name":"MyBenchmark",
        "path":"PathToDirectory",
        "inputVolumesList":"fileLists/DatabaseFileList.txt",
        "algorithmSets":"paramSets/all_algorithms.json",
        "maskList":["Organ","Vessels"],
        "enhancementMask":"",
        "nbThresholds":200,
        "removeResultsVolumes":false
    }
}
```

Code List. 5. Benchmark parameters.

In addition to the location of the benchmark output directory and the location of the required files, the benchmark includes several options. The first one is the list of areas of interest MaskList where the metrics will be computed. The number of masks in that list should match the number of masks added to the database listing. The option enhancementMask allows the user to choose one of the above ROIs as a mask for the enhancement filter (effects demonstrated on Zhang filter on Fig. 2 of Sect. 3.1). If the string is empty, then the metrics are computed on the whole input image. The number of thresholds (nbThresholds) allows to control the precision of the ROC curve. Finally, the benchmark is also designed for low disk memory usage with the option removeResultsVolume. If this option is set to true, only the resulting *csv* files will be kept and the vesselness filter outputs are removed as soon as the metrics are computed.

3.5 Extra Metrics

The addition of extra metrics requires to modify the C++ code. The benchmark is composed of two classes: the Benchmark class which manages I/O and launches the scripts according to the parameter files, and the Eval class that computes the metrics for a given binary image and the associated ground-truth, or a confusion matrix.

Adding a new metric is rather simple. It requires to implement it in the Eval class and overload the << operator so that the results are included with the rest of the metrics in the csv file. One should not forget to add the name of the metric in the header of the csv in the benchmark.cpp file.

The metrics already available are:

- true positives, true negatives, false positives, false negatives;
- accuracy, sensitivity, precision, specificity;
- Dice, Matthew's Correlation Coefficients (MCC).

3.6   Results Analysis

Since the outputs of the benchmark are *csv* files, the post-analysis can be done using tools such as *pandas*, *matlab* or any *csv* file reader. In the associated work [7], we were interested in measuring the most efficient filters when it comes to maximizing the mean MCC over the whole dataset. In other words, we aimed to determine the filter and parameter set that led to the best results in average, instead of seeking a per volume fine tuning.

4   Reproducibility of Benchmark Results

In this section, the focus is made on the reproducibility of the results presented in [7]. The reproducibility term follows the ACM definition: *"it consists of reproducing the results from a different research team by using the same experimental setup"* [3]. For this purpose of reproducibility, the requirements and main steps are presented in the following.

Requirements. The dependencies to construct the benchmark programs are the *ITK* library [10], the *JsonCPP* library (a C++ Json parser) [2] and the *cmake* (3.10.2 [1]) build architecture. Note that to improve the reproducibility success probability, a *git submodule* is integrated in the main repository to link to external library. The post-analysis script requires *python3* with *matplotlib*, *pandas* and *numpy*. Note that a *virtualenv* based configuration is also provided for this script analysis step.

Experiment Process. The experiments for the benchmark described in [7] follow two main steps. These experiments are relatively complex and some manual analyses are required. In particular, we chose to find optimal parameters with a two steps strategy. First, using default intrinsic parameters, we searched the best scale parameter set that maximizes the mean MCC over the whole dataset. Once these optimal scale parameters were found, a second run was performed to find the optimal intrinsic parameters. For instance, if we consider the Frangi algorithm, it means looking first in a three dimensions scale space, and then in a two dimensional intrinsic parameter space instead of handling a five dimensional space as a whole.

Step 1: scale search. For a chosen method, the first step is carried out by launching a scale parameter search, which can be done for all samples of the databases in one command line call (see CodeList 6). Approximately 24 h of computation are required to process a full database such as Ircad. However, it is possible to run several methods in parallel using a server with sufficient memory and computational power. At the end of this step, three *csv* files per method are produced, corresponding to each mask. Table 2 shows a sample of an aggregated result of this first step.

```
// To do for each method of the benchmark
./Benchmark -s scaleSearchIrcad<NameOfTheVesselnessFilter>.json
```

Code List. 6. Scale search command line.

Once the benchmark has been run for all the methods, a python script is in charge of summarizing the results in a pdf file. It gathers all the *csv* files in a folder and invokes **generatePDF.sh**. The produced pdf file will contain the top parameter set for each filters, and the top seven parameter sets per filters for each mask maximizing both MCC and Dice.

Table 2. Best scale parameter sets maximizing MCC.

Method	Ircad - Whole liver				Vascusynth - Whole volume			
	σ_{min}	σ_{max}	nb steps	Best MCC	σ_{min}	σ_{max}	nb steps	Best MCC
Sato *et al.* [13]	1.4	2.4	4	0.269 ± 0.065	1.4	2.8	4	0.541 ± 0.044
Frangi *et al.* [4]	1.4	3.0	4	0.344 ± 0.061	1.4	2.8	4	0.543 ± 0.040
OOF [8]	0.6	2.8	4	0.191 ± 0.039	0.6	1.6	4	0.382 ± 0.038
Meijering *et al.* [11]	1.2	2.2	4	0.138 ± 0.038	1.4	2.8	4	0.356 ± 0.040
Jerman *et al.* [5]	1.4	2.4	4	0.282 ± 0.063	1.4	2.6	4	0.612 ± 0.039
Zhang *et al.* [14]	1.4	2.4	4	0.344 ± 0.106	1.4	3.0	4	0.432 ± 0.040
Method	path size	factor	nb steps	Best MCC	path size	factor	nb steps	Best MCC
RORPO *et al.* [12]	60	1.2	3	0.384 ± 0.077	10	1.6	4	0.311 ± 0.032

Step 2: intrinsic parameter search. Once the scale search is done, we perform an intrinsic parameter search with the fixed best scale parameters. The results are summarized in Table 3.

Finally, the filtering results are shown in Table 4 and illustrated in Figs. 3 and 4.

5   Online Demonstration for Simple Custom Experiments

The different algorithms of the benchmark are available in the online demonstration mentioned in Sect. 2. The user can choose to apply a particular algorithm

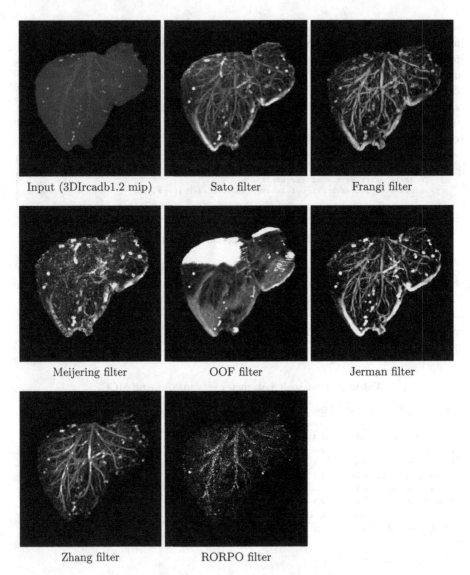

Input (3DIrcadb1.2 mip)   Sato filter   Frangi filter

Meijering filter   OOF filter   Jerman filter

Zhang filter   RORPO filter

Fig. 3. Results on the sample 3DIrcadb1.2 obtained for the parameter sets obtaining the best mean MCC.

and change the default parameters in order to assess the behavior and stability of the algorithm (see Fig. 5 (a)). He/she can also choose to apply the filter on a restricted area of interest around a particular organ by selecting predefined mask images such as liver, vessel or bifurcation areas (see Fig. 5 (a)). Moreover the

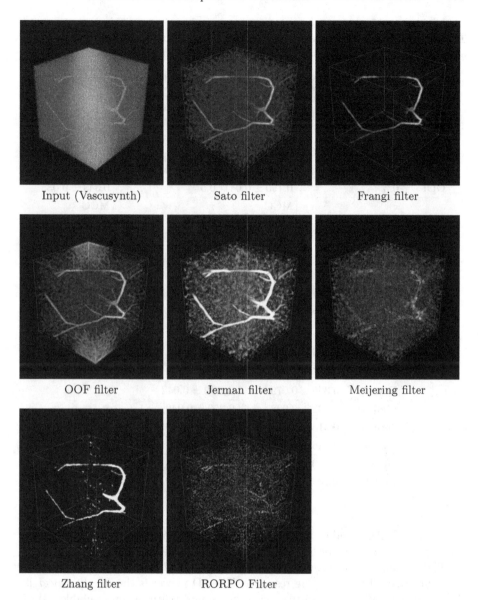

Fig. 4. Results on sample data 11 of group 4 obtained with the parameter set obtaining the best mean MCC.

user interface offers the possibility to upload new volume data and to check the response filter on any new images. In this case, the default mask images cannot be applied, but the user can choose to use his/her own custom mask before the

Table 3. Best parameter sets maximizing MCC. Note that the RORPO and Meijering methods are not mentioned here since they do not have intrinsic parameters.

	Ircad - Whole liver			Vascusynth - Whole volume		
	α	β	MCC	α	β	MCC
Sato	0.3	1	0.275 ± 0.066	0.9	2.8	0.544 ± 0.043
	α	β	MCC	α	β	MCC
Frangi	0.6	0.4	0.356 ± 0.079	0.2	0.8	0.602 ± 0.042
	σ (smoothing)		MCC	σ (smoothing)		MCC
OOF	0.5		0.190 ± 0.041	0.5		0.343 ± 0.035
	τ		MCC	τ		MCC
Jerman	0.2		0.318 ± 0.081	0.8		0.612 ± 0.040
	τ		MCC	τ		MCC
Zhang	1.0		0.346 ± 0.106	0.6		0.478 ± 0.041

Table 4. Results sum up table.

	Best MCC	
	Ircad - Liver mask	Vascusynth - Whole volume
Sato	0.275 ± 0.066	0.544 ± 0.043
Frangi	0.356 ± 0.079	$\mathbf{0.602} \pm 0.042$
Meijering	0.138 ± 0.038	0.356 ± 0.040
Jerman	0.318 ± 0.081	0.612 ± 0.040
Zhang	0.346 ± 0.106	0.478 ± 0.041
OOF	0.190 ± 0.041	0.343 ± 0.035
RORPO	$\mathbf{0.384} \pm 0.077$	0.311 ± 0.032

image upload. Any kind of 3D volumetric images supported by ITK can be used such as *.vol*, *.nii*, *.mhd*, or *.mha* and the maximal size is fixed to 50 MB.

The demonstration provides complementary feedback for the user through the 3D display of the resulting response. The 3D viewer is the *itk-vtk-viewer* [9] that provides a 3D volume display with the ground-truth (when available). With this viewer, the user can focus on the areas of interest directly from the interaction with the online demonstration. Figure 6 illustrates the viewer embedded in a web browser. Thanks to this advanced viewer, the result of any user upload volume data can be displayed (Fig. 6 (b)) and different display settings can be adjusted such as the contrast and filter intensity scale (Fig. 6 (c)), or the type of display by using 2D cutting planes.

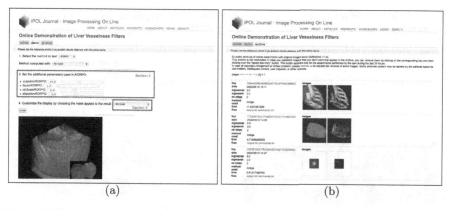

Fig. 5. Illustration of the online demonstration interface. (a) Main interface allowing to select and change the default parameters, including the intrinsic parameters and mask image (highlighted in blue). (b) Archive section of experiments given from user uploaded images. (Color figure online)

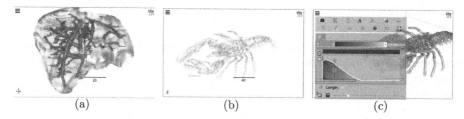

Fig. 6. Illustration of the 3D display obtained from the online demonstration. (a) Result of a filter displayed with ground-truth (in light red). Experiments with user's data can also be carried out (b) and the viewer allows to set the contrast display (c). (Color figure online)

The website interface also provides archives of the uploaded user's experiments (Fig. 5 (b)). The access to the user's results is interesting to highlight the domain of interest and to show the global weaknesses and strengths of a particular algorithm. For now, the volumetric source images are stored on the server but depending on the user's upload usage, the result archive could be restricted in the future to the image previews of experiments with the parameters used.

Filter Results Embedding in Other Web Pages. The online structure of the demonstrations allows the user to export the 3D view of the filter results in other web pages by simply relying on few lines of HTML code. A typical example is illustrated on the following *GitHub* repository:

https://kerautret.github.io/EmbeddingLiverFilterResViewer

The main instructions needed to embed a filter result are described in the example page. They consist of copying few lines of code and updating two links (one for the filter result and one for the mesh reference). An overview of a result view embedding is illustrated in Fig. 7. This behavior is possible thanks to *itk-vtk-viewer* and online demonstration archive coupled together. Such a feature can be useful to illustrate the performance of filter results in various conditions like in a research project web page and also for teaching activities.

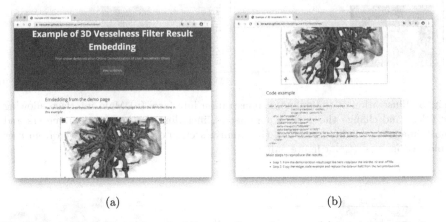

(a)   (b)

Fig. 7. Example of 3D result embedding in other web pages. (a) Interactive 3D viewer embedded in a *GitHub* web page. (b) HTML container source code with main steps to construct the given page.

Online Demonstration Repository Source. Following the purpose to integrate other future reference methods, the source code on the online demonstration is available in the following repository:

https://github.com/kerautret/LiverVesselnessIPOLDemo

The main idea is to invite authors to propose their new filter algorithms. The integration in the online demonstration can be done in two main steps (see `Readme.md` file of the above repository). The first step is to address the new source code to the main benchmark repository. Then, the authors can request an issue to integrate their new methods with the description of specific parameters (or propose directly the demonstration template edition through a *GitHub Pull Request*).

6   Conclusion

In this paper, the architecture of a fully reproducible benchmark experiment was presented including benchmark set up, use of different masks and databases. We also provided an online demonstration to perform quick tests and visualization without any software installation. We also took special care to design the benchmark so that the addition of new filters would be very easy both in the benchmark structure and on the online demonstration. We highly encourage the community to contribute to the algorithm pool through the different *GitHub* repositories so that future state of the art algorithms could be compared with existing literature.

References

1. Cmake. https://cmake.org. Accessed 14 Oct 2020
2. jsoncpp. https://github.com/open-source-parsers/jsoncpp. Accessed 14 Oct 2020
3. Artifact review and badging (2020). https://www.acm.org/publications/policies/artifact-review-badging. Revised 14 August. Accessed 14 Oct
4. Frangi, A.F., Niessen, W.J., Vincken, K.L., Viergever, M.A.: Multiscale vessel enhancement filtering. In: Wells, W.M., Colchester, A., Delp, S. (eds.) MICCAI 1998. LNCS, vol. 1496, pp. 130–137. Springer, Heidelberg (1998). https://doi.org/10.1007/BFb0056195
5. Jerman, T., Pernus, F., Likar, B., Spiclin, Z.: Enhancement of vascular structures in 3D and 2D angiographic images. IEEE Trans. Med. Imaging **35**, 2107–2118 (2016)
6. Johnson, H.J., McCormick, M., Ibáñez, L., Consortium, T.I.S.: The ITK Software Guide, 3rd edn. Kitware Inc. (2013). http://www.itk.org/ItkSoftwareGuide.pdf
7. Lamy, J., Merveille, O., Kerautret, B., Passat, N., Vacavant, A.: Vesselness filters: a survey with benchmarks applied to liver imaging. In: International Conference on Pattern Recognition (ICPR) (2020). https://hal.archives-ouvertes.fr/hal-02544493
8. Law, M.W.K., Chung, A.C.S.: Three dimensional curvilinear structure detection using optimally oriented flux. In: Forsyth, D., Torr, P., Zisserman, A. (eds.) ECCV 2008. LNCS, vol. 5305, pp. 368–382. Springer, Heidelberg (2008). https://doi.org/10.1007/978-3-540-88693-8_27
9. McCormick, M., et al.: Kitware/itk-vtk-viewer: v10.8.0, October 2020. https://doi.org/10.5281/zenodo.4064952
10. McCormick, M.M., Liu, X., Ibanez, L., Jomier, J., Marion, C.: ITK: enabling reproducible research and open science. Front. Neuroinform. **8**, 13 (2014)
11. Meijering, E., Jacob, M., Sarria, J.C., Steiner, P., Hirling, H., Unser, M.: Neurite tracing in fluorescence microscopy images using ridge filtering and graph searching: principles and validation. In: ISBI, pp. 1219–1222 (2004)
12. Merveille, O., Talbot, H., Najman, L., Passat, N.: Curvilinear structure analysis by ranking the orientation responses of path operators. IEEE Trans. Pattern Anal. Mach. Intell. **40**, 304–317 (2018)
13. Sato, Y., et al.: 3D multi-scale line filter for segmentation and visualization of curvilinear structures in medical images. In: Troccaz, J., Grimson, E., Mösges, R. (eds.) CVRMed/MRCAS 1997. LNCS, vol. 1205, pp. 213–222. Springer, Heidelberg (1997). https://doi.org/10.1007/BFb0029240
14. Zhang, R., Zhou, Z., Wu, W., Lin, C.C., Tsui, P.H., Wu, S.: An improved fuzzy connectedness method for automatic three-dimensional liver vessel segmentation in CT images. J. Healthcare Eng. **2018**, 1–18 (2018)

RRPR Short Papers

A Heuristic-Based Decision Tree for Connected Components Labeling of 3D Volumes: Implementation and Reproducibility Notes

Federico Bolelli$^{(\boxtimes)}$, Stefano Allegretti, and Costantino Grana

Dipartimento di Ingegneria "Enzo Ferrari",
Università degli Studi di Modena e Reggio Emilia, Modena, Italy
{federico.bolelli,stefano.allegretti,costantino.grana}@unimore.it

Abstract. This paper provides a detailed description of how to install, setup, and use the YACCLAB benchmark to test the algorithms published in "A Heuristic-Based Decision Tree for Connected Components Labeling of 3D Volumes," underlying how the parameters affect and influence experimental results.

1 Introduction

Although introduced many decades ago [31], the task of labeling objects inside binary images is still employed in several scenarios, whenever an identification of segmented visual objects or image regions is required. This procedure, usually identified as Connected Components Labeling or CCL in short, has a unique and exact solution which provides a description of the objects inside binary images, represented by an output symbolic image where pixels of a connected component are assigned the same integer identifier.

As a matter of fact, many state-of-the-art image processing and computer vision pipelines exploit CCL as a fundamental pre- or post-processing step. The fields of application of such an algorithm range from Object Tracking [18] to Document Restoration [10,25], including Image Segmentation [1,29], Medical Imaging [13,19,30] and many others [6,17]. For this reason, having a fast and efficient algorithm, able to minimize its impact on image analysis tasks, is undoubtedly very advantageous. This is why the research efforts in labeling techniques have such a very long story, full of different strategies and improvements targeting both sequential [8,9,20,22,23,34] and parallel architectures [2,3,5,24,28,32,35]. Among them, some of the most promising techniques that led to major breakthroughs in the field consist in the usage of Decision Trees (DTrees), combined with the 2 × 2 block-based approach. A detailed description of the algorithms based on these paradigms is provided in [7]. Moreover, algorithmic solutions relying on DTrees have demonstrated their effectiveness even when applied, with the necessary variations, to parallel architectures [4,12].

© Springer Nature Switzerland AG 2021
B. Kerautret et al. (Eds.): RRPR 2021, LNCS 12636, pp. 139–145, 2021.
https://doi.org/10.1007/978-3-030-76423-4_9

Unfortunately, existing techniques for the generation of DTrees become quickly unfeasible when the size of the mask used to scan the input image increases. This prevented the application of block-based trees to 3D scenarios. In order to compensate for this limitation a novel heuristic algorithm, based on decision tree learning and named Entropy Partitioning Decision Tree (EPDT), has been presented in [33]. This algorithm allows to compute near-optimal decision trees for large scan masks, overtaking the limitations of existing approaches.

This paper describes the benchmark used to evaluate the performance of EPDT-generated algorithms, focusing on how to configure it to reproduce the experiments reported in [33].

2   The Evaluation Framework

YACCLAB, Yet Another Connected Components Labeling Benchmark, has been originally released in [21] with the aim of providing a fair comparison and evaluation of CCL algorithms. The benchmark has been later improved with additional datasets, tests and with an extension to 3D and GPU algorithms [5,11]. After its first appearance in 2016, it has been used by many authors [14,15,36] to compare the performance of novel proposals with state-of-the-art solutions, thus setting a *de-facto* standard.

When measuring the performance of an algorithm several details should be taken into account, as they could significantly influence the performance. However, CCL is a well-defined problem and the burden of evaluation can be reduced to the measure of execution "speed".

The main elements that affect execution speed can be resumed as follows: data on which tests are performed, implementation details, hardware capabilities, and code optimization provided by the compiler. YACCLAB takes all these aspects into account; the benchmark is open-source and provides an implementation of state-of-the-art algorithms, directly including the source code released together with the scientific papers whenever available. Given its open-source nature, anyone can verify literature claims testing the algorithms with any combination of hardware architecture, operating system and build tools.

The public dataset provided with the benchmark covers most of CCL fields of application, including 2D images and 3D volumes of both real world and synthetically generated domains. A detailed description of the YACCLAB dataset is available in [5]. Because experimental results reported in [33] concern 3D EPDT-generated algorithms, the general properties of 3D datasets are summarized in Table 1 and a brief description follows:

– *OASIS* is a dataset of medical MRI data taken from the OASIS project [27], binarized with the Otsu threshold;
– *Mitochondria* is the Electron Microscopy Dataset [26], which contains binary sections taken from the CA1 hippocampus;
– *Hilbert* consists of the 3D Hilbert curve, which is a fractal space-filling curve, obtained at different iterations (1 to 6) of the construction method.

Table 1. Properties of 3D datasets in terms of foreground pixel density, number of connected components (objects), number of volumes, and resolution.

	Density		Objects		Volumes	Resolution
	μ	σ	μ	σ		
Hilbert	0.055291	0.0873024	1	0	373	$256 \times 256 \times 128$
Mitochondria	0.0588272	0.00599026	40	5.09902	3	$1024 \times 768 \times 165$
OASIS	0.198208	0.0245339	3199	1027.79	6	$128 \times 128 \times 128$

The source code of the EPDT-generated algorithms as well as the benchmarking suite is available at https://github.com/prittt/YACCLAB.

3 How to Test EPDT-Generated Algorithms

In order to correctly install and run the current version of the YACCLAB benchmark, the following packages, libraries and utilities are required:

- CMake 3.13 or higher (https://cmake.org);
- OpenCV 3.0 or higher (http://opencv.org);
- Gnuplot (http://www.gnuplot.info);
- A C++ compiler supporting C++14.

The installation procedure is well detailed in the aforementioned GitHub repository; the main steps can be resumed as follows:

- Clone the repository;
- Generate the YACCLAB project using CMake;
- Set the configuration file `config.yaml` placed in the installation folder;
- Open the project folder, build and run.

When configuring the project through CMake the flags `YACCLAB_ENABLE_3D` and `YACCLAB_ENABLE_EPDT_*` must be enabled in order to set-up the benchmark for 3D algorithms and to include EPDT implementations. The CMake file should automatically find the OpenCV installation path, otherwise it must be manually specified. The flag `YACCLAB_DOWNLOAD_DATASET_3D` must be enabled if the user wants CMake to automatically download the YACCLAB 3D dataset. CMake will automatically generate the C++ project for the selected compiler.

YACCLAB allows to perform multiple tests: *correctness* is an initial validation of the algorithms; *average* runs algorithms on every image of a dataset, measuring the average run-time; *average_with_steps* measures separated run-times for the different steps each algorithm is composed of, including multiple scans over the input image and allocation/deallocation of data structures; *granularity* uses synthetic images to evaluate the performance of different approaches in terms of scalability on the number of pixels, foreground density and pattern granularity; *memory* reports the expected number of memory accesses required by an algorithm on a reference dataset.

YACCLAB stores experimental results in the `output path` specified by the configuration file. Multiple output formats including plain text, bar chart and LᴬTᴇX table will be produced.

CCL algorithms are independent of the Union-Find strategy employed. For this reason YACCLAB provides a Union-Find templated implementation for most of the algorithms, thus being able to compare each algorithm (but those for which the label solver is built-in) with different label solving strategies: standard Union-Find (UF), Union-Find with Path Compression (UFPC) [34], Interleaved Rem's algorithm with splicing (RemSP) [16] and Three Table Array (TTA) [22]. This standardization reduces code variability, allowing to separate label solving data structures from CCL strategies, and provides fair comparisons without negatively impacting execution time.

4   Experiments Reproducibility

```
1  CPU 3D 26-way connectivity:
2    execute: true
3    perform:
4      correctness: true
5      average: true
6      average_with_steps: true
7      density: false
8      granularity: false
9      memory: true
10   algorithms:
11     - EPDT_3D_19c_RemSP
12     - EPDT_3D_22c_RemSP
13     - EPDT_3D_26c_RemSP
14     - LEB_3D_TTA
15     - RBTS_3D_TTA
```

Listing 1. Excerpt of the YAML configuration file.

The EDPT algorithms were tested on an Intel(R) Core(TM) i7-4790 CPU @ 3.60 GHz with Windows 10.0.17134 (64 bit) OS and the MSVC 19.15.26730 compiler. The benchmark was compiled for x64 architecture with optimizations enabled. It is worth noticing that most compilers need several minutes to build EPDT algorithms; in particular, some of them actually fail to compile EDPT_26c. For these reasons, aforementioned algorithms are optional and must be singularly enabled with CMake, as described in Sect. 3.

The performance of EPDT-generated algorithms have been compared to state-of-the-art solutions over the collection of 3D datasets included in YACCLAB and described in Sect. 2. In order to reproduce the same experiments reported in [33], the `CPU 3D 26-way connectivity` section of the configuration file must have its `execute`, `perform` and `algorithms` fields set as in Listing 1. The other fields can remain as default. Finally, 2D tests can be disabled to avoid useless experiments.

5   Conclusion

We described how to reproduce the experimental results reported in [33]. The environment employed for testing the algorithms can significantly affect performance. Cache size and RAM speed can change absolute results while preserving relative performance. Operative System and compiler are likely to heavily influence the outcome.

References

1. Abramov, A., Kulvicius, T., Wörgötter, F., Dellen, B.: Real-time image segmentation on a GPU. In: Keller, R., Kramer, D., Weiss, J.-P. (eds.) Facing the Multicore-Challenge. LNCS, vol. 6310, pp. 131–142. Springer, Heidelberg (2010). https://doi.org/10.1007/978-3-642-16233-6_14
2. Allegretti, S., Bolelli, F., Cancilla, M., Grana, C.: Optimizing GPU-based connected components labeling algorithms. In: 2018 IEEE International Conference on Image Processing, Applications and Systems (IPAS), pp. 175–180. IEEE (2018)
3. Allegretti, S., Bolelli, F., Cancilla, M., Grana, C.: A block-based union-find algorithm to label connected components on GPUs. In: Ricci, E., Rota Bulò, S., Snoek, C., Lanz, O., Messelodi, S., Sebe, N. (eds.) ICIAP 2019. LNCS, vol. 11752, pp. 271–281. Springer, Cham (2019). https://doi.org/10.1007/978-3-030-30645-8_25
4. Allegretti, S., Bolelli, F., Cancilla, M., Pollastri, F., Canalini, L., Grana, C.: How does connected components labeling with decision trees perform on GPUs? In: Vento, M., Percannella, G. (eds.) CAIP 2019. LNCS, vol. 11678, pp. 39–51. Springer, Cham (2019). https://doi.org/10.1007/978-3-030-29888-3_4
5. Allegretti, S., Bolelli, F., Grana, C.: Optimized block-based algorithms to label connected components on GPUs. IEEE Trans. Parallel Distrib. Syst. **31**, 423–438 (2019)
6. Berka, T.: The generalized feed-forward loop motif: definition, detection and statistical significance. Procedia Comput. Sci. **11**, 75–87 (2012)
7. Bolelli, F., Allegretti, S., Baraldi, L., Grana, C.: Spaghetti labeling: directed acyclic graphs for block-based connected components labeling. IEEE Trans. Image Process. **29**(1), 1999–2012 (2019)
8. Bolelli, F., Allegretti, S., Grana, C.: One DAG to rule them all. IEEE Trans. Pattern Anal. Mach. Intell. 1–12 (2021)
9. Bolelli, F., Baraldi, L., Cancilla, M., Grana, C.: Connected components labeling on DRAGs. In: International Conference on Pattern Recognition, pp. 121–126 (2018)
10. Bolelli, F., Borghi, G., Grana, C.: XDOCS: an application to index historical documents. In: Serra, G., Tasso, C. (eds.) IRCDL 2018. CCIS, vol. 806, pp. 151–162. Springer, Cham (2018). https://doi.org/10.1007/978-3-319-73165-0_15
11. Bolelli, F., Cancilla, M., Baraldi, L., Grana, C.: Toward reliable experiments on the performance of Connected Components Labeling algorithms. J. Real-Time Image Proc. **17**(2), 229–244 (2018). https://doi.org/10.1007/s11554-018-0756-1
12. Bolelli, F., Cancilla, M., Grana, C.: Two more strategies to speed up connected components labeling algorithms. In: Battiato, S., Gallo, G., Schettini, R., Stanco, F. (eds.) ICIAP 2017. LNCS, vol. 10485, pp. 48–58. Springer, Cham (2017). https://doi.org/10.1007/978-3-319-68548-9_5
13. Canalini, L., Pollastri, F., Bolelli, F., Cancilla, M., Allegretti, S., Grana, C.: Skin lesion segmentation ensemble with diverse training strategies. In: Vento, M., Percannella, G. (eds.) CAIP 2019. LNCS, vol. 11678, pp. 89–101. Springer, Cham (2019). https://doi.org/10.1007/978-3-030-29888-3_8
14. Chabardès, T., Dokládal, P., Bilodeau, M.: A labeling algorithm based on a forest of decision trees. J. Real-Time Image Proc. **17**(5), 1527–1545 (2019). https://doi.org/10.1007/s11554-019-00912-8
15. Chen, J., Nonaka, K., Sankoh, H., Watanabe, R., Sabirin, H., Naito, S.: Efficient parallel connected component labeling with a coarse-to-fine strategy. IEEE Access **6**, 55731–55740 (2018)

16. Dijkstra, E.W.: A Discipline of Programming. Prentice-Hall, Englewood Cliffs (1976)
17. Dinneen, M.J., Khosravani, M., Probert, A.: Using OpenCL for implementing simple parallel graph algorithms. In: Proceedings of the International Conference on Parallel and Distributed Processing Techniques and Applications (PDPTA) (2011)
18. Dubois, A., Charpillet, F.: Tracking mobile objects with several Kinects using HMMs and component labelling. In: Workshop Assistance and Service Robotics in a Human Environment, International Conference on Intelligent Robots and Systems, pp. 7–13 (2012)
19. Eklund, A., Dufort, P., Villani, M., LaConte, S.: BROCCOLI: software for fast fMRI analysis on many-core CPUs and GPUs. Front. Neuroinform. **8**, 24 (2014)
20. Grana, C., Baraldi, L., Bolelli, F.: Optimized connected components labeling with pixel prediction. In: Blanc-Talon, J., Distante, C., Philips, W., Popescu, D., Scheunders, P. (eds.) ACIVS 2016. LNCS, vol. 10016, pp. 431–440. Springer, Cham (2016). https://doi.org/10.1007/978-3-319-48680-2_38
21. Grana, C., Bolelli, F., Baraldi, L., Vezzani, R.: YACCLAB - yet another connected components labeling benchmark. In: 2016 23rd International Conference on Pattern Recognition (ICPR), pp. 3109–3114. Springer (2016)
22. He, L., Chao, Y., Suzuki, K.: A linear-time two-scan labeling algorithm. In: International Conference on Image Processing, vol. 5, pp. 241–244 (2007)
23. He, L., Zhao, X., Chao, Y., Suzuki, K.: Configuration-transition-based connected-component labeling. IEEE Trans. Image Process. **23**(2), 943–951 (2014)
24. Komura, Y.: GPU-based cluster-labeling algorithm without the use of conventional iteration: application to the Swendsen-Wang multi-cluster spin flip algorithm. Comput. Phys. Commun. **194**, 54–58 (2015)
25. Lelore, T., Bouchara, F.: FAIR: a fast algorithm for document image restoration. IEEE Trans. Pattern Anal. Mach. Intell. **35**(8), 2039–2048 (2013)
26. Lucchi, A., Li, Y., Fua, P.: Learning for structured prediction using approximate subgradient descent with working sets. In: Proceedings of the IEEE Conference on Computer Vision and Pattern Recognition, pp. 1987–1994. IEEE (2013)
27. Marcus, D.S., Fotenos, A.F., Csernansky, J.G., Morris, J.C., Buckner, R.L.: Open access series of imaging studies (OASIS): longitudinal MRI data in nondemented and demented older adults. J. Cognitive Neurosci. **22**(12), 2677–2684 (2010)
28. Perri, S., Spagnolo, F., Corsonello, P.: A parallel connected component labeling architecture for heterogeneous systems-on-chip. Electronics **9**(2), 292 (2020)
29. Pollastri, F., Bolelli, F., Paredes, R., Grana, C.: Improving skin lesion segmentation with generative adversarial networks. In: IEEE 31st International Symposium on Computer-Based Medical Systems (CBMS), pp. 442–443. IEEE (2018)
30. Pollastri, F., Bolelli, F., Paredes, R., Grana, C.: Augmenting data with GANs to segment melanoma skin lesions. Multimed. Tools Appl. **79**(21), 15575–15592 (2019). https://doi.org/10.1007/s11042-019-7717-y
31. Rosenfeld, A., Pfaltz, J.L.: Sequential operations in digital picture processing. J. ACM **13**(4), 471–494 (1966)
32. Spagnolo, F., Frustaci, F., Perri, S., Corsonello, P.: An efficient connected component labeling architecture for embedded systems. J. Low Power Electron. Appl. **8**(1), 7 (2018)
33. Söchting, M., Allegretti, S., Bolelli, F., Grana, C.: A heuristic-based decision tree for connected components labeling of 3D volumes. In: 2020 25th International Conference on Pattern Recognition (ICPR). IEEE (2021)

34. Wu, K., Otoo, E., Suzuki, K.: Two strategies to speed up connected component labeling algorithms. Technical report. LBNL-59102, Lawrence Berkeley National Laboratory (2005)
35. Zavalishin, S., Safonov, I., Bekhtin, Y., Kurilin, I.: Block equivalence algorithm for labeling 2D and 3D images on GPU. Electron. Imaging **2016**(2), 1–7 (2016)
36. Zhang, D., Ma, H., Pan, L.: A gamma-signal-regulated connected components labeling algorithm. Pattern Recogn. **91**, 281–290 (2019)

On the Implementation of Planar 3D Transfer Learning for End to End Unimodal MRI Unbalanced Data Segmentation

Martin Kolarik[1](✉) ⓘ, Radim Burget[1]ⓘ, Carlos M. Travieso-Gonzalez[2]ⓘ,
and Jan Kocica[3]ⓘ

[1] Department of Telecommunications, Brno University of Technology,
Brno, Czech Republic
martin.kolarik@vutbr.cz
[2] Department of Signals and Communications, IDeTIC,
University of Las Palmas de Gran Canaria, Las Palmas, Spain
[3] Masaryk University and University Hospital Brno, Brno, Czech Republic
https://www.utko.fekt.vut.cz/en

Abstract. This article describes detailed notes on the practical implementation of our paper Planar 3D transfer learning for end to end unimodal MRI unbalanced data segmentation (ICPR 2020, Milan), which deals with a problem of multiple sclerosis lesion segmentation from a unimodal MRI flair brain scan by applying a planar 3D transfer learning backbone weights to an autoencoder segmentation neural network. Our source code is published online under an open-source license, and we provide step-by-step instructions for the reproduction of our results.

Keywords: Multiple sclerosis · Reproducibility · Segmentation · Transfer learning

1 Introduction

Medical segmentation using deep 3D convolutional networks is an active research area with application in many problems, one of them being the segmentation of multiple sclerosis lesions. While it is obviously suitable for the natural 3D representation of medical MRI scans, the 3D data processing is often substituted by its 2D counterpart due to a sole availability of deep convolutional neural network transfer learning weights trained on the Imagenet dataset [4].

In our paper "Planar 3D transfer learning for end to end unimodal MRI unbalanced data segmentation" we propose a method for transformation of the 2D weights from the VGG network to planar 3D form. Then we study the effect of the transformed weights when used as a backbone of segmentation neural network for heavily unbalanced data processing. In the following sections, we

© Springer Nature Switzerland AG 2021
B. Kerautret et al. (Eds.): RRPR 2021, LNCS 12636, pp. 146–151, 2021.
https://doi.org/10.1007/978-3-030-76423-4_10

describe the software implementation details of the planar 3D weights preparation, dataset processing, and all details needed to reproduce our results in the aforementioned paper.

2   Implementation Details

The complete source code was published at **Github** [6] with instructions how to reproduce our experiments. The repository also contains code for generating the planar 3D VGG 16 weights for individual experimentation with this transfer learning method.

2.1   Dataset Pre-processing

We performed the experiment on the MSSEG 2016 multiple sclerosis lesion segmentation dataset [3]. Dataset example can be seen in Fig. 1. Although the data are originally in the axial view (top-down), we did rotate the scans to the sagittal view (left-right). This was done only due to our previous experience working with sagittal data. As the data are fully 3D, the evaluation metrics calculation was not affected by the rotation.

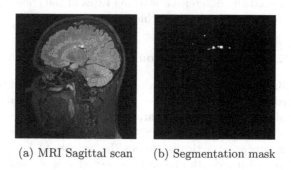

(a) MRI Sagittal scan   (b) Segmentation mask

Fig. 1. Dataset example MRI scan slice with corresponding segmentation mask

After the rotation, we did perform histogram normalization and scaling the data between intervals $[-1, 1]$ for scans and $[0,1]$ for masks. We have tested to scale the input scans to intervals of $[-127, 127]$, $[-1, 1]$, and $[0, 1]$, but the interval $[-1, 1]$ gave the best results and was the most stable during training. Our source code contains an automatic script to load the dataset and perform a complete pre-processing pipeline.

2.2   Hyperparameter Settings

Because of the heavily unbalanced dataset, where only 0.2% of the voxels were in a positive class, it was hard to find a hyperparameters combination, which resulted in a converged network. Most of the tested combinations resulted in a network predicting all voxels negative. This is obviously not a correct solution but a very probable one from the optimization point of view.

During the development and testing phase of our experiment, we tested various hyperparameters, and we selected the best performing combination to obtain the published results. Our tested loss functions included standard binary cross-entropy, Tversky loss, focal loss, and dice loss. The best results were acquired by the following loss function, which was a combination of dice coefficient and binary cross-entropy:

$$Loss(X, Y) = BC(X, Y) + 1 - D(X, Y) \tag{1}$$

As suggested in one of the reviews, it would be beneficial to implement weighted loss of Dice and cross-entropy as $Loss = (1 - \lambda) * BC(X, Y) + 1 - \lambda * D(X, Y)$ an study how different value of parameter λ affects the result.

We have tested Adam [5], Radam [7] and SGD optimizers. Optimizer Adam gave the best results with default settings from library Keras and value decay $= 1.99e - 7$. The learning rate proved to be the critical hyperparameter affecting the network convergence during training. We have tested values between $1e - 3$ to $1e - 6$. The network converged when trained with the learning rate values lesser than $1e - 4$, and the best results were obtained with the value of $5e - 5$. We also tested the differential learning rates in the encoder and decoder parts of the network, but we did not achieve better results.

2.3 Planar 3D Weights Generation

We used the VGG 16 as the base network for planar 3D weights generation. The weights were used from the default Keras [2] implementation as of October 2020. The process of planar 3D weights preparation is implemented as an addition of a dimension to a matrix of trained weights of convolutional layers of the VGG 16 network. This process practically shapes the weights to be used for the 3D convolutional layer with a depth of 1 in the selected axis as depicted in Fig. 2.

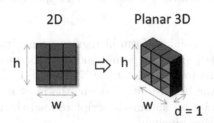

Fig. 2. Visualisation of 2D $\mapsto$ Planar 3D convolutional kernel transformation

We have also tested transforming the Resnet 18 neural network architecture to planar 3D, but we encountered problems mainly because the Resnet does not use pooling, but the convolutional kernel shapes to manipulate the feature size. Despite this, we managed to implement and test the planar 3D Resnet 18 backbone for segmentation. However, the network did not converge, and we were not able to successfully train it even after hyperparameter optimization.

2.4 Execution Environment

The experiments were carried out on a computer with 64 Gb of RAM and an Intel i7-8700. The GPU computations were done on GTX 1080ti and GTX 2080ti cards with 11 Gb of GPU memory. The computer was running an Ubuntu Linux 18.04.5. As for the software environment, the code is written in Python version 3.7.4. For deep learning computation, we used the libraries Keras [2] in version 2.2.4 and Tensorflow [1] in version 1.14.0. For GPU computations, the CUDA [8] in version 11 was used with Nvidia drivers in version 450.80.02.

3 Experiments Reproducibility

We published trained neural network weights from the first round of the cross-validation. The complete manual on reproducing the first round of cross-validation is at our **Github repository** [6].

3.1 Reproducing the MSSEG Results

After obtaining the data, it is important to pre-process and divide it into the scans and masks' testing and training set. The following Table 1 shows which of the MSSEG scans were used for testing in each of the cross-validation rounds. During each round, we selected 3 testing scans, one from each of the scanning center.

Table 1. Test data selection during cross-validation

K-fold	Test data		
	Center 1	Center 7	Center 8
1st fold	01042GULE	07043SEME	08037ROGU
2nd fold	01040VANE	07040DORE	08031SEVE
3rd fold	01039VITE	07010NABO	08029IVDI
4th fold	01038PAGU	07003SATH	08027SYBR
5th fold	01016SACH	07001MOE	L 08002CHJE

Validation data were selected as the last 8% of the training 3D volumes, which resulted in approximately one scan for validation in one cross-validation round. We tried to implement a better validation scheme with validation data from each of the training centers. Due to the small size of the MSSEG dataset (15 MRI scans) and the fact that other validation schemes required a larger portion of the training data to be used for validation, these experiments led to poorer results. In the following Table 2 you can see the results of the cross-validation rounds on each testing scan. The achieved Dice coefficients differ greatly due to the different progression of Multiple sclerosis within each scan. Early stages with small lesions are more difficult to segment, while later stages with severe lesions show much better segmentation results.

Table 2. Dice coefficient - results of 5-fold cross-validation

K-fold	Center 1	Center 7	Center 8	Average
1st fold	0.631	0.676	0.670	0.659
2nd fold	0.578	0.483	0.660	0.573
3rd fold	0.799	0.415	0.762	0.659
4th fold	0.609	0.529	0.492	0.542
5th fold	0.822	0.397	0.635	0.618
Result	0.69 ± 0.11	0.50 ± 0.11	0.64 ± 0.09	$\mathbf{0.61 \pm 0.05}$

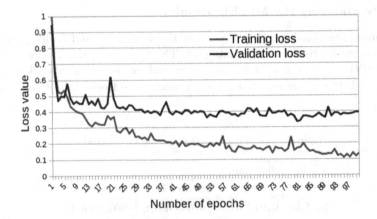

Fig. 3. Graph showing the training and validation loss during the training process. It is important to show that it is not easy to identify overfitting on multiple sclerosis data due to high fluctuations in accuracy on different brain scans.

3.2   Training Custom Neural Network

The planar 3D VGG 16 weights can be generated and used as a backbone for autoencoder segmentation neural networks using our code from the Github repository. Our data loading scripts are developed for loading the MSSEG dataset and a general dataset stored as PNG image slices. We have trained the neural network for 100 epochs, where each epoch denotes calculating the network error and updating its weights on each of the training samples. Depending on the chosen loss function and validation metrics, one epoch lasted between 100–120 s, which resulted in 2.5–3.5 h of training. The inference of a single 3D brain scan segmentation mask took approximately 15 s. The progress of the training and validation loss can be seen in Fig. 3. In a standard segmentation task, the results in Fig. 3 would be seen as overfitting. Our results, however, show a difference in the training and validation set. Similar differences can be seen in the results Table 2. It was difficult to pick a validation scan representing the training set in terms of Multiple sclerosis lesions severity, and we had to take this into account when trying to interpret the experiment results.

4 Conclusion

We have described the implementation of our paper Planar 3D transfer learning for end to end unimodal MRI unbalanced data segmentation in terms of software and hardware requirements. The Sect. 2 includes discussion on the selection of hyperparameters and the experiment implementation and the Sect. 3 the details on how to obtain and reproduce our results. Our source code is published online [6] under an open-source license with complete instructions on how to reproduce our experiments.

References

1. Abadi, M., Agarwal, A., Barham, P., et al., E.B.: TensorFlow: large-scale machine learning on heterogeneous systems (2015). https://www.tensorflow.org/, software available from tensorflow.org
2. Chollet, F.: keras (2015). https://github.com/fchollet/keras
3. Commowick, O., et al.: Objective evaluation of multiple sclerosis lesion segmentation using a data management and processing infrastructure. Sci. Rep. **8**(1), 1–17 (2018)
4. Deng, J., Dong, W., Socher, R., Li, L.J., Li, K., Fei-Fei, L.: ImageNet: a large-scale hierarchical image database. In: 2009 IEEE Conference on Computer Vision and Pattern Recognition, pp. 248–255. IEEE (2009)
5. Kingma, D.P., Ba, J.: Adam: a method for stochastic optimization. arXiv preprint arXiv:1412.6980 (2014)
6. Kolarik, M.: Github repository containing source code to this paper. https://github.com/mrkolarik/transfer2d3d
7. Liu, L., et al.: On the variance of the adaptive learning rate and beyond. arXiv preprint arXiv:1908.03265 (2019)
8. NVIDIA, Vingelmann, P., Fitzek, F.H.: Cuda, release: 10.2.89 (2020). https://developer.nvidia.com/cuda-toolkit

Reproducibility Aspects of Crack Detection as a Weakly-Supervised Problem: Towards Achieving Less Annotation-Intensive Crack Detectors

Yuki Inoue[✉]

Hitachi Ltd., Tokyo, Japan
yuki.inoue.wh@hitachi.com

Abstract. This paper focuses on the reproducibility aspects of our ICPR2020 paper titled *Crack Detection as a Weakly-Supervised Problem: Towards Achieving Less Annotation-Intensive Crack Detectors*. More specifically, we will describe our efforts in making the proposed framework reproducible, the dataset reproducible, and the experiments reproducible. In addition, we argue that reproducibility is a step toward adoptable research, which is something all researchers should strive for. To promote future research, the implementation of the paper is publicly made available at https://github.com/hitachi-rd-cv/weakly-sup-crackdet.

Keywords: Crack detection · Weakly-supervised learning · Reproducible research

1 Introduction

Ever since the epoch-making win by AlexNet in the ImageNet LSVRC-2012 competition [7], the field of machine learning and especially deep learning have garnered considerable attention. In fact, the booming corporate funding for AI-related research indicate that we are deep in the "AI spring" [9]. It feels as though everything new has "AI" sticker slapped on, even though their use of "AI" may widely widely.

The AI trend has also swept the floor in the academic realm as well. The number of submitted papers for premier machine learning conferences like NeurIPS has increased by 50% from 2018 to 2019 [11]. This sudden increase in the number of published paper further supports the claim that the AI field is popular and the field is progressing at a rapid pace. However, it also means that there is an increase in number of papers that are based on bad practices, such as over-aggressive hyperparameter tuning and lack of validation dataset. Also, recent culture of "publish or perish" in academia promotes research that are not thoroughly analyzed and tested. Unfortunately, the exploding volume of submitted papers has made it difficult for the review process to identify and remove such papers. As one of the main reasons why we publish papers is to learn from and

© Springer Nature Switzerland AG 2021
B. Kerautret et al. (Eds.): RRPR 2021, LNCS 12636, pp. 152–160, 2021.
https://doi.org/10.1007/978-3-030-76423-4_11

adopt each other's ideas, publishing ill-practiced papers is not only meaningless for the progress of the academia, but actually toxic, as we may learn erroneous information and be misguided. Therefore, we must try our best to promote publishing good papers.

One of the ways to judge the quality of a paper is to check if a paper is reproducible. Unfortunately, reproducibility does not come for free. In this paper, we will describe how our ICPR2020 paper *Crack Detection as a Weakly-Supervised Problem: Towards Achieving Less Annotation-Intensive Crack Detectors* [6] was designed for reproducibility, to showcase how one might conduct a reproducible research. In addition, we would also like to claim that the ultimate goal of any paper is to be adopted by others, as one of the basic principles of the progress within academia is adopting and building upon each other's work. On that note, we will describe reproducibility in a larger context of adoptability as well, by discussing how we designed our research for adoptability.

We hope that others will find some of our suggestions useful when they design their own research.

2 Overview of the Original Paper

Before we dive into the discussions on reproducibility, let us briefly review the contents of our original paper. In the paper, we tackled the problem of crack detection as a weakly-supervised problem. Because the crack detection task is formulated as a semantic segmentation task, it is very time-consuming to prepare the annotation. As it is ideal to have site-specific annotations to maintain high detection accuracy, the total annotation cost becomes very large. This motivated us to formulate the crack detection problem as a weakly-supervised problem, in which the annotations are approximately given.

As listed in the paper, the main contributions of the paper are three fold:

- Proposal of a framework that acts as a strong baseline for the task.
- Providing synthetic annotations as well as two manual annotations.
- Showing the effectiveness of the proposed framework under weakly-supervised settings.

In the next section we will detail our efforts on reproducibility of each of the items listed above.

3 Reproducible Research Design

3.1 Reproducible Proposal

In the paper, we proposed a simple framework for tackling weakly-supervised crack detection. In the proposal, we augment the traditional crack detection model with a rule-based, darkness calculation branch, conducting the inference

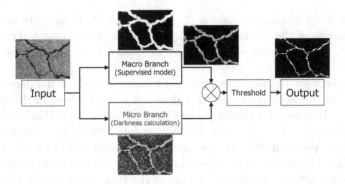

Fig. 1. Overview of the proposed framework with an example input. Taken from [6].

via two parallel branches. In the paper, we refer to the traditional crack detection model as the Macro Branch, and the new rule-based module as the Micro Branch. The final prediction is generated by multiplying the outputs of the two branches as shown in Fig. 1.

As one may notice, the configuration of the Micro Branch is kept very simple-it only calculates the pixel darkness. Adding other image processing techniques such as brightness equalization or pepper noise suppression could improve the detection accuracy, at least for some datasets. However, as the main goal of the paper is to show the strength of the framework structure (*i.e..* splitting the inference path into two branches), exploring the best performing module for the framework would ambiguate the main focus of the paper. Therefore, we decided to keep the Micro Branch as simple as possible. Moreover, we were concerned that adding extra processes to the Micro Branch would serve as a form of hyperparameter tuning, making the proposal appear more successful than it actually is, and potentially not be robust for new datasets.

To showcase this point, we tested the framework with various instantiations of the Micro Branch, as listed below.

- Basic: Uses a simple darkness calculation as proposed in the paper.
- Noise R: A pepper noise suppression operation is added as a postprocess to Basic. It is characterized by a tuple (t, s), where t is the threshold value to binarize the darkness output, and s is the maximum pixel size for noise suppression.
- CLAHE: Brightness equalizing operation called CLAHE [12] is used as a preprocess to Basic.

Table 1 shows the result of different Micro Branch applied to the Macro Branch output of the Inoue *et al.* model from the original paper. The bolded values correspond to cases in which the augmented Micro Branch performs better than the Basic Micro Branch. The sparsity of the bolded values indicate that the augmented Micro Branch does not perform better than the Basic Micro Branch in general. In addition, even for situations in which the augmented Micro

Table 1. Comparison of F-score for different augmentations of the Micro Branch. Basic corresponds to the Micro Branch used in the original paper. **Bold** values correspond to values better than that of the Basic Micro Branch.

	Aigle			CFD			DCD		
	R	R-er	Dil-4	R	R-er	Dil-4	R	R-er	Dil-4
Basic	0.816	0.802	0.775	0.631	0.597	0.558	0.836	0.813	0.813
Noise R (0.5, 4)	**0.817**	0.802	0.775	0.631	0.597	**0.561**	**0.837**	**0.814**	**0.814**
Noise R (0.7, 8)	0.814	0.797	**0.796**	0.617	0.582	0.543	0.835	0.813	0.812
CLAHE	0.810	0.797	**0.786**	0.623	0.595	**0.561**	0.835	0.805	0.808

Branch does perform better, the margins are very slim for most cases. The Noise R outputs also exhibit the hyperparameter tuning nature of introducing new modules to the Micro Branch as we mentioned earlier, as two different settings of the same method produces noticeably different outcomes.

In addition to the simplicity of the Micro Branch structure, its integration to the whole framework is kept simple. As mentioned earlier, the Macro Branch is a traditional crack detector without any modifications. Therefore, researchers can take any crack detectors of their choice and integrate the Micro Branch without major hacking. In other words, simple setup also implies simple implementation, and it encourages other researchers to adopt proposed method. One notable example of this point is the residual architecture introduced by the ResNet paper [4]. We believe that part of the reason for the wide acceptance of the residual idea owes to its simplicity and ease of implementation. Just like how the ResNet paper introduced the residual architecture to the existing feedforward networks, our paper introduced the Micro Branch to the existing semantic segmentation networks. We conclude that for reproducible and adoptable research, simpler is better.

3.2 Reproducible Datasets

To test the proposed framework under weakly-supervised settings, we prepared low quality annotations. Two types of annotations were prepared- namely, manual and synthetic annotations.

First important item for reproducible and fair dataset preparation is a solid annotation procedure. To see an example of this, let us discuss how we prepared the manual annotations. We prepared two sets of manual annotations, named *Rough* and *Rougher* annotations, where latter is of lower quality than the former. At first attempt, our instructions to the annotators were very vague. We just asked the annotators to annotate one dataset roughly, and another rougher. The result was chaotic as shown in Fig. 2, as different annotators had different understanding of the word "rough." Therefore we decided to define the annotation procedure more strictly. The final annotation procedures are outlined in Sec. A of the Appendix of the original paper. Of the many items we tried,

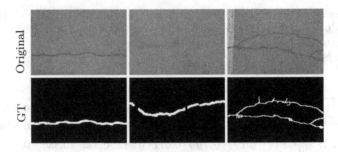

Fig. 2. Examples of annotations without specific annotation instructions. The annotation qualities greatly vary due to lack of solid instructions.

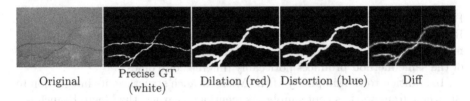

Original   Precise GT (white)   Dilation (red)   Distortion (blue)   Diff

Fig. 3. Example dataset synthesis procedure. Colors in the parenthesis correspond to the pixel colors in the "Diff" column. (Color figure Online)

specifying the pensize especially helped the annotators to solidify the definition of the rough and rougher annotation styles. After setting a strict instructions, the annotation process ended without any problems. Solid annotation procedure helps the annotators to be on the same page, and also helps future researchers to be on the same page when they decide to produce new annotations with similar standards. This makes it easier to reproduce the results on new datasets, and facilitates adoptation of the work.

In addition to manual annotations, we prepared a suite of synthetic annotations. This is done by applying the dilation operation to the precise annotation, and distorting the output using Elastic Transform [1]. The whole process is summarized in Fig. 3.

There are couple of reasons for deciding to synthesize annotations. First, if all we have is the results for the manual annotations, there is a possibility that there was an annotation bias that unfairly favors the proposed method. By making the annotation process automatic and transparent, we can claim that the evaluation results are fair. Second, automatic annotation synthesis means that annotations of same standard can be reproduced for different datasets, if we release the synthesis code.

Also, by varying the number of times the dilation operation is applied to the precise annotation, researchers can generate annotations of arbitrary quality. This means that in addition to being fair, researchers can easily adopt and extend our research at a small cost. This can be confirmed from the precision statistics of the synthesized annotations summarized in Table 2. As we increase

Table 2. Recall (left) and precision (right) statistics for the synthetic and the manual annotations. R and R-er stands for Rough and Rougher Annotations.

	Recall						Precision					
	Dil-1	Dil-2	Dil-3	Dil-4	R	R-er	Dil-1	Dil-2	Dil-3	Dil-4	R	R-er
Aigle	0.93	0.92	0.93	0.93	0.97	0.90	0.40	0.27	0.21	0.18	0.40	0.28
CFD	0.95	0.95	0.95	0.95	0.82	0.92	0.50	0.34	0.26	0.21	0.49	0.34
DCD	0.95	0.95	0.95	0.95	0.95	0.97	0.65	0.52	0.43	0.38	0.69	0.45

the number of dilation operations, the precision, which is in direct relationship with annotation quality, gets lowered.

To make the synthesized annotations as realistic as possible, we ensured that the synthesized annotation's crack regions has a target recall lower bound t_l against the true crack pixels when applying Elastic Transform, to prevent the annotations from being severely morphed. In addition, we set a target recall upper bound t_u as well to simulate rushed human annotators who are likely to miss parts of cracks during annotation. We decided to choose $t_l = 0.925$ and $t_u = 0.975$ in the paper to approximately match the recall values of the Rough and Rougher Annotations, shown in Table 2.

Our proposed framework performed well on the synthesized annotations, but we did not test for robustness against lower recall values. So we synthesized annotations with lower recall thresholds and evaluated our framework on the new annotations. For sake of time, the evaluation is only performed on DeepCrack [8] as the Macro Branch, but we believe it suffices since the proposed framework performed well for all Macro Branches tested. Table 3 shows the result. Since lower recall thresholds translate to degradation in annotation quality, lower F-scores for lower recall threshold range is expected. The important point is whether the benefit of introducing the Micro Branch is affected by the recall threshold. From Table 3 we can conclude that the Micro Branch is effective regardless of the recall threshold, as the F-score improves for all cases. In fact, the performance gap between the lowest recall threshold ($t_l = 0.85$, $t_u = 0.9$) and the highest recall threshold ($t_l = 0.925$, $t_u = 0.975$) shrinks when the Micro Branch is introduced. Therefore, we can conclude that our method is robust to annotations of varying recall values.

Finally, as manual and synthetic annotations approach the generation of low quality annotations differently, we can say that the two annotations present different annotation styles. Therefore, by evaluating the proposed framework with both manual and synthetic annotations, we also test the proposed framework for robustness against different annotation styles, further solidifying the method's reproducibility on new datasets.

Table 3. F-scores for the Dil-1 and Dil-4 Annotations under different lower and upper recall thresholds (t_l and t_u, respectively) during the synthesis process. $t_l = 0.925$, $t_u = 0.975$ is used in the original paper.

t_l	t_u	Dil-1			Dil-4		
		Aigle	CFD	DCD	Aigle	CFD	DCD
(a) Without micro branch							
0.85	0.9	0.532	0.579	0.814	0.296	0.389	0.716
0.9	0.95	0.562	0.589	0.792	0.335	0.410	0.727
0.925	0.975	0.579	0.603	0.799	0.323	0.445	0.749
(b) With micro branch							
0.85	0.9	0.755	0.625	0.844	0.746	0.564	0.815
0.9	0.95	0.771	0.625	0.829	0.772	0.561	0.822
0.925	0.975	0.772	0.636	0.831	0.775	0.574	0.823

3.3   Reproducible Experiments

When researchers hear the word "reproducible," they probably think about reproducing the experiments. One of the ways to prove reproducibility is to upload the codebase to a public repository as we have done. But is it possible to tell if an experiment is well designed an reproducible, without having to run the experiments yourself? We believe that the following are important items for reproducible experiment design:

- Is the method tested on multiple datasets?
- Does ablation study exist?
- Can the proposed method perform well even if some of its modules are replaced?

We tried to fulfill the above items when we designed the experiments.

First, we prepared three datasets, namely, Aigle [2], CFD [10], and DCD [8]. In addition, we prepared many versions of the low quality annotations for each dataset, as mentioned in Sect. 3.2.

Because each dataset is strongly biased, preparing many different dataset is important from the robustness standpoint. Table 4 summarizes the characteristics of the three datasets used in the experiments. As the table shows, the characteristics of the datasets vary greatly. For example, Aigle dataset is the smallest dataset with only 38 total image samples compared to over 500 images in DCD. The size of the cracks also greatly varies between those two datasets, with cracks in DCD occupying over 5 times the area as that of Aigle. In addition to difference in the characteristics of cracks, the quality of the Precise Annotation greatly varies among the datasets as well. As an example, Fig. 4 shows cropped samples from Aigle and CFD. Although it requires some familiarity with inspecting crack images, the image samples show that the annotations for Aigle

Table 4. Dataset information. Mean and standard deviation are for pixels values between 0 and 256.

Dataset	Sample counts		Crack Brightness		Crack width	Crack Area	Anno. quality
	Train	Test	Mean	Std			
Aigle	24	14	52	22.6	Narrow	0.71%	High
CFD	71	47	109	25	Medium	1.4%	Low
DCD	300	237	59	42	Wide	3.5%	Medium

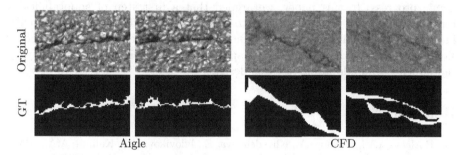

Fig. 4. Examples of variations in annotation quality. The annotation quality of CFD is significantly worse than that of Aigle. Evaluating with various datasets also tests against varying annotation quality.

is much more accurate than that of CFD. For example, in CFD, ring-shaped cracks are often completely filled, and faint lines that are probably artifacts of jpeg compression are annotated as cracks. Part of the reason why annotations on CFD is not very good is because its cracks are of lighter color- the mean value of the crack pixels is double that of the other datasets- making it difficult to identify the crack locations. This also caused problems for the performance of the proposed framework, as it performed poorly for CFD. Evaluating with various datasets allows for analysis from various angles, making it more likely that the proposed method is reproducible in a new environment.

Second item on the list of reproducible experiment design asks for ablation studies. We conducted ablation studies by evaluating the framework without Micro Branch, and showed that the inclusion of Micro Branch results in more robustness against annotation quality. We also showed that the Micro Branch alone is also not enough to achieve high detection accuracy.

Third item asks for the proposed method to be tested under different instantiations of the modules. The idea here is that a method's superior performance should be independent of the implementation details. For example, if a method uses a feature extracting backbone, does it perform well with different types of backbone networks? Also, can the proposed method perform well even if some of its layers are replaced with computationally lighter ones? In our case, we tested our framework with three different crack detectors [3,5,8] as the Macro Branch, and confirmed that the framework is effective regardless of the Macro Branch implementation. In addition, we also tested the proposed framework with a computationally lighter version of one of the networks to double check that the superior performance is reproducible regardless of the Macro Branch used.

4 Conclusion

The goal of a research paper is to encourage future researchers to adopt your work and expand the wealth of knowledge, not be a dead-end or misguide academic progress. In this paper, we argued that a first step of adoptability is reproducibility, and focused on how to secure adoptability and reproducibility in research by outlining our efforts in our ICPR2020 paper. Although the discussions were limited to our ICPR2020 paper, we hope that it helped demystifying reproducible and adoptable research designs.

References

1. Buslaev, A.V., Parinov, A., Khvedchenya, E., Iglovikov, V.I., Kalinin, A.A.: Albumentations: fast and flexible image augmentations. ArXiv e-prints (2018)
2. Chambon, S., Moliard, J.M.: Automatic road pavement assessment with image processing: review and comparison. Int. J. Geophys. **2011** (2011)
3. Chen, L.C., Zhu, Y., Papandreou, G., Schroff, F., Adam, H.: Encoder-decoder with atrous separable convolution for semantic image segmentation. In: Ferrari, V., Hebert, M., Sminchisescu, C., Weiss, Y. (eds.) ECCV 2018. LNCS, vol. 11211, pp. 833–851. Springer, Cham (2018). https://doi.org/10.1007/978-3-030-01234-2_49
4. He, K., Zhang, X., Ren, S., Sun, J.: Deep residual learning for image recognition. In: Proceedings of the IEEE Conference on Computer Vision and Pattern Recognition, pp. 770–778 (2016)
5. Inoue, Y., Nagayoshi, H.: Deployment conscious automatic surface crack detection. In: WACV, pp. 686–694. IEEE (2019)
6. Inoue, Y., Nagayoshi, H.: Crack detection as a weakly-supervised problem: towards achieving less annotation-intensive crack detectors. In: International Conference on Pattern Recognition (ICPR) (2020)
7. Krizhevsky, A., Sutskever, I., Hinton, G.E.: Imagenet classification with deep convolutional neural networks. Adv. Neural Inf. Proc. Syst. **25**, 1097–1105 (2012)
8. Liu, Y., Yao, J., Lu, X., Xie, R., Li, L.: DeepCrack: a deep hierarchical feature learning architecture for crack segmentation. Neurocomputing **338**, 139–153 (2019)
9. Mashable: Google's artificial intelligence chief says 'we're in an AI Spring' (2016). https://mashable.com/2016/05/20/google-ai-spring/
10. Shi, Y., Cui, L., Qi, Z., Meng, F., Chen, Z.: Automatic road crack detection using random structured forests. IEEE TITS **17**(12), 3434–3445 (2016)
11. Synced: NeurIPS 2019—the numbers (2019). https://syncedreview.com/2019/12/12/neurips-2019-the-numbers/
12. Zuiderveld, K.: Contrast limited adaptive histogram equalization. In: Graphics Gems IV, pp. 474–485. Academic Press Professional, Inc. (1994)

Reproducing the Sparse Huffman Address Map Compression for Deep Neural Networks

Giosuè Cataldo Marinò⬤, Gregorio Ghidoli⬤, Marco Frasca⬤,
and Dario Malchiodi(✉)⬤

Dipartimento di Informatica, Università degli Studi di Milano,
Via Celoria 18, 20133 Milan, Italy
{giosue.marino,gregorio.ghidoli}@studenti.unimi.it,
{marco.frasca,dario.malchiodi}@unimi.it

Abstract. Deploying large convolutional neural networks (CNNs) on limited-resource devices is still an open challenge in the big data era. To deal with this challenge, a synergistic composition of network compression algorithms and compact storage of the compressed network has been recently presented, substantially preserving model accuracy. The proposed implementation, which we describe in this paper, offers different compression schemes (pruning, two types of weight quantization, and their combinations) and two compact representations: the Huffman Address Map compression (HAM), and its sparse version $sHAM$. Taken as input a model, trained for a given classification or regression problem (as well as the dataset employed, which is necessary for the fine-tuning of weights after network compression), the procedure returns the corresponding compressed model. Our publicly available implementation provides the source code, two pre-trained CNN models (retrieved from third-party repositories referring to well-established literature), and four datasets. This implementation includes detailed instructions to execute the scripts and reproduce the obtained results, in terms of the figures and tables included in the original paper.

Keywords: CNN compression · Weight pruning · Weight sharing · Probabilistic quantization · Entropy coding

1 Introduction

This paper focuses on the reproducibility of results obtained in [5]. The aim of the original work is twofold: a) to evaluate the impact of lossy CNN compression techniques (pruning and quantization) on prediction accuracy, and b) to provide a compressed and compact representation of a given trained CNN for classification or regression problems. Step a) has been carried out by considering two publicly available CNNs (see Sect. 2.2) trained respectively for image classification and for protein-ligand affinity prediction (regression). The weights

© Springer Nature Switzerland AG 2021
B. Kerautret et al. (Eds.): RRPR 2021, LNCS 12636, pp. 161–166, 2021.
https://doi.org/10.1007/978-3-030-76423-4_12

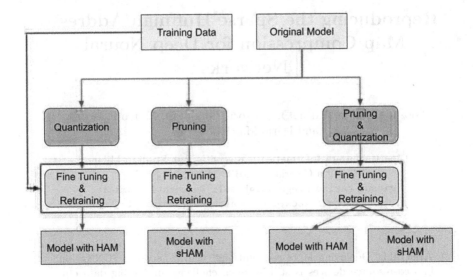

Fig. 1. Sketch of the proposed compression framework. The last level reports the best representation format for the corresponding weight compression strategy. For pruning and quantization both HAM and sHAM are shown, meaning that the format achieving the best compression rate depends on the proportion of original connection pruned (with low pruning HAM is preferred).

of these models have been pruned and/or quantized, considering in particular two different quantization procedures, namely weight sharing and probabilistic quantization (cfr. Sect. 2.3). The prediction performance of the compressed models has been assessed on four benchmark data sets: MNIST [4], CIFAR-10 [3], DAVIS [2] and KIBA [8] (see Sect. 2.1). Step b) leverages two novel compression formats specifically designed to benefit from the pruning and quantization of the connection weights, called HAM and sHAM, described in Sect. 2.4. Finally, Sect. 3 describes how to run the experiments discussed in the original paper, depicted in Fig. 1 and consisting of:

- input data retrieval (pre-trained CNN, as well as the corresponding training set);
- network pruning and/or quantization;
- model retraining;
- model transformation to HAM or sHAM formats;
- assessment of the compressed model performance.

2   Implementation

In this section we describe all stages of the processing pipeline underlying the results in [5]. Namely, Sect. 2.1 briefly introduces the processed datasets, while

Table 1. Structure of the processed datasets.

	Size	Resolution		Proteins	Ligands	Interactions
MNIST	70 k	28 × 28, grayscale	DAVIS	442	68	30056
CIFAR	60 k	32 × 32, color	KIBA	229	2111	118254
(a) Classification			(b) Regression			

Sect. 2.2 describes the models of neural networks used to test the performances of three compression schemes. The latter are detailed in Sect. 2.3, while Sect. 2.4 depicts the representation format of the compressed models.

2.1 Dataset

We validated our methodology on two problems, respectively in the classification and regression realms, employing in both cases two distinct datasets (see also Table 1).

Classification. The first application concerns the multiclass classification of handwritten digits, carried out on the MNIST [4] and CIFAR-10 benchmarks [3]. MNIST contains 70 k 28 × 28 grayscale images, whereas CIFAR-10 consists of 60 k 32 × 32 color images.

Regression. We considered the problem of predicting the affinity between drug (ligand) and targets (proteins), processing the DAVIS [2] and KIBA [8] datasets. Proteins and ligands are both represented through strings, respectively using the aminoacid sequence and the SMILES (Simplified Molecular Input Line Entry System) representation. DAVIS and KIBA contain, respectively: i) 442 and 229 proteins, ii) 68 and 2111 ligands, and iii) 30056 and 118254 total interactions.

2.2 State-of-the-art Models

We considered two state-of-the-art CNN models as part of the input of our processing pipeline:

– *VGG19* [7], containing 16 convolutional layers and a fully-connected block, trained on the CIFAR-10 and MNIST datasets; we assumed that this model is likely over-dimensioned for the digit classification task, and indeed we showed that we can obtain a succinct version (requiring significantly less than 1% of the original space) without accuracy loss;
– *DeepDTA* [6], composed of two convolutional blocks (three convolutional layers followed by a MaxPool layer) to process proteins and ligands separately, which are then joined through three fully-connected hidden layers; the network is trained in turn on the DAVIS and KIBA datasets: although the original network was specifically tailored for the considered problem, also in this case we obtained a remarkable compression rate, still preserving model performance.

2.3   Network Compression

In this section we shortly describe the considered compression schemes, namely pruning, weight sharing, and probabilistic quantization.

Pruning. Activation functions process the sum of the neuron inputs, each weighted according to its connection; a straightforward compression technique consists therefore in "cutting" all connections whose weight has a small absolute value. Indeed, nullifying such negligible weights should not sensibly change the above mentioned signal, as well as the global network output. We parameterized this technique on the threshold p used in order to deem a connection as negligible: in turn, this threshold was defined by considering a suitable set of empirical quantiles of connection weights. As a post-processing phase, we retrained the network, now ignoring the erased connections (that is, clamping the corresponding weights to zero).

Weight Sharing. In analogy with the observations at the basis of network pruning, when several weights are close one another, they can all be set to a common value without significantly affecting network performance. We clustered all learnt weights using the k-means algorithm, obtaining k representative centroids which we used to replace the weight values. Also in this case, we subsequently retrained the network, now updating centroids through cumulative gradient. Note that this algorithm, in its original form, outputs a table of representative weights, as well as a matrix storing indices to this table, rather than the weights themselves. We substituted this format with those described in the next section.

Probabilistic Quantization. An alternative approach to weight sharing is that of selecting the representative weights through a probabilistic algorithm. We adapted a technique used in the realm of bandwitdh reduction, having the desirable property that the above mentioned representative values can be thought as an unbiased estimate of the original weights. For this technique we used the same retraining process and parameterization used for the weight sharing technique.

2.4   Compact Network Representation

In order to appropriately exploit the characteristics of the compressed connection matrices, the latter are stored by means of two novel formats, respectively called HAM and sHAM. Both formats represent each matrix element through Huffman coding, subsequently concatenating the corresponding codewords by column order, thus obtaining a unique binary string. HAM encodes all weights, and the lower the number of distinct weights in the matrix, the lower the average codeword length. To benefit also from the matrix sparsity, sHAM applies Huffman coding only to non zero elements, stored through Compressed Sparse Column (CSC) format. In both HAM and sHAM cases, the generated bit sequence is organized as a succession of machine words, interpreted as an array of integers. Figures 2 and 3 show an example of encoding for both formats, highlighting the various phases of the involved conversion.

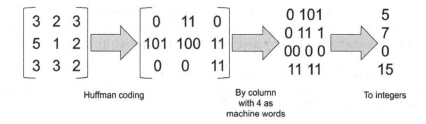

Fig. 2. Example of HAM storage format.

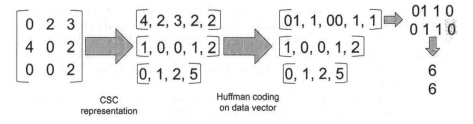

Fig. 3. Example of sHAM storage format. The additional 0 marked in red is the effect of padding required in order to work with machine words.

3   Reproducibility

The results illustrated in [5] can be fully replicated by running the code in the repository freely available on GitHub[1]. Once this repository has been cloned, the user can launch the **runner.sh** shell script (available in the root directory), which automatically creates a virtual environment within which all required libraries are installed, to subsequently run all the experiments. As a result, several text files are created in the **time_space/results/** directory. These files can be postprocessed by the notebook **time_space/plot_from_file.ipynb** to get the best compression results and to generate summary plots. It is worthy pointing out that, however, some small fluctuations in the results are inherently due to the GPU utilization [1]. Running the experiments requires the availability of at least 10 GB of RAM, in order to load the selected CNN models; the execution time took roughly two weeks using a computing environment equipped with an Nvidia RTX 2060 GPU and an i7-9750H CPU. Note, however, that this time refers to the execution more than 860 different experiments, each involving compression and retraining of a CNN. To reproduce a single compression experiment and to quickly check its reproducibility, the reader can refer to the script **runner_single_exp.sh** in the repository root. Whereas, the implementation of specific compression schemes is available in the **compressionNN_package/compressionNN** folder of the above mentioned repository. More precisely, the scripts in files **pruning.py**, **weightsharing.py**, and

---

[1] https://github.com/giosumarin/ICPR2020_sHAM.

stochastic.py, respectively implement pruning, weight sharing, and probabilistic quantization; analogously, the considered joint techniques are implemented in pruning_weightsharing.py and pruning_stochastic.py scripts.

Acknowledgements. This work has been supported by the Italian MUR PRIN project "Multicriteria data structures and algorithms: from compressed to learned indexes, and beyond" (Prot. 2017WR7SHH).

References

1. Cook, S.: CUDA Programming: A Developer's Guide to Parallel Computing with GPUs, 1st edn. Morgan Kaufmann Publishers Inc., San Francisco (2012)
2. Davis, M.I., et al.: Comprehensive analysis of kinase inhibitor selectivity. Nat. Biotech. **29**, 1046–1051 (2011)
3. Krizhevsky, A.: Learning multiple layers of features from tiny images. Master's thesis, University of Toronto (2009)
4. Lecun, Y., Bottou, L., Bengio, Y., Haffner, P.: Gradient-based learning applied to document recognition. Proc. IEEE **86**(11), 2278–2324 (1998)
5. Marinò, G., Ghidoli, G., Frasca, M., Dario, M.: Compression strategies and space-conscious representations for deep neural networks. In: International Conference on Pattern Recognition, ICPR 2020 (2020). arxiv:2007.07967
6. Öztürk, H., Özgür, A., Ozkirimli, E.: DeepDTA: deep drug-target binding affinity prediction. Bioinformatics **34**(17), i821–i829 (2018). https://doi.org/10.1093/bioinformatics/bty593
7. Simonyan, K., Zisserman, A.: Very deep convolutional networks for large-scale image recognition. In: International Conference on Learning Representations (2015)
8. Tang, J., et al.: Making sense of large-scale kinase inhibitor bioactivity data sets: a comparative and integrative analysis. J. Chem. Inf. Model. **54**(3), 735–743 (2014). https://doi.org/10.1021/ci400709d

Implementation of Genetic Pseudo Rehearsal

Bhasker Sri Harsha Suri and Kalidas Yeturu[✉]

Indian Institute of Technology Tirupati, Tirupati 517506, Andhra Pradesh, India
{cs18s506,ykalidas}@iittp.ac.in

Abstract. Deep neural networks suffer from catastrophic forgetting problem when they are deployed in a continual learning scenario. In our main work, we proposed *Genetic Pseudo rehearsal*, where we generated synthetic data of the previous task using Genetic Algorithms and *pseudo rehearsed* the neural network on it. We demonstrated the computational and memory efficiency offered by our proposed method. In this work, we discuss the implementation details of our proposed algorithm and the experimental setup in detail.

1 Introduction

1.1 Catastrophic Forgetting

Deep neural networks suffer from *Catastrophic forgetting* problem when deployed in a continual learning scenario [1]. Robins [3] proposed the concept of *pseudo rehearsal*, where a generator synthetically generates the data for the previous task on which the neural network is *rehearsed*. Generative replay [4] is a good example of *pseudo rehearsal* where the training data for the previous task is synthetically generated using a Generative adversarial network(GAN).

1.2 Genetic Pseudo Rehearsal

In our main work [5], we proposed to generate synthetic data using Genetic Algorithms instead of GANs. We demonstrated that we could achieve higher efficiencies in computational and memory resource consumption by forgoing the data's photo-realism. In this work, we try to explain the implementation details of our main work.

1.3 Organization of the Paper

The paper has been divided into five main sections. In Sect. 2, we give insights into the implementation of operations like Mutation, cross-over functions, which are an integral part of the Genetic algorithm. We also explain the *Enrichment function* used to enrich the data generated after the genetic algorithm phase.

© Springer Nature Switzerland AG 2021
B. Kerautret et al. (Eds.): RRPR 2021, LNCS 12636, pp. 167–172, 2021.
https://doi.org/10.1007/978-3-030-76423-4_13

To increase the work's availability to a broader audience, we implemented our work in 3 different formats. In the first format, the entire code has been made available in ready-to-run Google Colab notebooks. A detailed description of this implementation is provided in Sect. 3 of the paper. In the second format, the proposed algorithm has been implemented as a Python *function call*(.py file). A function called *Generate_Genetic_data* has been implemented where the user can pass their respective models and parameters as arguments, and the function returns the generated synthetic data as output. The file also gives access to other functions that are part of our main work, like *mutation, cross-over, and Enrichment phase* and *Agreement score*. A detailed description of this format is given in Sect. 4 of the paper.

In order to make our work available to users who build neural networks using frameworks other than Tensorflow, we implemented the work as an *service* as well. The proposed algorithm can be deployed on a local server, and users can generate synthetic data for neural networks that were implemented in any Deep learning framework. The description of this work is present in Sect. 5 of the paper.

2   Overview of the Code

The proposed algorithm was implemented in Python 3 with NumPy [2] library handling all the vector operations that arose at various points in the algorithm. The experiments in the main work used neural networks implemented using Keras with Tensorflow in the backend. The code is made available at the following Github link: https://github.com/BhaskerSriHarsha/Genetic-Pseudo-Rehearsal.

2.1   Representation of Images

The experimentation took place in an image classification setting; hence, it is essential to understand how images were represented in the Genetic Algorithm. The algorithm's crux lies in the process of evolving *genes* of organisms in a population through iterative selection using a fitness function. Each image was considered an organism, and the vector format representation of the pixel values of the generated images was considered the *genes* in the algorithm. So, instead of taking the images in standard picture formats like .jpg or .png, they were considered as *numpy arrays*.

2.2   Fitness Function

Each synthetically generated image was given to the neural network for classification. The softmax confidence of the neural network at the final layer for the target class was considered the *fitness score* of each organism. The fittest 25% of the organisms in a given generation were propagated to the next generation for evolution.

2.3   Mutation Function

The mutation function is responsible for perturbating the synthetic images' pixels with a probability *"p"*. To implement this, *np.random.choice()* function was used. The function generated a vector of size same as that of the given image, in which each element has a probability *p* of being a value between 0 and 1. The mutation magnitude of each pixel was decided using *np.random.normal()* function, which generated a value between 0 and 1 by sampling a normal distribution.

2.4   Crossover Function

In addition to the mutation function, the cross-over operation was also used to create the next generation of organisms. The cross-over function accepts two NumPy arrays as inputs and the index through which the arrays will be crossed over. The NumPy arrays (images) are clipped at the given *index* and the second half of the arrays are exchanged. The arrays that were passed as arguments are crossed over and ready to be used, and the function does not return anything as it uses the *"Call by Object reference"* property of the Python language.

2.5   Enrichment Phase

Sklearn package was used to implement the *Gaussian mixture models* that was critical in the enrichment phase of the algorithm. The *GaussianMixture* model can be imported from *sklearn.mixture* package and it accepts the *number-of-components* and *data* as arguments. The function fits N number of centers to the *data* where $N = number\text{-}of\text{-}components$. All the functions mentioned above were used in all the three formats in which our work was implemented. Though the environment changes for the three implementations, the core logic and code for the functions mentioned above remained constant.

3   Colab Notebooks

All the experiments that were reported in the main paper were run on Google Colab notebooks. The experiments used a Tesla P100 GPU and an Intel Xeon Dual Core 2.5 GHz processor. The Neural network was implemented in Keras with Tensorflow in the backend. Numpy was used to represent the images in a vector form; however, *Matploblib* library was used to display the images and generate the final graphs for the experiments. The experiments discussed in the main paper are made available in a ready-to-run form in the **Jupyter Notebooks** folder of our Github repository. The notebooks can be executed directly without any modifications on the Google Colaboratory platform. *Genetic_Rehearsal.py* file, which is also present in the folder, needs to be present in the working directory as it contains the supporting functions to run the algorithm. However, the main code to create the synthetic data using the Genetic algorithm and the

Enrichment phase is written in the notebook. It has to be noted that the purpose of these Google Colab notebooks is to aid in the reproducibility of experiments that were described in the main work. The notebooks generate the synthetic data for networks that are already declared in the notebooks. In case the reader wants to generate synthetic data for their neural network, it is required that the user swaps the default neural network in the notebook with their network.

4   Python Library Files

For users who wish to run the code on their local systems instead of Google Colab environment, the proposed algorithm has been implemented as a python library and can be accessed as a *function call*. To run it, visit the official GitHub repository and download the *Genetic_Rehearsal.py* file in the folder *.py files* to your working directory. A requirements file (*requirements.txt*) has been provided to aid the users in creating the virtual environment required to run the code. The main Genetic algorithm that generates the synthetic data is implemented in the function *Genetic_data_Generator()*. It accepts the *model, shape* of the image sample in the dataset, *target classes* for which the synthetic data is to be generated, *size of population* in a given generation, *number of cultures*, *number of generations* for which the evolution continues, pixel *mutation probability* and finally the pixel *mutation type* as input arguments. The function returns the generated synthetic data and the respective labels for the individual samples in the form of a list with the first element as data and the second element as labels.

The *Enrichment()* function performs the enrichment operation that was described in the main work using *Gaussian mixture models* from *Sklearn library*. The function takes the target *data, labels* of the data, target *model, number of centers* for the Gaussian mixture model, *number of classes* and *number of samples* to be generated as parameters. For Step 1 of the Enrichment phase, the number of centers is set equal to the number of classes, and for Step 2 of the Enrichment phase, the number of centers is set to 1. The explanation for this can be found in our main work. Please note that to avoid memory overflows, set the default datatype of the NumPy arrays as *float32* instead of the default *float64*. Since we are dealing with images in this particular application, a Numpy array with *float32* as datatype is sufficient and memory-efficient. In addition to the main functions, the file also has additional functions like *duplicate_remover()*, *duplicate_counter()*, *agreement_score()* etc. which were used in the *Ablation studies* section of the main paper.

An in-situ documentation of each function can be obtained using the *help()* function. For example, the command *help(duplicate_remover)* will print the documentation for the *duplicate_remover* function when executed.

5   Data Generation as a Service

To extend our algorithm's availability to users who have already developed their neural network models using frameworks other than Tensorflow, we are offering the proposed algorithm as a *service* which can be deployed on a local server. Neural networks developed using any deep learning framework can access our proposed algorithm as a service using HTTP methods.

The Genetic algorithm that generates synthetic data runs on a local server and will be referred to as *GA-service*. The Neural network is deployed on the local machine and will be called as *model-service* from here on. A continuous interaction between the *GA-service* and *model-service* generates the desired synthetic samples. The entire process of generating synthetic data has been split between the *GA service* and *model-service*. Whenever the *GA-service* requires the neural network predictions, the *model-service* requests the current generation of images and returns the softmax confidence for each image to the *GA-service* as a string. The predictions received by the *GA-service* are used by the fitness function to select the fittest individuals for the next generation. The whole process continues until the generated synthetic data reaches a threshold level of fitness.

The algorithm at the *model-service* is described in Algorithm 1. The "/" symbol describes the path from where the server-side script was deployed.

Algorithm 1: Algorithm at the *model-service*

---

status_flag = 0;
target_labels = "1,2,3";
POST('/', data = target_labels, timeout = 1);
status_flag = GET('/training');
while *status_flag == 1* **do**
    images_flag = GET("/flag");
    if *images_flag == 1* **then**
        images = GET('/images');
        predictions = model(images);
        POST('/predictions',data = predictions);
        POST('/reset_flag',data = 0);
        POST('/ready',data = 1);
    end
    status_flag=GET('/training');
end
synthetic_data=GET('/synthetic_data');

The synchronization between the two services is achieved by monitoring three variables: *status_flag, images_flag* and *ready_flag* on the server by the client. *status_flag* is responsible for letting the *model-service* know that the generation of synthetic images is still active and on-going. When the *GA-service* flips the status_flag to 0, it means that the required synthetic data is ready, and the evolution procedure can be stopped. *images_flag* variable says that the *GA-service* has prepared the current generation of images, and the *model-service* can acquire them using the GET method. *ready_flag* is used by *GA-service* to know whether predictions for the previously sent images are ready to be collected by the *GA-service* from the *model-service*.

The *model-service* starts the synthetic data generation process by sending POST command to the *GA-service*. The POST command carries the *target labels* for which the synthetic data is to be generated as data. The *model-service* then monitors the *status_flag* on the *GA-service* using the GET command. As soon as the *status_flag* is set to 1, the procedure to generate the synthetic images begins. The *GA-service* begins by generating random images as the first generation. It then sets the *images_flag* variable to 1, indicating the *model-service* to collect the images. The *model-service* collects those images using a GET command and returns the softmax predictions of each image to the *GA-service* in the form of a string. This process continues till a generation reaches a certain threshold level of fitness. The *GA-service* ends the procedure by setting the *status_flag* back to 0. Finally, the *model-service* collects the generated synthetic data using a GET method.

To install the setup, download the *GA-service.py* file available in the *API* folder of the Github repository. The requirements file (*requirements.txt*) is also provided in the folder, which can be used to set up the virtual environment required to run the *GA-service* and *model* side codes. A template (*model-service.py*) for the *model-service* side is provided, which can be used by any deep learning framework in Python. If the user uses any language other than Python, the reference algorithm (Algorithm 1) provided on the Github page can be used to write the *model-service*'s code. Currently, the *target labels* can be sent as parameters to the *GA-service* from the *model-service*. The package will be updated to send more parameters concerning the genetic algorithm soon.

6   Conclusion

In this work, we discussed the implementation details of Genetic Pseudo Rehearsal. The proposed algorithm was implemented in three different formats to increase the work's availability to the research community. All the formats were discussed in the current work to aid the reproducibility of the research.

References

1. French, R.M.: Catastrophic forgetting in connectionist networks. Trends Cogn. Sci. **3**(4), 128–135 (1999)
2. Harris, C.R., et al.: Array programming with NumPy. Nature **585**(7825), 357–362 (2020)
3. Robins, A.: Catastrophic forgetting, rehearsal and pseudorehearsal. Connect. Sci. **7**(2), 123–146 (1995)
4. Shin, H., Lee, J.K., Kim, J., Kim, J.: Continual learning with deep generative replay. In: Advances in Neural Information Processing Systems, pp. 2990–2999 (2017)
5. Suri, B.S.H., Yeturu, K.: Pseudo rehearsal using non photo-realistic images. In: International Conference on Pattern Recognition (ICPR) (2020)

Author Index

Printed in the United States
by Baker & Taylor Publisher Services